MILITARY AIRCRAFT

1914 TO THE PRESENT DAY

MILITARY AIRCRAFT

1914 TO THE PRESENT DAY

ROBERT JACKSON AND JIM WINCHESTER

CHARTWELL
BOOKS, INC.

This edition published by
CHARTWELL BOOKS, INC.
A Division of
BOOK SALES, INC.
114 Northfield Avenue
Edison, New Jersey 08837

ISBN 0-7858-1895-2

Editorial and design by:
Amber Books Ltd
Bradley's Close
74–77 White Lion Street
London N1 9PF
www.amberbooks.co.uk

Artworks © Art-Tech/Aerospace

Printed in Singapore

CONTENTS

INTRODUCTION

THE BEAUTIFUL ILLUSTRATIONS of military aircraft contained in this book were all created in the 1980s and 1990s for Aerospace Publishing, a London-based company that specialized in high-quality aviation publications.

Many Aerospace publications were partworks, a term which might require some explanation. A partwork is published in (normally weekly) instalments like a magazine, which builds up into a comprehensive and fully indexed reference work. A partwork's first few issues are normally available on news-stands, after which readers subscribe to subsequent issues until the partwork is complete, after a given number of issues – normally 100 or more. Readers are encouraged to file issues in specially produced binders, available from the publishers.

Beginning with weekly partworks such as *The Illustrated Encyclopedia of Aircraft* and later the quarterlies *World Air Power Journal* and *Wings of Fame,* Aerospace gained a reputation for the quality of its illustrations: cutaway drawings, colour profiles, three-view paintings and the spectacular artworks seen here. All

but the latter were well-established forms in aviation books and magazines, but the perspective paintings against a white background used as the magazine's gatefold centrepiece were all new.

The first gatefolds were painted by Keith Fretwell for the new partwork *Warplane* in 1985. The very first to appear was the Tornado GR.1 of No. 617 Squadron and the second was the Lockheed SR-71. The successful launch of this partwork, which was eventually to run to 120 issues, required a new gatefold of a current military aircraft each week, and soon more talented artists were recruited to meet the demand. Generally speaking, one gatefold represented one month to six weeks of work for the artist. Up to a dozen different artists produced gatefolds for *Warplane*

A Panavia Tornado GR.Mk.1A of No. 13 Squadron, Royal Air Force, based at Marham, Norfolk, in the early 1990s.

and later products, of which three – Keith Fretwell, Chris Davey and Iain Wylie – contributed the majority.

The need for the *Warplane* artworks to feature aircraft currently in service (in the 1980s) dictated the colours and markings of many aircraft featured here. Thus the Douglas C-47, Cessna A-37 and Grumman Tracker, to name but three examples, are depicted in service with Latin American air arms, not in their more familiar World War II or Vietnam-era colours.

Warplane was followed by 132 issues of *Take-Off*, which covered a broader spectrum of aviation, from interwar airliners to fighters of the 1950s. The style of illustration was adapted to fit a two-page (rather than four) format. To fit the reduced space and reflect a different readership, the

compositions were often in a more vertical format or with a more 'head-on' aspect. Multiple aircraft often appeared and their markings complemented the narrative – whether it be extracts from a Sabre pilot's memoirs or an account of the special operations of Luftwaffe unit KG200.

In 1990 the encyclopedia-style partwork *Airplane* appeared and again ran to 132 issues, each featuring a gatefold. Many of these were modern civil aircraft, mostly done by Mike Badrocke, who also painted a number of the military subjects featured here.

In the same year, Aerospace launched *World Air Power Journal*, a quarterly reference series with unprecedented depth of coverage of modern military aviation. Further new gatefolds were commissioned for many of the first 37 of the eventual 43 volumes. Each was the centrepiece of the main

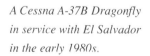

A Cessna A-37B Dragonfly in service with El Salvador in the early 1980s.

feature, which was normally on a single aircraft type. Two exceptions were the Altenburg MiG-29, which illustrated an article on Russian forces in East Germany, and the Cannon AFB F-111F, which accompanied a feature on the USAF bomber force. In 1995 *Wings of Fame* (twenty volumes) applied the same formula to historic military aviation, featuring subjects from the Messerschmitt 109 to the Convair F-106.

Although both *World Air Power Journal* and *Wings of Fame* reused some of the older artworks alongside new commissions, each gatefold was enhanced by new detailed captions and annotations about units, weapons, engines and other details. Several factors, including the passing of Keith Fretwell, led to an end to commissioning of new gatefold pages for *World Air Power Journal*, the last, an AV-8B started by Keith but completed by John Weal, appearing in Volume 37. *Wings of Fame* carried a few

new artworks after this time, the last being Iain Wylie's TBM Avenger in Volume 13.

The author of this introduction commissioned some of the gatefolds and more of the three-view aircraft illustrations for *Wings of Fame,* and it was a most enjoyable process liaising with the artist to achieve the most accurate possible representation of an aircraft at a particular time and place. The company's huge photo and cuttings archive was a main source of reference material as were the artist's own resources. Period photographs, models and 'life' sketches of preserved aircraft all contributed to the final result.

The artworks were mostly airbrushed gouache, although some were airbrushed using inks. Details were hand-brushed and drawn with pens and pencil. Before painting began, the artists submitted full-sized pencilled roughs of different viewpoints of the subject aircraft from which the editors chose that which they liked best.

A Soviet Mikoyan MiG-29 Fulcrum-A based at Nobitz (Altenburg) in the GDR.

A Messerschmitt Bf 109K-4 of Jagdgeschwader 27, as it would have appeared in 1944.

An unusual aspect of painting against a white background was that the perspectives had to be much more accurate than for a traditional painting against background of scenery. If the perspective was copied from a projection of a photograph, the distortions caused by the lens would be very apparent. The more experienced artists could create a proportionally correct depiction from almost any angle, and create images which would be impossible to capture in a photograph. The fine detail in these artworks is astonishing and stands up to the closest scrutiny. Each original was painted on a piece of high quality art board well over a metre (3 ft) long and would only fit inside a standard plan chest if two corners were lopped off and the painting inserted diagonally.

Much excitement ensued when the latest artwork arrived from the artist in its stiff board packaging. Many of these boards must have travelled thousands of miles all told between the artist's drawing board, Aerospace's office in west London, the photographers in Covent Garden and all the way back again to be reused for the next one.

Choice of subject for the gatefold treatment followed several paths. The first subjects for *Warplane* needed to be those which would appeal to the greatest audience and thus attract subscriptions. As the form became more established, the subjects, or at least the colour schemes, became more open to the whim of the editors. Pilots who had helped the company on other products often found 'their' aircraft illustrated, the Gulf War Jaguar being an example. Several gatefolds and three-views depicted aircraft from the varied RAF career of one editor's father.

Others simply depicted important units, weapons or variants which were otherwise difficult or impossible to illustrate in colour.

Each particular artist had a distinct and recognisable style and many readers will find a favourite in this collection. Some preferred historical aircraft and others modern warplanes. One artist based his pilots and groundcrew on familiar faces. Tennis player Ivan Lendl appears in this volume, as does a well-known singer.

Despite all the research, errors did creep in, albeit very rarely. One modern naval fighter included here has a serial number that belongs rightfully to a Marine Corps helicopter. Coming to caption a World War II fighter for *Wings of Fame*, this author began to panic when the serial did not match the particular variant depicted. After some research using unpublished original photographs, things were put straight by simply having the Roman numeral 'II' added to the nose-art, which had otherwise been the same on two successive airframes flown by the same pilot. Researching the individual aircraft in this book has thrown up instances where an initial suspicion that the variant did not match the serial have proved on closer examination to be unfounded, proving the depth of research that has gone into each of these paintings.

Sadly, in the spring of 2001, flooding caused by a nearby burst water main inundated the archive where the artworks were stored. Although protected from normal wear and tear by fixatives and cover sheets, the gatefolds proved particularly susceptible to water and many were irretrievably damaged. Fortunately, each had

A Jaguar GR.Mk.1A of the Royal Air Force, based at Muharraq, Bahrain, during the 1991 Gulf War.

already been photographed onto 10 x 8-inch transparency film as part of the reproduction process, and most had been further backed-up onto electronic media, and thus survived to be presented here.

Although Aerospace no longer commissions this style of artwork, the style has been adapted for the computer age by other publishers (usually with less success), and this traditional painted form flourishes with Russian artists. This volume collects almost all of the military aircraft gatefolds together for the first time and should stand as a tribute to the many thousands of hours of research, sketching and painting that helped create some of the most distinctive aviation magazines ever published.

Jim Winchester

Manfred von Richthofen, the 'Red Baron', scored 20 of his 80 kills in a Fokker Dr.I Triplane. One of the three aircraft piloted by Richthofen is pictured in action here.

Keith Fretwell

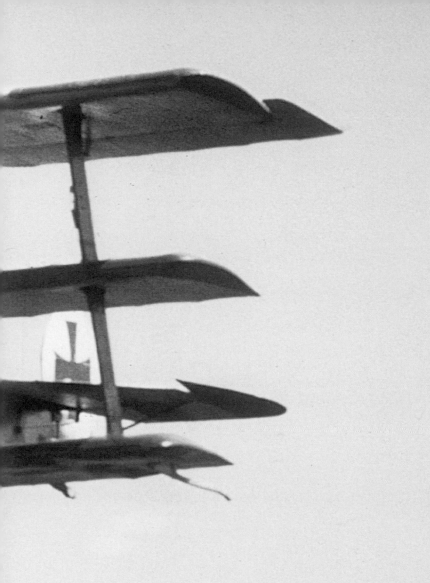

THE BIPLANE ERA: 1914–1939

As World War I began, the aircraft employed as scouts over the battlefields were flimsy, unreliable, and often unarmed. The invention in 1915 of the synchronized machine gun led to the development of the first air combat tactics, and further technological developments ushered in the fast, heavily armed biplane fighters of the 1920s and '30s.

A replica Fokker Dr.I triplane, the type flown by legendary World War I ace Manfred von Richthofen. The Dr.I was ordered into production as a result of the success of the British Sopwith Triplane.

AVRO 504N

No. 601 (County of London) Squadron, Royal Auxiliary Air Force, Northolt, Middlesex, 1929

AVRO 504N

Specification
- **Type** biplane trainer
- **Crew** 2
- **Powerplant** one 134kW (180hp) Armstrong-Siddeley Lynx III radial engine
- **Performance** max speed 161km/h (100mph); service ceiling 4450m (15,000ft); endurance 8 hours
- **Dimensions** wing span 10.97m (40ft); length 8.79m (28ft 10in); height 3.17m (10ft 5in)
- **Weight** 1016kg (2240lb) loaded
- **Armament** none

The Avro 504 was introduced as a fighter, reconnaissance aircraft and light bomber in 1914, having first flown in July the previous year. As a bomber, the 504 could carry only four 20lb (9.1kg) bombs, and the advent of better aircraft meant it saw little action. By mid-1915 it was considered obsolete for a frontline role, but its stability and docile handling made it an ideal training aircraft. Large numbers were ordered as the 504K, with a mounting that could take a variety of engines. Like most of its predecessors, it featured long skids beside the undercarriage wheels to prevent it nosing over when landing on soft ground. A total of 5440 Avro 504s was built during the war.

The design was modernized after the war with a revised undercarriage and an Armstrong-Siddeley Lynx radial engine. This was larger than the original Clerget rotary and had no cowling. Avro 504s were sold to many countries after the war, including Australia, New Zealand and Norway. Greece received 30 504Ns and 12 504Ks; some were still in service at World War II's outbreak. The 504N was sometimes called the Avro Lynx. Avro 504N J8504 was delivered to No. 601 Squadron in July 1929. It moved to the RAF College at Cranwell, Lincolnshire, in March 1931. On 5 September 1932, it hit a wall on landing and was wrecked.

No. 601 Squadron was formed at Northolt in October 1925 as a light-bomber unit of the Auxiliary Air Force, but did not begin flying until May 1926. It used Avro 504s to gain experience before DH.9A bombers arrived in 1927, but kept flying Avros alongside the de Havillands. During the war, No. 601 flew Hurricanes in the Battle of France and Battle of Britain. After a brief period with P-39 Airacobras, the squadron flew Spitfires in North Africa and Italy. Re-formed in 1946, it flew Spitfires, Meteors and Vampires until disbandment in 1957.

BRISTOL BULLDOG II

No. 23 Squadron,
Royal Air Force Fighter Command,
RAF Biggin Hill, Kent, 1932

BRISTOL BULLDOG II

Specification
- **Type** single-seat day fighter
- **Crew** 1
- **Powerplant** one 440kW (330hp) Bristol Jupiter VIIF radial piston engine
- **Performance** max speed 280km/h (174mph); service ceiling 8930m (29,300ft); range 563km (350 miles)
- **Dimensions** wing span 10.31m (33ft 10in); length 7.62m (25ft); height 2.99m (9ft 10in)
- **Weight** 1601kg (3530lb) loaded
- **Armament** two 7.7mm (0.303in) Vickers machine guns

Together with the Hawker Fury, the Bristol Bulldog epitomized Royal Air Force (RAF) Fighter Command in the 1930s. The prototype Bristol Type 105 Bulldog flew as a contender for an RAF fighter specification in May 1927. A 'fly-off' was arranged between the Bristol and the slightly superior Hawker Hawfinch, and the modified Type 105A was selected as the Bulldog II in 1928. Two factors in its favour were its more modern steel tube structure and cheaper Jupiter radial engine. The 92 Mk IIs were followed by 268 of the Mk IIA with a more powerful Jupiter as its powerplant.

Although possessing better handling than its predecessor, the Sopwith Snipe, the Bristol Bulldog was not very much faster or better climbing, and its armament of two machine guns was the same. The Bulldog did, however, introduce a radio and oxygen supply for the first time in an RAF fighter. Due to the conservative approach of the Air Ministry, which issued overcautious specifications, British fighter development was to progress little in the 1920s. The RAF's fighters remained biplanes with two or four rifle-calibre machine guns until the Hurricane and Spitfire entered service in 1937–38.

No. 23 Squadron was one of 10 frontline units that operated the Bulldog between 1929 and 1937. No. 23's Bulldog era in fact only lasted from 1931 to 1933. This aircraft, K1678, served with the squadron throughout this period, before going to No. 2 Aircraft Servicing Unit (ASU) until it was struck off charge in August 1938. The squadron flew multi-place fighters into the 1960s when it received the single-seat Lightning. Returning to two-seaters with the Phantom and Tornado F.3, No. 23 Squadron exists today as the operator of some of the RAF's Sentry AEW.1 AWACS aircraft at RAF Waddington.

CURTISS P-6E HAWK

33rd Pursuit Squadron,
8th Pursuit Group,
United States Army Air Corps,
Langley, Virginia, 1933

CURTISS P-6E HAWK

Specification
- **Type** biplane pursuit fighter
- **Crew** 1
- **Powerplant** : one 522kW (700hp) Curtiss V-1570C Conqueror V-12 piston engine
- **Performance** max speed 311km/h (193mph); service ceiling 7285m (23,900ft); range 393km (244 miles)
- **Dimensions** wing span 9.60m (31ft 6in); length 7.67m (25ft 2in); height 2.82m (8ft 7in)
- **Weight** 1439kg (3172lb) loaded
- **Armament** two 7.62mm (0.30in) machine guns in wings

The Curtiss Hawk family of fighters for the US Army Air Corps (USAAC) and US Navy (USN) originated with racing aircraft of the early 1920s. None was ordered in huge numbers, but they helped to keep a cadre of experienced pilots active through the lean years of the Depression. The main model was the radial-engined P-1 Hawk, also bought by the Navy as the F6C. Testing of P-1s with the new V-12 Curtiss Conqueror engine resulted in the P-6 through P-6D, the latter having a turbo supercharger, and glycol as coolant. The XP-6E was derived from this and other experimental versions. It was tested by the Army and proved capable of just under 320km/h (200mph), at least in part because of much better streamlining than its predecessors. Faster than the contemporary radial-engined Boeing P-12, but not as manoeuvrable, it had longer range due to its large additional external fuel tank under the mid-fuselage. Armament was only two machine guns, mounted behind the engine and firing along troughs under the exhaust pipes.

The P-6E was the last biplane fighter ordered by the US Army; only 45 were built. They served with the 1st Pursuit Group, comprised of the17th, 27th and 94th Pursuit Squadrons at Selfridge Field, Michigan, and the 8th PG (33rd, 35th and 36th PS) at Langley Field, Virginia. Production began in 1931, and the P-6E's US career was over by 1939. P6E's were initially delivered in olive drab with yellow wings and elaborate white markings around the nose and wheel spats, but a 1934 order saw P-6E fuselages painted in overall blue; it was some years before all aircraft were in the new colours. A total of 27 of the Army's P-6E Hawks were written off in accidents, and the survivors were mainly issued as training aids to civilian flying schools. Eight had been supplied to the Netherlands East Indies and one sold to Japan. Only one P-6E aircraft survives today, at the US Air Force Museum.

FOKKER DR.1

Jasta 11, Jagdgeschwader 1, Luftstreikräfte, Cappy, France, 1918

FOKKER DR.1

Specification

- **Type** triplane fighter
- **Crew** 1
- **Powerplant** one 82.1kW (110hp) Oberursel UR.II, nine-cylinder rotary piston engine
- **Performance** max speed 185km/h (115mph); service ceiling 6100m (20,013ft); endurance 1 hour 30 minutes
- **Dimensions** wing span 7.19m (23ft 7in); length 7.19m (18ft 11in); height 2.9m (9ft 8in);
- **Weight** loaded 586kg (1292lb)
- **Armament** two synchronized 7.92mm (0.31in) LMG 08/15 machine guns

The success of the British Sopwith Triplane impressed the German High Command, and all the German aircraft makers were ordered to produce a triplane, or *dreidecker*, design. Of all the designs that emerged, only two, the Pfalz Dr.I and the Fokker Dr.I, entered production, and only 10 of the former were built. Anthony Fokker was reluctant to spend time on a triplane, but produced an aircraft based around the fuselage of an experimental biplane named the V4. To this was added three fabric-covered wings and an aerofoil-section wheel axle. Two pre-production V4s were shipped to the front for evaluation in late August 1917 as the F.I, and these were evaluated by ace World War I pilots Manfred von Richthofen and Werner Voss. Richthofen's machine, F.1 102/17, was soon painted overall red, and he rapidly scored his sixtieth victory in it.

Werner Voss was shot down and killed on 23 September 1917 after an epic dogfight, and the 'Red Baron's F.1 was lost with another pilot at the controls. Production Fokker Dr.Is entered service with JG 1, Richthofen's 'Flying Circus' in October. Only 320 production aircraft were built, and peak strength in the German Imperial Army Air Service (*Luftstreikräfte*) never exceeded 170 aircraft. The Dr.I was very successful in the German spring offensive of 1918 and achieved lasting fame in the hands of Richthofen, the 'Red Baron', who scored 20 of his 80 kills in at least three different examples, including 425/17 shown here. Richthofen himself was shot down in this aircraft on 21 April 1918, either by Canadian pilot Roy Brown or by Australian machine-gunners. The remains of the Red Baron's Fokker Triplane were displayed in Berlin after World War I, but were destroyed by Allied bombing in 1944 during World War II.

HAWKER FURY MK II

No. 25 Squadron,
Royal Air Force Fighter Command,
RAF Hawkinge, Kent, 1937

HAWKER FURY MK II

Specification
- **Type** single-seat interceptor fighter
- **Crew** 1
- **Powerplant** one 477kW (640hp) Rolls-Royce Kestrel VI V-12 piston engine
- **Performance** max speed 359km/h (223mph); service ceiling 8990m (29,500ft); range 492km (305 miles)
- **Dimensions** wing span 9.14m (30ft); length 8.15m (26ft 9in); height 3.02m (10ft 2.5in)
- **Weight** 1637kg (3609lb) loaded
- **Armament** two Vickers 7.7mm (0.303in) Mk V machine guns

The Hawker Fury was the Royal Air Force's first dedicated interceptor fighter, its predecessors being intended for long-standing patrols, rather than optimized for speed and climb. Due to its greater sophistication and higher cost, the Fury initially equipped only three 'elite' squadrons of the Royal Air Force (RAF). The Fury fighter was one of a number of successful aircraft to stem from the Hart bomber of 1928, all of which were based around the Rolls-Royce Kestrel V-12 engine. The Hart and its bomber and trainer derivatives could outperform most RAF fighters of the day, so Hawker developed a single-seat fighter of the same basic configuration, but which was smaller and structurally different to its progenitors. Of mixed metal, wood and fabric construction, the Fury had a tightly cowled water-cooled engine with a radiator slung between the undercarriage legs.

In order to increase the number of fighter squadrons in the RAF prior to the arrival of the new Spitfire and Hurricane monoplanes, a batch of 99 Fury Mk IIs was delivered in July 1936. These differed in having the more powerful Kestrel VI and greater fuel capacity. The first batch had wheel spats as seen here, but these were later removed because they tended to clog with grass and mud. The other main distinguishing feature was a tailwheel rather than a skid, and this was only found on some later aircraft. The Fury II entered service in November 1936 with No. 25 Squadron, which was the only unit to receive this version as new, although it later passed its aircraft to No. 41 Squadron. The example depicted at right followed that route, before being allocated to No. 6 Maintenance Unit as an instructional airframe in June 1939.

SPAD XIII

*Escadrille SPA.48,
Escadrille de Chasse, Aviation Militaire
Western Front, 1917*

SPAD XIII

Specification
- **Type** scouting biplane
- **Crew** 1
- **Powerplant** one 164 kW (220hp) Hispano-Suiza 8BEc eight-cylinder Vee-type engine
- **Performance** max speed 224km/h (139mph); service ceiling 6650m (21,815ft); endurance 2 hrs
- **Dimensions** wing span 8.1m (26ft 7in); length 6.3m (20ft 8in); height 2.35m (7ft 8in)
- **Weight** 845kg (1863lb) loaded
- **Armament** two 7.62mm (0.303in) machine guns

In May 1917, the French *Escadrilles de Chasse* on the Western Front began to standardize on a new type, the SPAD XIII. Like its predecessor, it was an excellent gun platform and was extremely strong, although it was tricky to fly at low speeds. Powered by a Hispano-Suiza 8Ba engine and armed with two forward-firing Vickers guns, it had a maximum speed of nearly 225km/h (140mph) – quite exceptional for that time – and was capable of climbing to 6710m (22,000ft). The SPAD XIII subsequently equipped more than 80 *escadrilles*, and 8472 were built. The type also equipped 16 squadrons of the American Expeditionary Force, which purchased 893 examples, and was supplied to Italy, which still had 100 in service in 1923. After World War I, surplus French SPAD XIIIs were sold to Belgium (37), Czechoslovakia, Japan and Poland (40).

The SPAD XIII was described by American air ace Captain Eddie Rickenbacker as 'the best ship I ever flew'. A rugged aircraft, well able to withstand the stresses of a dogfight, the SPAD XIII had a higher speed than any rotary-egined aircraft at the front during World War I. What the machine lacked in manoeuvrability, it more than made up for in rate of climb and maximum speed.

The example of the SPAD XIII illustrated here bears the crowing cockerel emblem of SPA.48, derived from the unit's motto '*Chante et Combat*' ('Sing and Fight'). SPA.48 also used SPAD S.VIIs, which were generally uncamouflaged. This type was flown by French air ace Georges Guynemer, who scored 54 victories before being shot down and killed in September 1917. An example is preserved at the French Air Force Academy, Salon-de-Provence.

WORLD WAR II: 1939–1945

At no other time in history did science and technology make faster progress than in the years between 1939 and 1945, and in no area was progress swifter and more dramatic than in the design of military aircraft, some of them developed in response to requirements that had scarcely been envisaged in the years prior to World War II.

The last flying Avro Lancaster. The aircraft forms part of the Royal Air Force Battle of Britain Memorial Flight, performing at air shows alongside a Supermarine Spitfire and Hawker Hurricane.

ARADO AR 234B-2 BLITZ

9th Staffel, III Gruppe,
Kampfgeschwader 76, Luftwaffe,
Achmer, Germany, March 1945

ARADO AR 234B-2 BLITZ

Specification
- **Type** twin-engined jet bomber
- **Crew** 1
- **Powerplant** two 9.1kN (1962lb thrust) Junkers Jumo 004B axial turbojet engines
- **Performance** max speed 742km/h (461mph); service ceiling 10,000m (32,800 ft); range 1630km (1013 miles)
- **Dimensions** wing span 14.2m (46ft 3.5in); length 12.65m (41ft 5.5in); height 4.3m (14ft 1.25in)
- **Weight** 8410kg (18,541lb) loaded
- **Armament** up to 1500kg (3300lb) bomb load

Although Arado's Ar 234 'Blitz' (Lightning) was the first jet bomber to see operational service, it was designed as a reconnaissance aircraft, with work beginning as early as 1940. The prototype first flew in June 1943. In place of a conventional undercarriage, it had a wheeled dolly, which was dropped on take-off; for landing there was a metal skid. The pilot's cockpit was pressurized, and he sat on a primitive ejection seat. The original Ar 234A reconnaissance version provided valuable intelligence on Allied movements in Normandy after the D-Day landings. The Ar 234 was intended to have a pair of rearward-firing 20-mm cannon in fuselage blisters, but these were not fitted to production aircraft.

On the Ar 234B bomber, the periscopic sight above the cockpit was used for dive-bombing, but could also be turned backwards for sighting the cannon on those few test aircraft fitted with it. Another bombsight between the pilot's feet worked in conjunction with a sophisticated autopilot to allow level bombing attacks.

The 9th *Staffel* of *III Gruppe* of *Kampfgeschwader (KG) 76* was re-equipped with Ar 234s in January 1945, having previously flown the Junkers Ju 88A, mainly in the Mediterranean theatre. Its first jet sorties were flown during the Ardennes campaign, but were hampered by lack of fuel. More active during February, the Arados flew sorties against British troops around Cleve. The most significant Ar 234 operation was against the Ludendorff bridge over the Rhine at Remagen, on 7 March 1945. The Americans had captured this, the last intact bridge, and were crossing it in large numbers. KG 76 Arados, accompanied by Me 262 fighters, were ordered to destroy the bridge. Jumped by RAF Tempests, their attack was thwarted, but some hits were made on the bridge; it collapsed several days later. This was the last major attack recorded by the Ar 234.

AVRO LANCASTER B.MK I

*No. 9 Squadron, Royal Air Force,
RAF Bardney, Lincolnshire, 1945*

AVRO LANCASTER B.MK I

Specification
- **Type** four-engined heavy bomber
- **Crew** 7
- **Powerplant** four 1233kW (1640hp) Rolls-Royce Merlin 24 V-12 piston engines
- **Performance** max speed 462km/h (287mph); service ceiling 7467m (24,500ft); range 2675km (1660 miles)
- **Dimensions** wing span 31.1m (102ft); length 21.1m (69ft 4in); height 5.97m (19ft 7in)
- **Weight** 31,750kg (71,000lb) loaded
- **Armament** eight 7.7mm (0.303in) Browning machine guns, up to 6350kg (14,000lb) of conventional bombs or one 5443kg (12,000lb) 'Tallboy' or one 10,000-kg (22,000lb) 'Grand Slam' bomb

The Avro Lancaster is the most famous of the Royal Air Force's 'heavies' of World War II, being able to carry a greater load at higher altitude than its contemporaries, the Halifax and Stirling. The Lancaster was derived from the unsuccessful Manchester, which had two Rolls-Royce Vulture engines and a three-fin tail section. The Manchester was redesigned to take four Merlins, and the central fin was removed. The first Lancaster was originally known as the Manchester III and flew in January 1941.

Making its first (daylight) raids in April 1942, the Lancaster went on to become the backbone of RAF Bomber Command's night-bomber force. The Lancaster also proved adaptable to carry various weapons for special operations, the most famous of which was the Dams Raid carried out by No. 617 Squadron in May 1943. The 'Dambusters' squadron was often partnered by No. 9 Squadron, which also conducted precision attacks with modified aircraft.

'Getting Younger Every Day' was normally flown by Flight Lieutenant Douglas Tweddle and crew of No. 9 Squadron. The aircraft was an Armstrong Whitworth–built Lancaster B.I (Special), which was modified to carry the 5443kg (12,000lb) Tallboy bomb designed by Barnes Wallis, who had also invented the 'bouncing bomb' used against the Ruhr dams. It is depicted dropping a Tallboy on the U-boat pens at Bergen, Norway, during a raid on 11/12 January 1945. Thirty-two Lancasters of Nos. 9 and 617 Squadrons were despatched and three, including one from No. 9 Squadron, lost. The U-boat pens were damaged, but not destroyed. A minesweeper in the harbour was sunk by a Tallboy while trying to escape. No. 9 Squadron went on to fly the Canberra and Vulcan bombers, and today flies the Tornado GR.4 from Lossiemouth, Scotland.

BOEING B-17G FLYING FORTRESS

322nd Bombardment Squadron, 91st Bomber Group, United States Eighth Air Force, RAF Bassingbourn, England, 1944

BOEING B-17G FLYING FORTRESS

Specification

- **Type** four-engined heavy bomber
- **Crew** usually 10
- **Powerplant** four 895kW (1200hp) Wright R-1820-97 Cyclone nine-cylinder radial piston engines
- **Performance** max speed 475km/h (295mph); service ceiling 10,850m (35,600ft); range 5085km (3160 miles)
- **Dimensions** wing span 31.62m (103ft 9in); length 22.80m (74 ft 9in); height 5.85m (19ft 2in)
- **Weight** 29,710kg (65,500lb) loaded
- **Armament** 13 x 12.7mm (0.50in) machine guns; bomb load of up to 6169kg (13,600lb)

The Flying Fortress was the best-known US bomber of Word War II and symbolized American air power for a decade from the late 1930s. The Boeing Model 299 flew in July 1935 and was followed by 13 pre-production Y1B-17s and then the B-17B, C and D. All of these had limited defensive armament, slim rear fuselages and a 'shark' fin. None of these versions was particularly successful in combat, having many troubles with superchargers and oxygen systems at altitude.

The B-17E introduced the familiar outline of the majority of Flying Fortresses, over 12,000 of which were eventually built by several contractors. The B-17F and the B-17G were the main versions used in Europe by the Eighth Air Force from 1942–45. The chin turret was introduced on late-model B-17Fs and was fitted to all production Gs. Enclosed waist windows made life less uncomfortable for the gunners and a new tail turret, not fitted to the aircraft illustrated, provided better visibility and an improved gunsight.

B-17G serial No 42-31367 was built by the parent factory in Washington State, ferried to England and assigned to Lieutenant Jerry Newquist and crew, who christened it 'Chow-Hound'. The aircraft flew over 30 missions, and its gunners were credited with 19 aerial victories. The original crew flew their assigned missions and returned to the United States in mid-1944.

Lieutenant Jack Thompson and crew took over 'Chow Hound', flying an additional dozen missions in the aircraft. On their thirteenth mission, a raid on Caen supporting the Normandy campaign carried out on 8 August 1944, the aircraft was shot down over France by a direct flak hit. Thompson was the only survivor and became a prisoner of war.

BOEING B-17G FLYING FORTRESS

Kommando Olga,
2nd Staffel, Kampfgeschwader 200,
Luftwaffe, Wackersleben,
Germany, 1944–45

BOEING B-17G FLYING FORTRESS

Specification
- **Type** four-engined heavy bomber/special operations aircraft
- **Crew** usually 10
- **Powerplant** four 895kW (1200hp) Wright R-1820-97 Cyclone nine-cylinder radial piston engines
- **Performance** max speed 475km/h (295mph); service ceiling 10,850m (35,600ft); range 5085km (3160 miles)
- **Dimensions** wing span 31.62m (103ft 9in); length 22.80m (74 ft 9in); height 5.85m (19ft 2in)
- **Weight** 29,710kg (65,500lb) loaded
- **Armament** (in USAAF service) 13 x 12.7mm (0.50in) machine guns; bomb load of up to 6169kg (13,600lb)

German and Italian forces captured more than 40 airworthy or potentially airworthy B-17s and at least four B-24s during World War II. By early May 1944, at least four Flying Fortresses and two or three Liberators were in service with the clandestine *Luftwaffe* unit *Kampfgeschwader* (KG) 200. The 2nd *Staffel* (squadron) of the first *Gruppe* (group), headquartered at Finow, was assigned the larger captured aircraft for a variety of secret missions. These included shadowing US Army Air Forces (USAAF) bomber formations and reporting on their altitude and heading, and dropping agents over occupied territory. Some of these were dropped in metal and plywood pods containing three agents and their equipment. *Kommando* (or detachment) *Olga* was the sub-unit tasked with these missions and moved between many airfields, some little more than forest clearings.

It is likely that this aircraft was originally a Lockheed-Vega–built B-17G-4-VE 42-39974 of the 731st Bomb Squadron of the 452nd Bomb Group based at Deopham Green, Norfolk, and named 'Punchboard'. It was hit by flak on its thirteenth mission to the Heinkel aircraft plant at Warnemunde on 9 April 1944 and belly-landed at Vaerlose airfield, Denmark, one of 86 USAAF bombers lost that day. The crew members were taken prisoner, and the aircraft was repaired for use by KG 200. It is believed to have worn the code letters A3+BB and also no codes, as depicted here.

There are two stories about its fate: one that it exploded on take-off on 9 February 1945 at Echterdingen (Stuttgart) with the loss of its crew and 10 Vichy French agents, the other than it was mistakenly shot down by German flak while moving bases (or trying to escape to Spain) in an attempt to avoid advancing Allied ground forces.

BOEING B-29 SUPERFORTRESS

421st Bombardment Squadron,
504th Bomb Group, 20th Air Force,
United States Army Air Force,
Tinian, Marianas Islands, 1945

BOEING B-29 SUPERFORTRESS

Specification
- **Type** four-engined heavy bomber
- **Crew** 11
- **Powerplant** four 1641kW (2200hp) Wright R-3350-23 Cyclone 18-cylinder turbocharged radial piston engines
- **Performance** max speed 576km/h (358mph); service ceiling 9710m (31,850ft); range 5230km (3250 miles)
- **Dimensions** wing span 43.05m (141ft 3in); length 30.18m (99ft); height 9.02m (29ft 7in)
- **Weight** 56,245kg (124,000lb) loaded
- **Armament** 12 12.7mm (0.50in) Browning machine guns; bomb load of up to 9072kg (20,000lb)

Even before the United States had entered the war, the US Army Air Corps (USAAC) – US Army Air Forces (USAAF) from March 1942 – sought a new bomber much more capable than the relatively new B-17 and B-24. Boeing's Model 345 design was selected (as was the Consolidated XB-32) for further development, and an XB-29 prototype was ordered. Even before it flew, in September 1942, an order for 1500 B-29s was made. The B-29 was notable for its tubular-section fuselage and centrally controlled, remotely operated gun turrets. The manned tail turret initially had a 20-mm cannon as well as two machine guns, but this was later deleted.

The B-29s were built in four massive plants: Renton, near Seattle; Wichita, Kansas; Atlanta, Georgia; and Omaha, Nebraska. This extremely complex aircraft was beset with teething troubles and engine fires, and its combat debut was delayed until May 1944. The first pressurized bomber, it was able to fly over the 'Hump' of the Himalayan mountains from bases in India to attack Japan. As the islands south of Japan fell, they became available as bases to attack the Home Islands themselves.

Depicted here dropping bundled M47 incendiary bombs, Wichita-built B-29 'Dina Might' (serial number 44-69936) was the first B-29 to make a landing on Iwo Jima after it had been taken by US forces in March 1945. Assigned to the 504th Bomb Group (Very Heavy), it was flown by Captain William Pitts and crew of the 421st Bombardment Squadron. On the crew's twenty-fifth mission, the B-29 was shot down by Japanese fighters during a daylight raid on the Osaka Army Arsenal. Four B-29s from the group were lost that day, one of them to a ramming attack. Four of the crew of 'Dina Might' were killed and seven, including Pitts, survived, at least one being picked up by a US submarine.

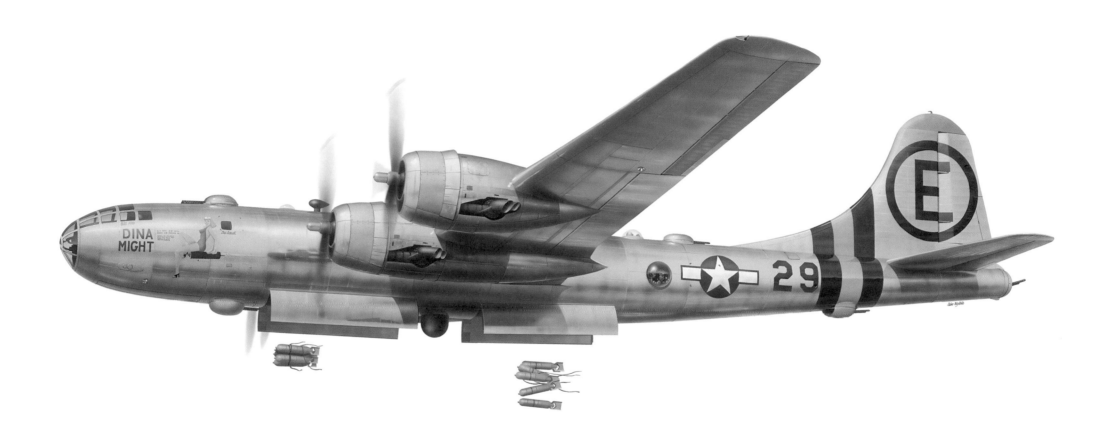

BRISTOL BEAUFIGHTER MK 21

No. 22 Squadron, No. 77 (Attack) Wing,
Royal Australian Air Force,
Morotai, Moluccan Islands, 1945

BRISTOL BEAUFIGHTER MK 21

Specification
- **Type** twin-engined attack aircraft
- **Crew** 2
- **Powerplant** two 1294kW (1735hp) Bristol Hercules XVII radial engines
- **Performance** max speed 514km/h (320mph); service ceiling 8839m (29,000ft); range 2400km (1500 miles)
- **Dimensions** wing span 17.64m (57ft 10in); length 12.59m (41ft 4in); height 4.84m (15ft 10in)
- **Weight** 11,521kg (25,400lb) loaded
- **Armament** four 12.7mm (0.5in) machine guns in wings, four 20-mm Hispano cannon in forward fuselage; eight rocket projectiles under wings

In the remarkably quick time of six months from concept to completion of the prototype, Bristol created the Type 156 Beaufighter, a powerful fighter with twin Hercules engines and a narrow fuselage housing the pilot at the front and the crewman in the mid-fuselage under a Perspex dome. Rapid development was aided by using the general layout of the Type 152 Beaufort torpedo bomber and many parts from it, namely the wings, tail group and undercarriage. The Type 156 prototype first flew in July 1939, and the Mk IF night-fighter entered service in September 1940. The Beaufighter TF.X was developed as a long-range strike fighter, armed with rockets, torpedoes or bombs, as well as cannon and machine guns. Used mainly by RAF Coastal Command, the TF.X wreaked havoc on German shipping in Norway and against enemy patrol aircraft in World War II.

The Australian Department of Aircraft Production (DAP) produced 364 Beaufighter Mk.21s, based on the TF.10, from 1944. Originally intended to have Wright R-2600 engines, they were actually produced with the standard Hercules. The Australian 'Beaus' were distinguished by a prominent hump in front of the windscreen intended to house a Sperry Autopilot, which was never fitted, and by use of 12.7mm (0.50in) rather than 7.7mm (0.303in) machine guns.

A8-186 was delivered in early 1945 and joined No. 22 Squadron in New Guinea in July, flying several operations including the last flown by the squadron. It became an instructional airframe in 1947, and in 1950 was sold to a farmer as a children's plaything. Recovered in 1965, it was restored by the private Camden Museum of Aviation at Camden, New South Wales, where it is preserved today.

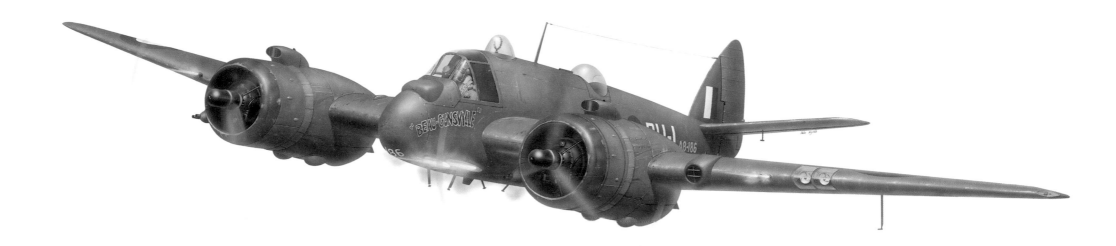

BRISTOL BLENHEIM MK IV

No. 88 Squadron,
Royal Air Force Bomber Command,
RAF Attlebridge, 1941

BRISTOL BLENHEIM MK IV

Specification
- **Type** twin-engined light bomber
- **Crew** 3
- **Powerplant** two 742kW (995hp) Bristol Mercury XV radial piston engines
- **Performance** max speed 428km/h (266mph); service ceiling 8300m (27,280ft); range 1810km (1215 miles)
- **Dimensions** wing span 17.22m (56ft 6in); length 12.98m (42ft 7in); height 2.99m (9ft 10in)
- **Weight** 6532kg (14,400lb) loaded
- **Armament** one 7.7mm (0.303in) machine gun in port wing and one in rear turret; up to 601kg (1325lb) of bombs

A privately funded prototype of the aircraft which was to evolve into the Bristol Blenheim, named 'Spirit of Britain', was first was flown in 1935. The aircraft proved 80km/h (50mph) faster than the fighters of the day and was adopted by the Royal Air Force (RAF) as the basis of a new light bomber. The first Blenheim I flew in September 1936 and was ordered by several European nations in addition to Britain.

A number of the exported aircraft fell into Axis hands in the early years of World War II. By the time the production Blenheim was equipped with guns, armour plate and other military equipment, it had lost the edge it once had over fighters, which in turn had become faster. The snub-nosed Blenheim I was the first production model, some of which were built as Mk IF fighters. The Mk IV with an elongated nose was the most numerous version, with more than 3000 produced. Used in small numbers on daylight raids in 1939–41, the Mk IV bombers were easy prey for German flak and Messerschmitts. The last examples in regular RAF Bomber Command squadrons were retired in October 1942. They proved adequate with other commands in the night-fighter and anti-shipping roles, and later provided useful trainers for new bomber crews.

Blenheim Z7427 is illustrated here in the colours of No. 88 Squadron at Attlebridge in Norfolk, where they were based from August 1941 to September 1942. It served with No. 105 Squadron before and after its time with No. 88. After that the aircraft went to No. 21 Squadron, and ended its days with an Operational Training Unit (OTU) in Scotland before being struck off charge as surplus in December 1943.

CONSOLIDATED
B-24H LIBERATOR

726th Bombardment Squadron,
451st Bomb Group, 49th Bomb Wing,
15th Air Force, United States Army Air
Forces, Italy, 1944

CONSOLIDATED B-24H LIBERATOR

Specification
- **Type** four-engined heavy bomber
- **Crew** 10
- **Powerplant** four 895kW (1200hp) 14-cylinder R-1830-43 Twin Wasp radial piston engines
- **Performance** max speed 483km/h (300mph); service ceiling 8534m (28,000ft); range 2735km (1700 miles)
- **Dimensions** wing span 33.52m (110ft 0in); length 20.47m (67ft 2in); height 5.48m (18ft)
- **Weight** 32,295kg (71,200lb) loaded
- **Armament** 10 12.7mm (0.5in) machine guns, up to 5806kg (12,800lb) of bombs

Although less famous than either the B-17 or the P-51, the B-24 Liberator was the most numerous US combat aircraft ever built. The first of 18,188 Liberators flew in March 1939, and the first production aircraft were issued to the Royal Air Force (RAF) in 1941. Although the early models had large, glazed nose sections with flexibly mounted machine guns, the B-24G and subsequent versions had various models of rotating gun turret mounted above the bombardier's position. The B-24H had the Emerson A-15 electrically operated turret. Later production H-models had glazed windows for the waist gun positions, which improved the gunners' comfort greatly. During the run of B-24H production camouflage paint was omitted, and the remainder of Liberators were delivered in natural metal finish to save weight.

The 'Stork' was one of 1580 B-24Hs built by Ford at Willow Run, Detroit, amounting to about half total production of this model. Others were assembled by Douglas at Tulsa, Oklahoma, and Consolidated at Fort Worth, Texas. It was assigned to the 726th Bombardment Squadron of the 451st Bomb Group, 49th Bomb Wing. The 451st moved between bases in Italy in 1944, arriving at Gioia del Colle, in the Bari province of Apulia, in January, moving to San Pancrazio, Brindisi province, also in Apulia, in March, then on to Castelluccio, in the Potenza province of Basilicata, a month later.

The pilot of the 'Stork' was Lieutenant Robert Blair, although the aircraft is believed to have been known as 'Cave Girl' at another time when flown by a different crew. The 451st was known as one of the most accurate bomb groups in the Mediterranean theatre, but also one of the hardest hit – in 216 missions flown during World War II, 135 of the group's B-24s were lost in combat.

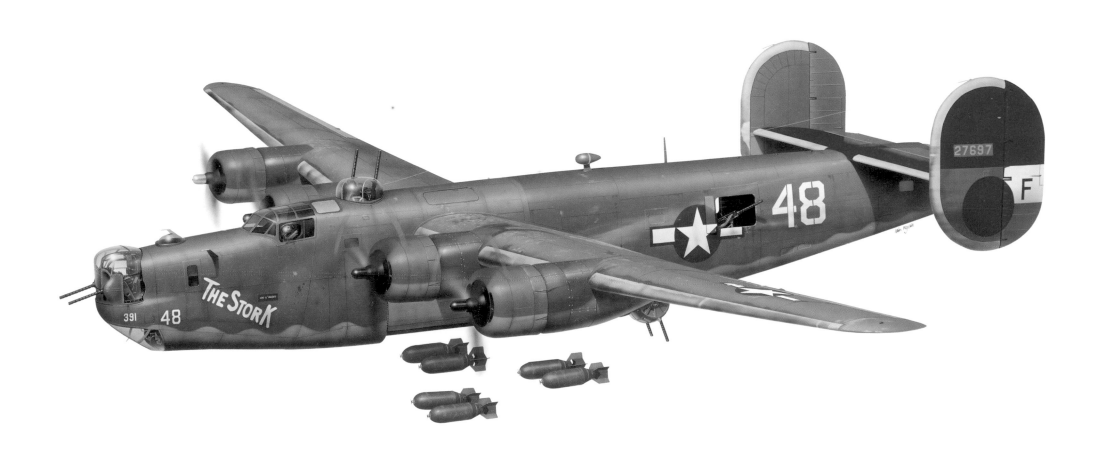

CONSOLIDATED CATALINA MK IVA

No. 202 Squadron Coastal Command,
Royal Air Force, Castle Archdale,
Fermanagh, Northern Ireland, 1944

CONSOLIDATED CATALINA MK IVA

Specification
- **Type** twin-engined patrol bomber
- **Crew** 7
- **Powerplant** two 895kW (1200hp) Pratt & Whitney R-1830-82 Twin Wasp engines
- **Performance** max speed 322km/h (200mph); service ceiling 6584m (21,600ft); range 3049km (1894 miles)
- **Dimensions** wing span 31.7m (104 ft); length 19.45m (63ft 9in); height 5.76m (18ft 10in)
- **Weight** 15,145kg (33,380lb) loaded
- **Armament** One 12.7mm (0.5in) machine gun in nose turret and two in beam blisters; up to four depth charges, two torpedoes or four 454kg (1000lb) bombs could be carried under the wings

With over 4000 built by Consolidated in San Diego, Boeing and Vickers in Canada, and several factories in the Soviet Union, the Consolidated Catalina was built in greater numbers than any other flying boat or amphibian. The prototype was designated XP3Y-1 and first flew in March 1935. Entering service as the PBY-1 the following year, its production was planned to cease in 1939, but the outbreak of war saw it resumed, and an amphibian version with retractable wheels was introduced. The Royal Air Force (RAF) ordered over 600 PBYs of various marks and gave the aircraft the name that stuck – Catalina. The first RAF Catalinas entered service in the spring of 1941 and, on 26 May, a No. 209 Squadron aircraft located the German battleship *Bismarck* in the Atlantic, an event which led to its sinking the next day.

No. 202 Squadron was based at Gibraltar at the beginning of World War II. It was re-equipped with Catalina Mk Is in April 1941. During 1941–42 the squadron also flew Sunderlands. A squadron Catalina sank *U-620* north-west of Lisbon in February 1943. A year later, on 24 February 1944, a US Navy Catalina detected *U-761* attempting to cross the Strait of Gilbraltar. A US Navy Ventura and Catalina 'G' of No. 202 Squadron attacked the submarine. *U-761* suffered nine casualties and had to be scuttled, the survivors being rescued by British destroyers.

The Mk IVA was equivalent to the US PBY-5 flying-boat model, and JX202 was built by Consolidated Vultee at San Diego in the spring of 1941. Delivered to the RAF's Marine Aircraft Experimental Establishment at Felixstowe, then to Nos. 190, 210 and finally 202 Squadrons, it survived the war and was struck off RAF charge in March 1947. The squadron disbanded in June 1945, but was later reformed as a search-and-rescue unit and today flies Sea King helicopters.

CURTISS P-40E WARHAWK

76th Fighter Squadron,
23rd Fighter Group, 14th Air Force,
United States Army Air Forces,
Kunming, China, 1942

CURTISS P-40E WARHAWK

Specification
- **Type** single-seat fighter
- **Crew** 1
- **Powerplant** one 857kW (1150hp) Allison V-1710 V-12 piston engine
- **Performance** max speed 589km/h (366mph); service ceiling 8839m (29,000ft); range 563km (360 miles)
- **Dimensions** wing span 11.36m (37ft 3.5in); length 9.69m (31ft 9in); height 3.75m (12ft 4in)
- **Weight** 3756kg (8,280lb) loaded
- **Armament** six 12.7mm (0.50in) machine gun; one 227kg (500lb) bomb

The P-40 was derived from the radial-engined P-36/Hawk 75 fighters built mainly for export by Curtiss before World War II. A few of these were in US service in December 1941, but by then had largely been replaced by the P-40B and C Tomahawk with Allison V-1710 liquid-cooled inline engine. Like the P-36, they featured guns mounted atop the cowling and firing through the propeller arc.

These were the most numerous fighters in the US arsenal at the time of the Pearl Harbor attack. By mid-1942, they were replaced by the new P-40E. This featured the longer 'F-series' V-1710 engine with a single-stage supercharger and saw the nose lengthened and deepened. Cowl guns were dispensed with, the armament consisting of six 12.7mm (0.50in) machine guns in the wings. The British called this new model the Kittyhawk, as did the Commonwealth nations which procured it in large numbers, including Canada, Australia and New Zealand. The Kittyhawks were called Warhawks by Curtiss and the US Army.

This P-40E, named 'Holdin' My Own', was the personal mount of First Lieutenant Dallas A. Clinger. Not one of the original 'Flying Tigers' pilots of the American Volunteer Group (AVG) who flew against the Japanese in China from late 1941, Clinger scored five aerial victories against the Japanese while flying with the 23rd Fighter Group, which succeeded the AVG in July 1942. The distinctive 'shark's-mouth' marking was copied by the AVG from illustrations of RAF Tomahawks in the Western Desert and was used by the 23rd Fighter Grouop on P40s and P-51s for the rest of the war. The 23rd went on to fly A-7 and A-10 attack aircraft in post-war years. The 76th Squadron is now the 76th Space Control Squadron (SPCS), 'America's first counterspace squadron', a non-flying unit based at Peterson Air Force Base, Colorado.

DOUGLAS A-20G HAVOC

647th Bomb Squadron, 410th Bomb Group, 97th Bomb Wing (Light), Ninth Air Force, United States Army Air Forces, Gosfield, Essex, 1944

DOUGLAS A-20G HAVOC

Specification
- **Type** twin-engined attack bomber
- **Crew** 2
- **Powerplant** two 1193kW (1600hp) Wright R-2600-23 Cyclone supercharged 14-cylinder radial piston engines
- **Performance** max speed 510km/h (317mph); service ceiling 7225m (23,700ft); range 1603km (996 miles)
- **Dimensions** wing span 18.67m (61ft 3in); length 14.32m (47ft); height 4.83m (15ft 10in)
- **Weight** 10,964kg (24,127lb) loaded
- **Armament** six 12.7mm (0.50in) Browning machine guns in nose, two in mid-upper turret and one in ventral position; bomb load of up to 2722kg (6000lb)

A 1938 US Army requirement for a twin-engined light bomber was met by Douglas with its Model 7, or DB-7, design, a high-winged single-tail aircraft which first flew in October that year. The French initially showed more interest in the DB-7 than the United States, ordering nearly 200. About half of these reached France before June 1940, and the rest were delivered to the United Kingdom as the Boston, as were a further 200 examples, some of which became Havoc night-fighters.

The first US Army Air Forces (USAAF) version was the A-20, with a glazed nose like the French and British aircraft, but a strengthened airframe. The next important version and the first with a solid nose rather than a glazed bomb-aimer's position was the A-20G. The flexible gun mount in an open position was replaced with a powered Martin gun turret during A-20G production. The wings were strengthened to allow up to four 227kg (500lb) bombs under the wings. The Royal Air Force's Bostons were reasonably effective as low-level bombers, but the USAAF used them either at medium altitude or as low-level strafers, particularly in the Pacific. To this end, some had additional 'package' guns on the fuselage sides, like the nose guns fired by the single pilot.

'Joker' was an A-20G-35-DO of the 647th Bomb Squadron, known as 'Beaty's Raiders'. The squadron and its parent group, the 410th Bomb Group (Light), were formed in July 1943 and entered combat in May 1944 as part of the Ninth Air Force, which was mainly used on tactical missions to support the advancing troops. In September 1944, the group moved to forward airfields in France. Just at the end of the European war, the 410th made the transition to the A-26 Invader, Douglas's own successor to the A-20.

DOUGLAS SBD-1 DAUNTLESS

VMB-2, Marine Air Group 11, US Marine Corps, Quantico, Virginia, 1941

DOUGLAS SBD-1 DAUNTLESS

Specification
- **Type** carrier-based dive bomber
- **Crew** 2
- **Powerplant** one 746kW (1000hp)Wright R-1820-32 Cyclone radial piston engine
- **Performance** max speed 427km/h (266mph); service ceiling 9175m (31,000ft); range 972km (604 miles)
- **Dimensions** wing span 12.65m (41ft 6in); length 9.68m (31ft 9in); height 3.91m (12ft 10in)
- **Weight** 3183kg (7018lb) loaded
- **Armament** two 12.7mm (0.50in) Browning machine guns in the nose and one 7.62mm (0.30in) in the rear cockpit; bomb load of one 454kg (1000lb) bomb under centre fuselage and two 45kg (100lb) bombs under wings

The Douglas Dauntless was developed from the Northrop BT-1 light bomber. At the time Northrop was a subsidiary of Douglas, and, when the parent company absorbed it in 1939, Ed Heinemann revised the design to meet a US Navy requirement for a carrier-based dive bomber. The prototype XSBD-1 was a conversion from a BT-1 and flew in early 1939. In April, the US Marine Corps (USMC) and US Navy placed orders for the SBD-1 and SBD-2, respectively, the latter having increased fuel capacity and twin rear guns, rather than the single weapon of the USMC version.

There were 57 examples of the SBD-1 built, and they entered service with Marine dive-bomber squadron VMB-2 in late 1940. The first SBD-2s joined the US Navy in early 1941. Sometimes called the 'Barge' or the 'Clunk', or the 'Speedy One' (an ironic reading of SBD-1), the nickname that stuck was 'Slow but Deadly'. Using its swinging bomb cradle to make high-angle dive attacks, the Dauntless was a very accurate bomber and could defend itself well with its fixed and flexible armament.

In the colour-coded US Navy and USMC of the 1930s, the full red cowling, red bands and code letters on the SBD-1 illustrated all indicated the first aircraft of the first section, which was flown by the squadron commander. This in fact is the second production Dauntless, Bureau Number 1597. Its fate is unknown, but is not believed to have been lost in an accident or to enemy action.

Most of the SBD-1s were used for training, but some were lost during the attack on Hawaii on 7 December 1941. The later SBD-3 was vital in the Battle of Midway in June 1942 and played an important role at Guadalcanal and in other island campaigns in the early part of the Pacific war.

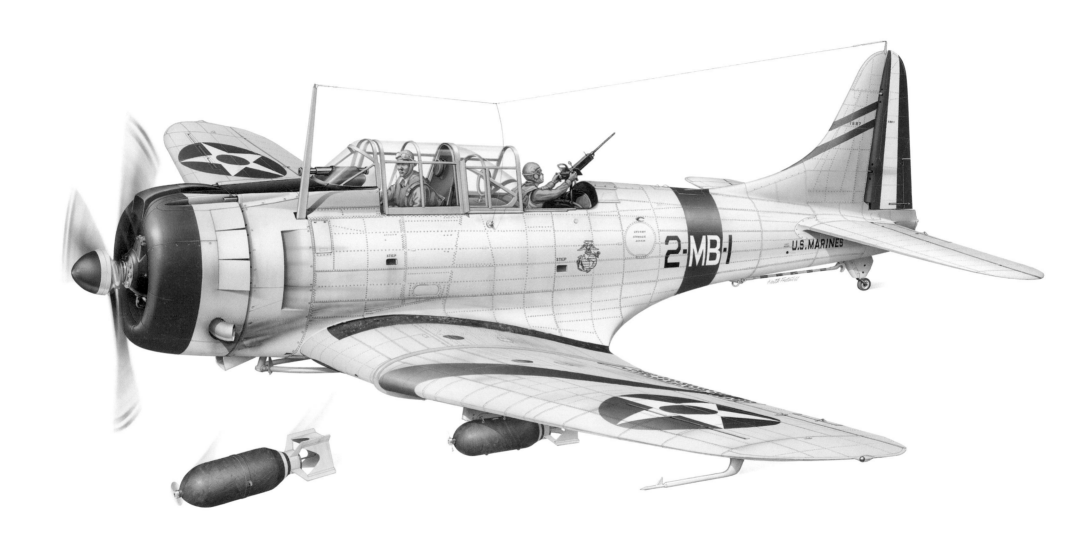

FOCKE-WULF FW 190F-2

5th Staffel, II Gruppe,
Schlachtgeschwader 1,
Luftwaffe, Kharkov, Soviet Union, 1943

FOCKE-WULF FW 190F-2

Specification
- **Type** single-engined ground-attack fighter
- **Crew** 1
- **Powerplant** one 1567kW (2100hp) BMW 801D-2 14-cylinder radial piston engine
- **Performance** max speed 634km/h (394mph); service ceiling 13,410m (44,000ft); range 750km (466 miles)
- **Dimensions** wing span 10.51m (34ft 5.5 in); length 8.95m (29ft 4.25in); height 3.95m (12ft 11.5in)
- **Weight** 4400kg (9700lb) loaded
- **Armament** two 7.9mm (0.31in) MG 17 machine guns in upper fuselage, with 1000 rounds each and two 20mm MG151/20 cannon with 200 rounds each in wings; bomb load of up to 350kg (802lb)

The Focke-Wulf Fw 190 arose from a 1937 German Air Ministry requirement for a new single-seat fighter. Designer Kurt Tank took up the challenge and produced a compact fighter around the most powerful engine available. The prototype Fw 190V1 first flew in June 1939, powered by a BMW 139 air-cooled radial. Production aircraft had the 1193kW (1600hp) BMW 801 14-cylinder engine. The first Fw 190As saw combat over the Channel front in September 1941, completely surprising Allied intelligence, who until then had no inkling of the new fighter's development. The early 190s were superior to the Spitfire V, setting in train a seesaw of development that was to last throughout the war.

The Fw 190A-8 was the principal early version, with 1334 built. Armament was two machine guns and four cannon. The Fw 190F was a dedicated fighter-bomber with provision for a 500kg (1102lb) bomb under the fuselage and two 250kg (551lb) bombs under the wings. The F-2 subtype was based on the A-8 and introduced a new blown canopy. On the Eastern Front, the ground-attack units (*Schlachtgeschwadern*, literally 'slaughter wings') equipped with the Fw 190 were mainly used against Soviet armour, vehicles, outposts and troops, using a wide variety of anti-personnel and anti-armour weapons. Russian fighters were often encountered and a number of *Schlacht* pilots scored over 20 aerial victories.

The second *Gruppe* of *Schlachtgeschwader* 1 (II./SG 1) converted from the Ju 87 Stuka to the Fw 190F2 at Deblin-Irena, Poland in March 1943. The 5th *Staffel* (squadron) used red spinners and code letters with white trim, but it was thought that red could be mistaken for Soviet markings, and these were changed to black before the unit entered combat. The black triangle was a symbol of the *Luftwaffe*'s ground attack arm.

FOCKE-WULF FW 200C-1 CONDOR

I./KG 40 IV Fliegerkorps,
Luftflotte 3, Bordeaux-Mérignac,
France, 1940

Initially designed and flown as an airliner, the Focke-Wulf Condor first flew in July 1937, after a remarkably quick development. The Japanese were impressed by the Condor, and ordered several airliner versions. Additionally, the tenth development aircraft was completed as a prototype maritime patrol aircraft for the Imperial Japanese Navy. Japan's Condors were never delivered.

On Hitler's orders, in the spring of 1939 the *Luftwaffe* Chief of Staff directed a young officer, *Oberstleutnant* Edgar Petersen, to establish a new unit to attack ships in the Bay of Biscay. To fulfil this role, the Condor was adapted as the Fw 200C-0, and entered service with the 1st *Gruppe* of *Kampfgeschwader* 40 (I.KG 40) in 1940, initially with limited armament. The first true production model was the Fw 200C-1, armed with one cannon and four machine guns, and racks for bombs and mines under the wings and central fuselage. The Condor was not stressed for all this extra weight, and many suffered structural failure on landing.

Later versions had more guns and could even carry guided anti-ship missiles. Until the Allies introduced long-range patrol aircraft of their own and were able to base fighters in Iceland, the Condor was the 'scourge of the Atlantic' and took a heavy toll of shipping from bases all the way from Norway to southern France.

Fw 200C-1 F8+AH was normally flown by *Gruppe* commander Edgar Petersen and his crew, who were quite successful judging by the ship kill markings on the aircraft's tailfin. On 5 February 1941, while flown by another pilot, this aircraft's luck ran out. During an attack on a British convoy to the west of Ireland, it was hit and damaged by return fire. While attempting to reach its base near Bordeaux, the aircraft encountered dense fog and flew into Cashelfeane Hill, in County Cork. Five of the six crew aboard were killed; the sixth was badly burnt but survived.

FOCKE-WULF FW 200C-1 CONDOR

Specification
- **Type** four-engined maritime patrol bomber
- **Crew** 5
- **Powerplant** four 619kW (830hp) BMW 132H radial piston engines
- **Performance** max speed 360km/h (224mph); service ceiling 6000m (19,685ft); range 4440km (2795 miles)
- **Dimensions** wing span 32.82m (107ft 8in); length 23.46m (76ft 11.5in); height 6.3m (20ft 8in)
- **Weight** 22,700kg (50,045lb) loaded
- **Armament** three 7.92mm (0.31in) MG 15 machine guns and one 20-mm MG FF cannon; bomb load of up to four 250kg (551lb) bombs or two 1000kg (2205lb) mines

GRUMMAN F4F-3 WILDCAT

VMF-121, United States Marine Corps, Tafuna, Samoa, 1941

GRUMMAN F4F-3 WILDCAT

Specification

- **Type** single-seat carrier/land-based fighter
- **Crew** 1
- **Powerplant** one 895kW (1200hp) Pratt & Whitney R-1830-76 nine-cylinder radial engine
- **Performance** max speed 534km/h (332mph); service ceiling 10,577m (34,700ft); range 1448km (900 miles)
- **Dimensions** wing span 11.58m (38ft); length 8.81m (28ft 11in); height 3.02m (9ft 11in)
- **Weight** 3396kg (7847lb) loaded
- **Armament** four 12.7mm (0.50in) Browning machine guns

Grumman's Wildcat was the most important early-war US Navy and US Marine Corps (USMC) fighter and could trace its lineage back to the 'flying barrel' biplanes of the 1930s. Following the FF, F2F and F3F designs, a contract for a smaller biplane prototype designated XF4F-1 was awarded in 1936. Almost as soon as work began, it was realized that the biplane was becoming uncompetitive. The other fighters in the race were all-metal monoplanes, and Grumman scrapped the original XF4F-1 design and went ahead with a monoplane, designated XF4F-2, although it owed little to its precursor.

September 1937 saw the first flight of the XF4F-2, but an accident and failure to win the US Navy's competition saw the aircraft redesigned and rebuilt as the XF4F-3, which flew in February 1939 and formed the basis of the production Wildcat. The F4F-3 did not have folding wings and was just able to fit into carrier elevators. The later F4F-4 and the General Motors–built FM-1 and FM-2 had wings that folded back alongside the fuselage, as on the TBF/TBM Avenger.

This F4F-3 was flown by First Lieutenant R. Bruce Porter, who flew Wildcats with VMF-121, VMF-141 and VMF-111. He was reassigned to VMF-121 shortly before the squadron made the transition to the F4U Corsair. VMF-121 was credited with downing 208 Japanese planes, more than 160 of them with Wildcats; however, Porter flew his first combat mission and scored his first kill on 12 June 1943 in an F4U Corsair flying from Guadalcanal. Eventually he was to score five victories by day and night, and became the only Marine aviator to score kills in both the Corsair and the Hellcat.

GRUMMAN F6F-5P HELLCAT

VF-84, CVG-84, United States Navy,
USS **Bunker Hill,** *1945*

GRUMMAN F6F-5P HELLCAT

Specification
- **Type** single-seat carrier-based fighter
- **Crew** 1
- **Powerplant** one 1492kW (2000hp) Pratt & Whitney R-2800-10W 18-cylinder radial piston engine
- **Performance** 612km/h (380mph); service ceiling 11370m (37,300 ft); range 1674km (1040 miles)
- **Dimensions** 13.05m (42ft 10in); length 10.23m (33ft 7in); height 3.99m (13ft 1in)
- **Weight** 6991kg (15,413lb)
- **Armament** six 12.7mm (0.50in) Browning machine guns in wings and up to two 454kg (1000lb) bombs or six 127mm (6in) rockets

In 1938, the airframe of the XF4F-2, predecessor of the Wildcat, was to be modified with the 1492kW (2000hp) R-2600 radial, but it was soon realized that this was impractical, not least because the necessarily larger propeller would not clear the ground. A complete redesign was begun, but this was put on hold as development of the Wildcat progressed. It was dusted off to produce a new fighter to replace the Wildcat in US Navy and US Marine Corps (USMC) service.

The XF6F-1 first flew in October 1942 and was broadly similar to the F4F, but was much larger (with the largest wing area of any US single-seat fighter), and its undercarriage retracted into the rearwards-folding wing. The armament was six machine guns. Deliveries of the production F6F-3 started in early 1943, and the Hellcat first saw combat on the Marcus Island raid, site of a Japanese naval base, which took place in August 1943.

The F6F-5 appeared from 1944 with relatively few changes to the F6F-3. The canopy glazing was altered and provision for bombs and rockets was added. This was the main production version, with more than half the 12,275 Hellcats being F6F-5s. A subvariant was the F6F-5P, which could carry cameras for the tactical reconnaissance role.

This F6F-5P was based aboard the USS *Bunker Hill* in February 1945 during a series of raids over Tokyo alongside two Marine Corsair units. VF-84 also flew some of the F6F-5N night-fighter model. The unit lost many aircraft and pilots when the *Bunker Hill* was hit by a Kamikaze attack on 11 May 1945. The squadron was disestablished on 8 October 1945. Later its nickname ('Jolly Rogers') and traditions were adopted by a new VF-84 and carried through to the modern era with the F-14 Tomcat.

GRUMMAN TBM-3 AVENGER

VT-4, CVG-4, United States Navy,
USS Essex, 1945

GRUMMAN TBM-3 AVENGER

Specification
- **Type** carrier-based torpedo bomber
- **Crew** 3
- **Powerplant** one 1417kW (1900hp) Wright R-2600-20 Cyclone 14-cylinder twin-row radial piston engine
- **Performance** max speed 414km/h (257mph); service ceiling 6523m (21,400ft); range 4321km (2685 miles)
- **Dimensions** wing span 16.51m (54ft 2in); length 12.42m (40ft 9in); height 4.19m (13ft 9in)
- **Weight** 7215kg (15,905lb) loaded
- **Armament** two forward-firing 12.7mm (0.5in) machine guns in wings, one in dorsal turret and one 7.62mm (0.30in) machine gun in ventral position; bomb load of up to 907kg (2000lb) or one 1383kg (3050lb) torpedo

---

The Avenger was the largest single-engined aircraft of World War II. Its combat debut at the Battle of Midway was a disaster, with all but one aircraft lost, but with improved tactics the Avenger became extremely effective as a torpedo bomber and a level bomber against ground targets. In 1939, the US Navy issued a requirement for a replacement for the TBD Devastator, capable of 483km/h (300mph) and 1600km (1000 miles) range with a 908kg (2000lb) payload. This was met by Grumman with its TBF design. This carried its torpedoes internally and had more defensive armament, as well as better all-round performance due to its huge Wright R-2600-20 14-cylinder double-row radial engine.

The XTBF-1 flew in August 1941 and was named Avenger following the Pearl Harbor attack on 7 December. The Royal Navy had nearly 1000 TBFs, which they named the Tarpon, and New Zealand was another wartime user. Nearly 3000 TBF-1s were built by the parent company, but General Motors Eastern Aircraft Division produced over 7500 as the TBM, most of which were the TBM-3 model. There were over 20 subvariants of the Avenger, including those with specialized anti-submarine equipment and search radar. Post-war, others became transports, ambulances and fire-fighting aircraft.

This TBM-3 was assigned to Torpedo Squadron 4, part of Air Group 4 (CVG-4) aboard the USS *Essex* at the time of a series of attacks on Japanese shipping off the coast of Indochina (Vietnam) in January 1945. These were some of the last attacks made by fixed-wing torpedo-carrying aircraft against ships. CVG-4 was only aboard *Essex* for a few weeks in January and February 1945 before the carrier was hit by a Kamikaze and had to withdraw for repairs. VT-4 with 22 Avengers was partnered by two Marine Corsair squadrons and one Navy SB2C Helldiver unit.

HANDLEY PAGE HALIFAX B.MK VII

No. 408 'Goose' Squadron, No. 6 Group, Royal Canadian Air Force, Linton-on-Ouse, Yorkshire, 1944

HANDLEY PAGE HALIFAX B.MK VII

Specification
- **Type** four-engined heavy bomber
- **Crew** 7
- **Powerplant** four 1231kW (1650hp) Bristol Hercules XVI air-cooled 14-cylinder radial engines
- **Performance** max speed 460km/h (285mph); service ceiling 5669m (18,600ft); range 1657km (1030 miles)
- **Dimensions** wing span 31.76m (104ft 2in); length 21.82 m (71ft 7in); height 6.32m (20ft 9in)
- **Weight** 29,448kg (65,000lb) loaded
- **Armament** two 12.7mm (0.50in) Browning machine guns in tail turret, four 7.7mm (0.303in) Browning machine guns in mid upper turret and one in nose; bomb load of up to 5895kg (13,000lb)

Like the Avro Lancaster, the Halifax began as a twin-engined design, although it was revised to take four Merlins before the first example flew in October 1939. The Mk I and Mk II versions with various armament layouts had Merlins, while the Mk III introduced the Bristol Hercules radial. The Mk VII was essentially similar, but was fitted with lower powered versions of the Hercules and a glazed dome in place of the rotating front turret. Subvariants were used to drop agents and commandos, and as troop transports, glider tugs and freighters. The Halifax had lesser performance than the Lancaster and usually flew at a lower altitude. The Canadian squadrons in No. 6 Group of Bomber Command were largely equipped with the Halifax for much of the war.

'Vicky the Vicious Virgin' is a rare example of a Royal Air Force (RAF) bomber with large and vivid nose art. The Canadian squadrons were less restrained than their British colleagues in this respect. PN230 was one of a batch of 150 B.IIIs and B.VIIs built under contract by Fairey Aviation at Stockport. Its only operational unit was No. 408 'Goose' Squadron, and it survived the war, being sold for scrap in 1949.

No. 408 Squadron received Halifaxes in September 1942, flying the Mk V and then the Mk II until October 1943. From then until September 1944 the squadron flew the radial-engined Lancaster Mk II, but reverted to the Halifax Mks III and VII in September 1944 and flew them until the end of the war. In post-war years, No. 408 became a transport squadron, flying Dakotas and C-119 Boxcars. The squadron is still in existence with the modern Canadian Armed Forces, flying the CH-146 Griffon helicopter from CFB Edmonton, Alberta.

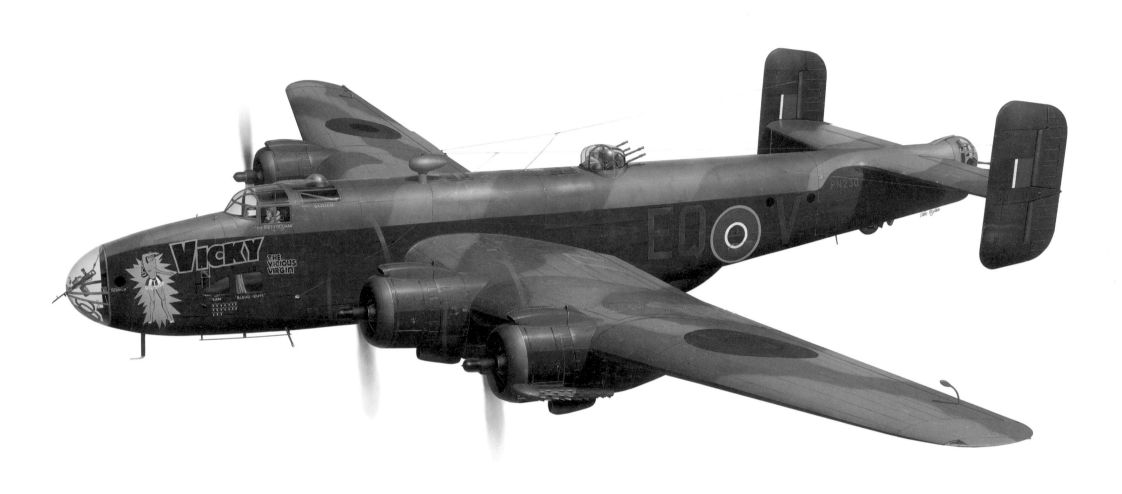

HAWKER HURRICANE MK IID

*No. 6 Squadron, Desert Air Force,
Royal Air Force, Tunisia, 1943*

HAWKER HURRICANE MK IID

Specification
- **Type** single-seat ground-attack fighter
- **Crew** 1
- **Powerplant** one 955kW (1280hp) Rolls-Royce Merlin XX V-12 piston engine
- **Performance** max speed 460km/h (286 mph); service ceiling 10,365m (34,000ft); range 740km (460 miles)
- **Dimensions** wing span 12.19m (40ft 0in); length 9.81m (32ft 2in); height 3.95m (12ft 11.5in)
- **Weight** 3719kg (8200lb) loaded
- **Armament** two 40mm Vickers S guns in underwing pods and two 7.7mm (0.303in) Browning machine guns in wings

Built to essentially the same specification as the Spitfire and fitted with the same Merlin engine, the Hawker Hurricane was slower and less manoeuvrable, but was a more stable gun platform and was often available where and when Spitfires were not. The Hurricane prototype flew in November 1935 and was the most numerous and effective fighter in Royal Air Force (RAF) service during the Battle of Britain.

Although thereafter quickly replaced on home defence duties, the Hurricane was issued to units in the Mediterranean, North Africa and Far East, where it was often the best Allied fighter available. Hurricanes distinguished themselves in the defence of Malta, in North Africa and on the Burma front.

The Hurricane Mk II had a Merlin XX with two-stage supercharger and spawned many subvariants, differing mainly in their armament. The IID was a dedicated ground-attack version, armed with two heavy cannon for the tank-busting role and fitted with additional armour on the undersides.

HV663 was built in late 1943 and shipped to North Africa, where it was initially used at No. 71 Operational Training Unit (OTU) at Carthago, Sudan. It was the assigned to No. 6 Squadron, nicknamed the 'Flying Can-Openers', which had operated the Hurricane Mk IID from June 1942. The squadron moved from Egypt into the combat zone in February 1943, and supported the Eighth Army all the way to Tunisia, taking a large toll of *Afrika Korps* vehicles with their powerful 40-mm cannon.

Success with the Mk IID led to the Hurricane Mk IV, which possessed the same gun armament as the Mk IID, but was capable of exchanging the cannon pods for rockets or bombs.

HAWKER TYPHOON Mk 1B

No. 175 Squadron, 2nd Tactical Air Force, Royal Air Force, Normandy, 1944

HAWKER TYPHOON Mk 1B

Specification
- **Type** low-level interceptor and ground-attack aircraft
- **Crew** 1
- **Powerplant** one 1566kW (2100hp) Napier Sabre 24-cylinder in-line engine
- **Performance** max speed 663km/h (412mph); service ceiling 10,730m (35,200ft); range 1577km (980 miles)
- **Dimensions** wing span 12.67m (41ft 7in); length 9.73m (31ft 11in); height 4.67m (15ft 4in)
- **Weight** 5171kg (11,400lb) loaded
- **Armament** four 20mm (0.79in) cannon in wing; external bomb load of up to 907kg (2000lb) or eight 27kg (60lb) rocket projectiles

The Hawker Typhoon was designed in response to a 1937 Air Staff requirement for an aircraft capable of taking on heavily armed and armoured escort fighters such as the Messerschmitt Bf 110. The first of two prototypes flew for the first time on 24 February 1940. The first production aircraft, however, did not fly until May 1941.

Delays in production were blamed on the unreliability of the massive Sabre engine, but there were other problems, including structural failures of the rear fuselage. These had still not been cured when the Royal Air Force's No. 56 Squadron at Duxford was issued with the Typhoon in September 1941, and several pilots were lost in accidents. Moreover, although the aircraft was fast and handled well at medium and low altitudes, its performance at high altitude was inferior to that of both the Focke-Wulf 190 and the Messerschmitt Bf 109F, and its rate of climb was poor. In fact, only its success at intercepting German low-level intruders saved its from being cancelled.

By the end of 1943, with the aircraft's technical problems cured and a growing number of Typhoon squadrons striking hard at the enemy's communications, shipping and airfields, the Typhoon was heading for its place in history as the most potent Allied fighter-bomber of all. After the Allied landings in Normandy, the name of the rocket-armed Typhoon became synonymous with the destruction of enemy armour, especially in the Falaise Gap during the German retreat from Normandy. In all, 3330 Typhoons were built. The Mk 1B was the major production version, with more than 3000 being completed.

HEINKEL HE 111H-22 AND FIESELER FI 103

III/Kampfgeschwader 3, Luftwaffe, Venlo, The Netherlands, 1944

HEINKEL HE 111H-22 AND FIESELER FI 103

Specification
- **Type** bomber and missile combination
- **Crew** 5
- **Powerplant** two 1007kW (1350hp) Junkers Jumo 211F inverted V-12 engines
- **Performance** max speed 436km/h (271mph); service ceiling 6700m (21,980ft) range 1950km (1212 miles)
- **Dimensions** wing span: 22.60m (74ft 1in); length 16.40m (53ft 9|in); height 3.40m (13ft 1in)
- **Weight** 14,000kg (30,865lb) loaded
- **Armament** one 20mm (0.79in) MG FF cannon in nose, one 13mm (0.51in) MG131 gun in dorsal position, two 7.92mm (0.31in) MG15 guns in rear of ventral gondola and two 7.92mm (0.31in) MG81 guns in each of two beam positions; one Fieseler Fi.103 flying bomb

The most fascinating of all the varied operations carried out by the versatile Heinkel He 111H bomber were those undertaken by the *Luftwaffe*'s *Kampfgeschwader* (G) 3, which was equipped with the Heinkel He 111H-22 variant. Following experiments at Peenemünde, the German secret weapons research establishment, in 1943, several He 111H-6s, H-16s and H-21s were modified to carry a Fieseler Fi 103 (V-1) missile under the starboard wing and given the new designation He 111H-22. The type was assigned to the newly formed III/*Kampfgeschwader* (KG) 3, which became operational at Venlo and Gilze-Rijn in the Netherlands in July 1944.

By the end of August 1944, the unit had launched 300 V-1s against London, 90 against Southampton and 20 against Gloucester. In October 1944 the unit, now redesignated II/KG 53 and substantially reinforced, was operating from bases in Germany. With a strength of about 100 He 111H-22s, KG 53's principal target was London, but it also launched V-21 attacks on other UK cities towards the end of the year. Perhaps the most notable was the launching of 50 V-1s against Manchester on 24 December 1944.

Despite the development of special night-attack techniques by the Germans, the lumbering combination of He 111 and the V-1 proved easy prey for the Royal Air Force's Mosquito night fighters, which patrolled constantly over the sea on the bombers' approach routes, often directed to their targets by radar picket ships. By the time operations ceased on 14 January 1945, KG 53 had lost 77 aircraft, 41 of them on operations.

ILYUSHIN IL-2M3

*566th Shturmovik Aviation Squadron,
277th Shturmovik Aviation Division,
Soviet Frontal Air Forces, 1944*

ILYUSHIN IL-2M3

Specification
- **Type** armoured ground-attack aircraft
- **Crew** 2
- **Powerplant** one 1320kW (1770hp) Mikulin AM-38F liquid-cooled in-line engine
- **Performance** max speed 404km/h (251mph); service ceiling 6000m (19,685ft); range 800km (497 miles)
- **Dimensions** wing span 14.60m (47ft 10in); length 11.60m (38ft); height 3.40m (11ft 2in)
- **Weight** 6360kg (14,021lb) loaded
- **Armament** (typical) wing-mounted armament of two 37mm (1.46in) and two 7.62mm (0.30in) guns, and one 12.7mm (0.50in) machine gun in the rear cockpit; 200 PTAB hollow-charge anti-tank bombs, or eight RS-82 or RS-132 rocket projectiles

The Ilyushin Il-2 Shturmovik assault aircraft was ordered into full production By March 1941, before the German invasion of June of the same year, 249 examples had been produced. The lack of a rear gun position proved to be a serious drawback, however, and losses in action were heavy.

A modified single-seat Il-2M, with a boosted engine and new armament, began to reach Soviet frontline units in the autumn of 1942, and this version was used in considerable numbers during the battle for Stalingrad that winter. Meanwhile, further modifications were under way. The armoured forward section was extended rearwards to accommodate a rear gunner's cockpit. The new two-seater variant, the Il-2m3, entered service in August 1943, and thereafter played a prominent and often decisive part in the campaigns on the Eastern Front.

The Il-2 is probably best remembered for its part in the great armoured battle of Kursk in July 1943. Following a series of experiments, Il-2s were fitted with two long-barrelled anti-tank cannon, and these were used with devastating effect at Kursk on the latest German Tiger and Panther tanks. The number of Il-2s built reached the staggering total of 36,183 in all, more than any other type of aircraft in history.

The Il-2m3 illustrated here was flown by Lieutenant V.I. Mykhlik, officer commanding the 566th Squadron. The slogan on the rear fuselage aft of the red star reads 'Revenge for Khrishtenko' (a squadron pilot who had been killed earlier), while the legend forward of the star reads 'For Leningrad'.

JUNKERS JU 52/3M

*I Gruppe, Kampfgeschwader zbV
(Transport Wing) 172, Luftwaffe
Italy, 1943*

JUNKERS JU 52/3M

Specification
- **Type** transport aircraft
- **Crew** 2/3, plus 18 troops or 12 stretcher cases
- **Powerplant** three 544kW (730hp) BMW 132T-2 nine-cylinder radial engines
- **Performance** max speed 286km/h (178mph); service ceiling 5900m (19,360ft); range 1305km (811 miles)
- **Dimensions** wing span: 29.20m (95ft 10in); length 19.90m (62ft); height 4.52m (14ft 10in)
- **Weight** 11,030kg (24,317lb) loaded
- **Armament** four 7.92mm (0.31in) machine guns

The story of the Junkers Ju 52/3m, one of the most famous transport aircraft in history, began on 13 October 1930, with the maiden flight of the single-engined Ju 52/1m commercial transport. Eighteen months later, a new variant of the basic design appeared: this was the Ju 52/3m, fitted with three 429kW (575hp) BMW 132A radial engines (licence-built Pratt & Whitney Hornets). In 1934, a military version of the civil Ju 52/3m airliner was produced for use by the still-secret *Luftwaffe*. Designated Ju 52/3mg3e, the aircraft was designed as a heavy bomber. In 1934–35, no fewer than 450 Ju 52/3ms were delivered to the *Luftwaffe*. The type featured prominently in the Spanish Civil War, flying 5400 sorties for the loss of eight aircraft.

In April 1940, the Ju 52 was at the forefront of the invasions of Denmark and Norway. About 475 Ju 52s were available for the invasion of the Netherlands, and 493 took part in the invasion of Crete in May 1941. By the end of the year, around 300 Ju 52s were operating in the Mediterranean theatre. Between 5 and 22 April 1943, no fewer than 432 German transport aircraft, mostly Ju 52s, were destroyed as they tried to fly in supplies to Axis forces trapped in Tunisia. On the Russian front, five Ju 52 *Gruppen* took part in the Stalingrad airlift. Total production of the Ju 52/3m between 1939 and 1944, including civil models, was 4845 aircraft.

The example illustrated here is a Junkers Ju 52/3mg5e of KGzbV 172. On its nose and tailfin, the aircraft carries a badge depicting Iolanthe, a flying cartoon pig popular in Germany.

JUNKERS JU 87B-2 STUKA

I Gruppe, Stukageschwader 76, Luftwaffe, France, July 1940

JUNKERS JU 87B-2 STUKA

Specification
- **Type** dive-bomber
- **Crew** 2
- **Powerplant** one 895kW (1200hp) Junkers Jumo 211D inverted-Vee engine
- **Performance** max speed 380km/h (237mph); service ceiling 8000m (26,248ft); range 600km (372 miles)
- **Dimensions** wing span 13.80m (45ft 3.33in); length 11.00m (37ft 1in); height 3.88m (12ft 9in)
- **Weight** 4250kg (9321lb) loaded
- **Armament** three 7.92mm (0.31in) machine guns; external bomb load of up to 1000kg (2205lb)

Although the word Stuka – an abbreviation of *Sturzkampfflugzeug*, which literally translates as 'diving combat aircraft' – was applied to all German bomber aircraft with a dive-bombing capability during World War II, it will forever be associated with the Junkers Ju 87. The first prototype Ju 87V1 was flown for the first time in the late spring 1935, powered by a 477kW (640hp) Rolls-Royce Kestrel engine. In December 1937, three production Ju 87A-1s were sent to Spain for operational trials with the *Kondor* Legion, the German units flying in support of the Spanish Nationalists.

The Ju 87A-2 subseries, the next to appear, was succeeded on the production line in 1938 by an extensively modified version, the Ju 87B. By the outbreak of World War II, first-line Stuka units had standardized on the Ju 87B-1, which was fitted with the more powerful 820kW (1100hp) Junkers Jumo 211A 12-cylinder engine with fuel injection. The most important external change was the replacement of the A model's 'trousered' undercarriage by a 'spatted' one, with close-fitting streamlined oleo covers and streamlined wheel spats. The Ju 87B-2 was similar, but was powered by a 895kW (1200hp) Junkers Jumo 211D engine with moveable radiator flaps. An anti-shipping version of the Ju 87B-2 was known as the Ju 87R. The next production model was the Ju 87D, several subseries of which were produced in some quantity. The last Stuka variant was the Ju 87G, a standard Ju 87D-5 converted to carry two BK37 cannon (37mm Flak 18 guns) under the wing.

The aircraft pictured at right is a Junkers Ju 87B-2 Stuka of I *Gruppe*, *Stukageschwader* 76, France, July 1940, flown by Hauptmann Walter Siegel.

JUNKERS JU 88A-4

I Gruppe, Kampfgeschwader 30, Luftwaffe, Netherlands, 1940

JUNKERS JU 88A-4

Specification
- **Type** bomber
- **Crew** 4
- **Powerplant** two 999kW (1340hp) Junkers Jumo 211J inverted V-12 engines
- **Performance** max speed 450km/h (280mph); service ceiling 8200m (26,900ft); range 2730km (1696 miles)
- **Dimensions** wing span 20.00m (65ft 7|in); length 14.40m (47ft 3in); height 4.85m (15ft 11in)
- **Weight** 14,000kg (30,865lb) loaded
- **Armament** up to seven 7.92mm (0.31in) MG15 or MG81 machine guns; maximum internal and external bomb load of 3600kg (7935lb)

One of the most versatile and effective combat aircraft *ever* produced, the Junkers Ju 88 remained of vital importance to the Luftwaffe throughout World War II, serving as a bomber, dive bomber, night fighter, close support aircraft, long-range heavy fighter, reconnaissance aircraft and torpedo bomber. A pre-series batch of Ju 88A-0s was completed during the summer of 1939, the first production Ju 88A-1s being delivered to a test unit, *Erprobungskommando* 88.

In August 1939, this unit was redesignated I *Gruppe, Kampfgeschwader* 25 (I/KG 25), and soon afterwards it became I/KG 30, carrying out its first operational mission – an attack on British warships in the Firth of Forth – in September, making it the first unit to use the type in action. The same target was attacked on 16 October, when two Ju 88s were shot down by Spitfires.

The Ju 88A was built in 17 different variants up to the Ju 88A-17, with progressively uprated engines, enhanced defensive armament and improved defensive capability. The most widely used variant was the Ju 88A-4, which served in both Europe and North Africa. Twenty Ju 88A-4s were supplied to Finland, and some were supplied to Italy, Romania and Hungary. Some 7000 examples of the Ju 88A series were delivered.

The Ju 88As saw considerable action in the Balkans and the Mediterranean, and on the Eastern Front. They operated intensively during the German invasion of Crete, and were the principal threat to the island of Malta and its supply convoys. Some of their most outstanding service, however, was in the Arctic, where aircraft of KG 26 and KG 30, based in northern Norway, carried out devastating attacks on Allied convoys to Russia.

LAVOCHKIN LA-5FN

159th Fighter Aviation Regiment, Soviet Air Force, 1944

LAVOCHKIN LA-5FN

Specification

- **Type** fighter
- **Crew** 1
- **Powerplant** one 1230kW (1650hp) Ash-82FN radial engine
- **Performance** max speed 647km/h (402mph); service ceiling 11,000m (36,090ft); range 765km (475 miles)
- **Dimensions** wing span 9.80m (32ft 1in); length 8.67m (28ft 6in); height 2.54m (8ft 4in)
- **Weight** 3402kg (7500lb) loaded
- **Armament** two 20mm (0.79in) or 23mm (0.91in) cannon, plus provision for four 82mm (3.23in) RS-82 rockets or 150kg (330lb) of bombs or anti-tank mines

The Lavochkin La-5 was a radial-engined development of the earlier LaGG-3. The first combat formation to equip with the new fighter was the 287th Fighter Air Division, commanded by Colonel S.P. Danilin, which was assigned to the 8th Air Army on the Volga Front, in the defence of Stalingrad.

Early combats showed that the La-5 was a better all-round performer than the Messerschmitt 109G, although its rate of climb was inferior. Lavochkin therefore undertook some redesign work to reduce the fighter's weight and re-engined it with the 1126kW (1510hp) M-82FN direct-injection engine, which endowed the La-5 with better climbing characteristics and manoeuvrability than either the Bf 109G or the Focke-Wulf FW 190A-4.

In addition to Soviet Air Force units, the La-5FN also equipped the 1st Czech Fighter Regiment, the pilots of which scored some notable successes. A variant of the La-5, the La-7, had a similar engine to the La-5 and differed only in minor design detail. A two-seat trainer version, the La-5UTI, was also produced, bringing total production of the La-5/La-7 series to 21,975 examples by the end of the war. Although the primary role of the La-5/La-7 series was that of low- and medium-level fighter, it was occasionally assigned ground-attack missions.

This Lavochkin La-5FN was flown by Kapitan Petr Yakovlevich Likholetov of the 159th Fighter Aviation regiment. Petr Likholetov's final score was 30 enemy aircraft destroyed. Seriously injured in a car crash at the end of 1944, he died of his injuries on 13 July 1945.

LOCKHEED HUDSON

No. 48 Squadron, RAF Coastal Command, Royal Air Force, Gibraltar, 1943

LOCKHEED HUDSON

Specification
- **Type** twin-engined maritime patrol bomber
- **Crew** 4
- **Powerplant** two 895kW (1200hp) Pratt & Whitney R-1830-67 air-cooled radial engines
- **Performance** max speed 420km/h (261mph); service ceiling m (27,000ft); range 8230km (2160 miles)
- **Dimensions** wing span 19.96m (65ft 6in); length 19.96m (44ft 4in); height 3.63m (11ft 10in)
- **Weight** 8399kg (18,500lb) loaded
- **Armament** two forward-firing 7.62mm (0.303in) machine guns, two in dorsal turret and one in ventral position; up to 726kg (1600lb) bombs or depth charges

A conversion of Lockheed's Model 14 Super Electra design was ordered by the Royal Air Force (RAF) to fulfil its needs for a modern patrol bomber and navigation trainer in 1938. The prototype Hudson Mk I flew in December that year, and the initial order of 250 was completed by October 1939. The Hudson had a bomb bay instead of a freight hold and a Boulton-Paul defensive turret. There was also a ventral gun position, and two more forward-firing guns operated by the pilot. The airliner-type windows were retained and Hudsons saw much service as transports, as well as patrol aircraft with RAF Coastal Command and other users such as the Royal Australian Air Force and Royal New Zealand Air Force.

Development continued, and aircraft powered by both Wright Cyclone and Pratt & Whitney Twin Wasp engines rolled off the production lines in their hundreds with the designations A-28 and A-29. The Hudson VI was the A-28A. A total of 410 examples of the Hudson VI went to the RAF and others to Canada.

FK395 was delivered to No. 48 Squadron of Coastal Command, then used for a time by the Air Transport Auxiliary, presumably as a crew ferry. It was returned to No. 48 Squadron and finally ended up with the Airborne Forces Experimental Establishment at Ringway, Manchester. It was struck off charge in June 1946. No. 48 itself was based at North Front airfield on Gibraltar from December 1942 to February 1944, when it was reassigned to Transport Command and swapped its Hudsons for Dakotas. Equipped with ASV sea search radar and armed with bombs and depth charges, the Gibraltar-based Hudsons hunted German U-boats in the Mediterranean. On 28 March 1943, a No. 48 Squadron Hudson attacked and damaged *U-77* with depth charges east of Cartagena, Spain. The U-boat was finished off by another Hudson from No. 233 Squadron.

MACCHI MC.202

151 Squadriglia, 20 Gruppo, 51 Stormo, Regia Aeronautica, Sicily, 1942

MACCHI MC.202

Specification
- **Type** fighter
- **Crew** 1
- **Powerplant** one 802kW (1075hp) Alfa Romeo RA 1000 RC.411 12-cylinder inverted V-type
- **Performance** max speed 600km/h (373mph); service ceiling 11,500m (37,730ft); range 610km (379 miles)
- **Dimensions** wing span 10.58m (34ft 8|in); length 8.85m (29ft); height 3.50m (11ft 6in)
- **Weight** 2930kg (5490lb) loaded
- **Armament** two 12.7mm (0.5in) Breda-SAFAT and two 7.7mm (0.303in) machine guns; late-production aircraft, two 20mm (0.79in) cannon in wings

The Macchi MC.202 Folgore (Thunderbolt) was a direct descendant of the MC.200 Saetta (Lightning), the second of Italy's monoplane fighters, which was powered by a Fiat A74 radial engine and which first flew on 24 December 193. Deliveries to the *Regia Aeronautica* began in October 1939, and about 150 aircraft were in service by June 1940.

Attempts to improve the performance of the MC.200 began in 1938, but it was not until early in 1940 that a suitable engine became available in the shape of the German Daimler-Benz DB 601A-1 liquid cooled in-line engine. This was installed in a standard Saetta airframe and flown on 10 August 1940. The subsequent flight tests produced excellent results, and the aircraft, designated MC.202 Folgore, was ordered into production fitted with the licence-built DB 601, the engine being produced by Alfa Romeo as the RA.1000 RC.411.

The type entered service with the 1st *Stormo* at Udine in the summer of 1941, moving to Sicily to take part in operations over Malta in November. The Folgore remained in production until the Italian armistice of September 1943, although the rate of production was always influenced by the availability of engines. Macchi built 392 MC.202s, and around 1100 more were produced by other companies, mainly Breda.

The Macchi MC.202 Serie VII illustrated here was flown by Sergeant Ennio Tarantola of 151 *Squadriglia*, 20 *Gruppo*, 51 *Stormo* of the *Regia Aeronautica*. One of Italy's air aces, Tarantola had eight victories to his credit. His aircraft was named 'Dai Banana' ('Go, Banana!'), Tarantola having been a banana importer before the outbreak of World War II.

MESSERSCHMITT BF 109E-4

I Gruppe, Jagdgeschwader 3,
Luftwaffe, Grandvillier, France,
August 1940

MESSERSCHMITT BF 109E-4

Specification
- **Type** fighter
- **Crew** 1
- **Powerplant** one 876kW (1175hp) Daimler-Benz DB 601Aa
  12-cylinder inverted-Vee engine
- **Performance** max speed 560km/h (348mph); service ceiling 10,500m (34,450ft);
  range 660km (410 miles)
- **Dimensions** wing span 9.87m (32ft 4.5in); length 8.64m (28ft 4.5in);
  height 2.50m (8ft 2.33in)
- **Weight** 2665kg (5875lb) loaded
- **Armament** two 20mm (0.79in) cannon and two 7.92mm (0.31in) machine guns

The prototype Messerschmitt Bf 109V-1 flew for the first time in September 1935, and by the time World War II began in September 1939, 1060 Bf 109s of various subspecies were in service with the *Luftwaffe*'s fighter units. These included the Bf 109C and Bf 109D, which were already being replaced by the Bf 109E series; this model was to be the mainstay of the *Luftwaffe*'s fighter units throughout 1940. The series extended to the E-9, including models built as fighters, fighter-bombers and reconnaissance aircraft. Ten Bf 109Es were converted for operations from Germany's planned aircraft carrier, the *Graf Zeppelin*, under the designation Bf 109T.

The Bf 109E-3, the Royal Air Force's principal fighter opponent in the Battle of France, featured four MG17 machine guns, two mounted in the nose and two in the wings, and an engine-mounted FF cannon firing through the propeller boss; however, complaints about this arrangement led to the deletion of the nose-mounted cannon, two Oerlikons being installed in the wings of the Bf 109E-4 variant, which equipped most German fighter units during the Battle of Britain.

The Bf 109E-4 seen here was the personal aircraft of *Gruppenkommandeur* Hans von Hahn, and displays the emblem of I *Gruppe, Jagdgeschwader* (I/JG 3), a *Tatzelwurm* (serpent with claws), on its nose. The emblem was applied in green to *Stab* (staff flight) aircraft, in white to aircraft of the 1st *Staffel*, in red to aircraft of the 2nd *Staffel*, and in yellow to aircraft of the 3rd *Staffel*. Hans von Hahn ended the war with 34 kills.

MESSERSCHMITT BF 109K-4

III Gruppe, Jagdgeschwader 27, Luftwaffe, 1944

MESSERSCHMITT BF 109K-4

Specification
- **Type** fighter
- **Crew** 1
- **Powerplant** one 1100kW (1475hp) Daimler-Benz DB 605DCM 12-cylinder inverted-Vee engine
- **Performance** max speed 608km/h (378mph); service ceiling 11,550m (37,890ft); range 1000km (620 miles)
- **Dimensions** wing span 9.92m (32ft 6in); length 8.85m (29ft); height 2.50m (8ft 2in)
- **Weight** 3370kg (7438lb) loaded
- **Armament** one 20mm (0.79in) or 30mm (1.18in) cannon and two 12.7mm (0.50in) machine guns; external bomb load of 250kg (551lb)

The Messerschmitt Bf 109E was replaced by the best of all Bf 109 variants, the Bf 109F, which began to reach *Luftwaffe* units in France in May 1941 and which was superior in most respects to the principal Royal Air Force (RAF) fighter of the time, the Spitfire Mk V. The Bf 109F differed from the Bf 109E in having a generally cleaned-up airframe, redesigned engine cowling, wing, radiators and tail assembly.

The Bf 109F was succeeded in turn by the Bf 109G, which appeared late in 1942. The last operational versions of the Bf 109 were the K-4 and K-6, which both had DB 605D engines with MW 50 power boost. The last variant was the Bf 109K-14, with a DB-605L engine, but only two examples saw service, with *Jagdgeschwader* (JG) 52. The Bf 109G was built in both Spain (as the Hispano Ha-1109) and Czechoslovakia (as the Avia S-199). The Spanish aircraft, some of them re-engined with Rolls-Royce Merlins, served for many years following World War II, and some of the Czech-built aircraft were acquired by Israel in 1948, equipping No. 101 Squadron. In all, Bf 109 production reached a total of approximately 35,000 aircraft.

The Bf 109K was first issued to III/JG 27 and III/JG 77, the type entering combat on 2 November 1944, when JG 27 attacked P-51 Mustangs escorting American bombers bear Leipzig. The German unit suffered its worst single-day loss of the war in this engagement, wih 27 pilots killed and 11 wounded.

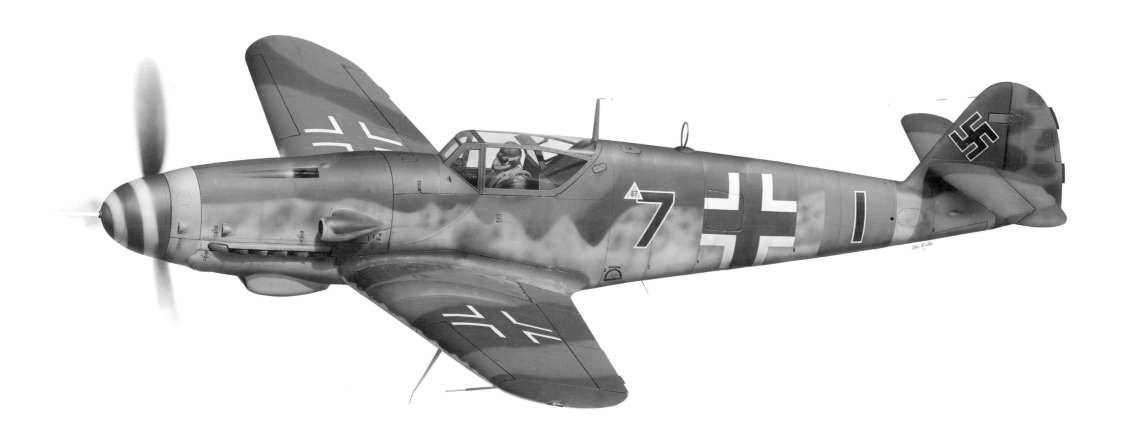

MESSERSCHMITT BF 110C-4/B

II Gruppe, Erprobungsgruppe 210, Luftwaffe, Summer 1940

MESSERSCHMITT BF 110C-4/B

Specification
- **Type** fast fighter-bomber
- **Crew** 2
- **Powerplant** two 1475hp Daimler-Benz DB 605B-1 12-cylinder inverted-Vee type engines
- **Performance** Max speed 550km/h (342mph); service ceiling 8000m (26,245ft); range 1300km (808 miles)
- **Dimensions** Wing span 16.25m (53ft 3in); length 13.05m (42ft 9in) including SN-2 radar antenna; height 4.18m (13ft 8|in)
- **Weight** 9888kg (21,799lb) loaded
- **Armament** two 20mm (0.79in) cannon and four 7.92mm (0.31in) machine guns in the nose and one 7.92mm (0.31in) machine gun in the rear cockpit; two 250kg (550lb) bombs

The first of three Bf 110 long-range escort fighter prototypes flew on 12 May 1936, with deliveries of the production Bf 110C-1 being made in 1938. The Bf 110C-2 differed from the C-1 only in its radio equipment. The C-2 and C-3 had modified 20mm (0.79in) cannon. A fighter-bomber version, the Bf 110C-4/B, carried two 250kg (550lb) bombs under the centre section. This variant was first issued to *Zerstörergeschwader* (ZG) I, and then to *Erprobungsgruppe* 210, formed to carry out attacks on Britain's coastal radar stations and other precision targets. The Bf 110C-5 was a special reconnaissance version.

Numerous other variants appeared, including the Bf 110C-6, with additional firepower, and the Bf 110C-7 specialized bomber, which could carry two 500kg (1100lb) bombs, making it necessary to strengthen the undercarriage. The Bf 110D and E could be used in either the fighter or bomber roles. The Bf 110F-1 (bomber), F-2 (heavy fighter), F-3 (long-range reconnaissance aircraft) and F-4 (night fighter) had 970kW (1300hp) DB 601F engines; however, the final major production aircraft, the Bf 110G, produced in larger numbers than any other variant, adopted the 1007kW (1350hp) DB 605 engine. It was as a night fighter, equipped with Lichtenstein AI radar, that the Bf 110 truly excelled.

The Messerschmitt Bf 110C-4/B seen here carries the *Wespe* (Wasp) insignia of ZG I, the 1st *Staffel* of which formed the nucleus of II/*Erprobungsgruppe* 210. The distinctive wasp marking was retained when the surviving aircraft were returned to their original unit in 1942.

MESSERSCHMITT ME 163

I Gruppe, Jagdgeschwader 400, Luftwaffe, Brandis, near Leipzig, Autumn 1944

MESSERSCHMITT ME 163

Specification
- **Type** rocket-powered interceptor
- **Crew** 1
- **Powerplant** one 1700kg (3748lb) thrust Walter 109-509A-2 rocket motor
- **Performance** max speed 955km/h (593mph); service ceiling 12,000m (39,370ft); range 35.5km (22 miles)
- **Dimensions** wing span 9.33m (30ft 7in); length 5.85m (19ft 2in); height 2.76m (9ft)
- **Weight** 4310kg (9502lb) loaded
- **Armament** two 30mm (1.18in) Mk 108 cannon in wing roots

The Me 163 Komet was based on the experimental DFS 194, designed in 1938 by Professor Alexander Lippisch and transferred, together with its design staff, to the Messerschmitt company for further development. The first two Me 163 prototypes were flown in the spring of 1941 as unpowered gliders, with the Me 163V-1 being transferred to Peenemünde later in the year to be fitted with its 750kg (1653lb) thrust Walter HWK R.II rocket motor. The fuel used was a highly volatile mixture of T-Stoff (80 per cent hydrogen peroxide; 20 per cent water) and C-Stoff (hydrazine hydrate, methyl alcohol and water).

The first rocket-powered flight was made in August 1941. During subsequent trials the Me 163 broke all existing world air speed records, reaching speeds of up to 1000km/h (620mph).

In May 1944, an operational Komet unit, *Jagdgeschwader* (JG) 400, began forming at Wittmundhaven and Venlo. Many Me 163s were lost in landing accidents. About 300 Komets were built, but JG 400 remained the only operational unit. The rocket fighter recorded only nine kills during its brief career, while at the same time losing 14 of its own aircraft in combat. All the victories were credited to I/JG 400, which ended the war at Nordholz in northern Germany and continued operating until the cessation of hostilities.

This Me 163 displays the emblem of I *Gruppe*, *Jagdgeschwader* 400 (I/JG 400), depicting the notorious liar Baron Münchausen riding a cannonball. I/JG 400 was formed at Bad Zwischenahn in February 1944, II *Gruppe* being formed later at Wittmundhaven.

MESSERSCHMITT ME 262

III Gruppe, 9th Staffel, Jagdgeschwader 3, Luftwaffe, Parchim, Northeast Germany, April 1945

MESSERSCHMITT ME 262

Specification
- **Type** jet fighter
- **Crew** 1
- **Powerplant** two 900kg (1984lb) thrust Junkers Jumo 109-004B turbojets
- **Performance** max speed: 870km/h (541mph); service ceiling 11,450m (37,565ft); range 1050km (652 miles)
- **Dimensions** wing span 12.51m (41ft); length 10.60m (34ft 9in); height 73.83m (11ft 6in)
- **Weight** 7130kg (15,720lb) loaded
- **Armament** four 30mm (1.18in) MK108 cannon in nose; 24 R4M unguided air-to-air missiles on underwing racks

---

Delays in the development of satisfactory engines, the massive damage caused by Allied air attacks and Hitler's later obsession with using the aircraft as a bomber rather than a fighter all meant that six years elapsed between the Me 262 taking shape on Messerschmitt's drawing board and its entry into *Luftwaffe* service. The jet fighter presented a serious threat to Allied air superiority during the closing weeks of 1944.

Two versions were developed in parallel: the Me 262A-2a Sturmvogel (Stormbird) bomber variant and the Me 262A-1a fighter. The Sturmvogel was issued to *Kampfgeschwader* (KG) 51 'Edelweiss' in September 1944; other bomber units that armed with the type at a later date were KG 6, 27 and 54. Problems encountered during operational training delayed the aircraft's combat debut, but in the autumn of 1944 the 262s began to appear in growing numbers, carrying out low-level attacks on Allied targets, mainly moving columns. There were also two reconnaissance versions, the Me 262A-1a/U3 and Me 262A-5a.

Towards the end of 1944, a new Me 262 fighter unit, *Jagdgeschwader* (JG) 7 'Hindenburg' was formed under the command of Johannes Steinhoff. Later, authority was also given for the formation of a second Me 262 jet-fighter unit, known as *Jagdverband* 44 and commanded by Adolf Galland. It comprised 45 highly experienced pilots, many of them Germany's top-scoring aces. Its principal operating base was München-Riem.

Sixteen German pilots became history's first jet-fighter aces. Foremost among them was *Oberst* Heinz Bär, who claimed 16 of his 220 victories while flying the Messerschmitt Me 262.

MITSUBISHI A6M2 REISEN

*2nd Sentai, 1st Koku Kentai
(Air Fleet), Hiryu Carrier Air Wing,
Imperial Japanese Navy, May 1942*

MITSUBISHI A6M2 REISEN

Specification
- **Type** carrier-borne fighter
- **Crew** 1
- **Powerplant** one 708kW (950hp) Nakajima NK1C Sakae 12 14-cylinder radial engine
- **Performance** max speed 534km/h (332mph); service ceiling 10,000m (32,810ft); range 3104km (1929 miles)
- **Dimensions** wing span 12.00m (39ft 4in); length 9.06m (29ft 8in); height 3.05m (10ft)
- **Weight** 2796kg (6164lb) loaded
- **Armament** two 20mm (0.79in) cannon and two fixed 7.7mm (0.303in) machine guns; external bomb load of 120kg (265lb)

One of the finest aircraft of all time, the Mitsubishi A6M Reisen (Zero fighter) first flew on 1 April 1939, powered by a 582kW (780hp) Zuisei 13 radial engine; after 15 aircraft had been evaluated under combat conditions in China, the type was accepted for service with the Japanese Naval Air Force in July 1940, entering full production in November that year as the A6M2 Model 11. Sixty-four Model 11s were completed, these being powered by the more powerful Sakae 12 engine, and were followed by the Model 21 with folding wingtips. This was the major production version at the time of the attack on Pearl Harbor in December 1941.

The A6M2 soon showed itself to be clearly superior to any fighter the Allies could put into the air in the early stages of the Pacific war. In 1942, the Americans allocated the code name 'Zeke' to the A6M, but as time went by the name 'Zero' came into general use. During the first months of the conflict, the Zeros carved out an impressive combat record. In the battle for Java, which ended on 8 March 1942, they destroyed 550 Allied aircraft. These remarkable victories earned enormous prestige for the Japanese Navy pilots and tended to overshadow the achievements of their Army colleagues.

The Zero depicted here is in the colours of an aircraft that fought at the crucial Battle of Midway in June 1942, when the sinking of four Japanese aircraft carriers, including the *Hiryu*, effectively turned the tide of the Pacific war.

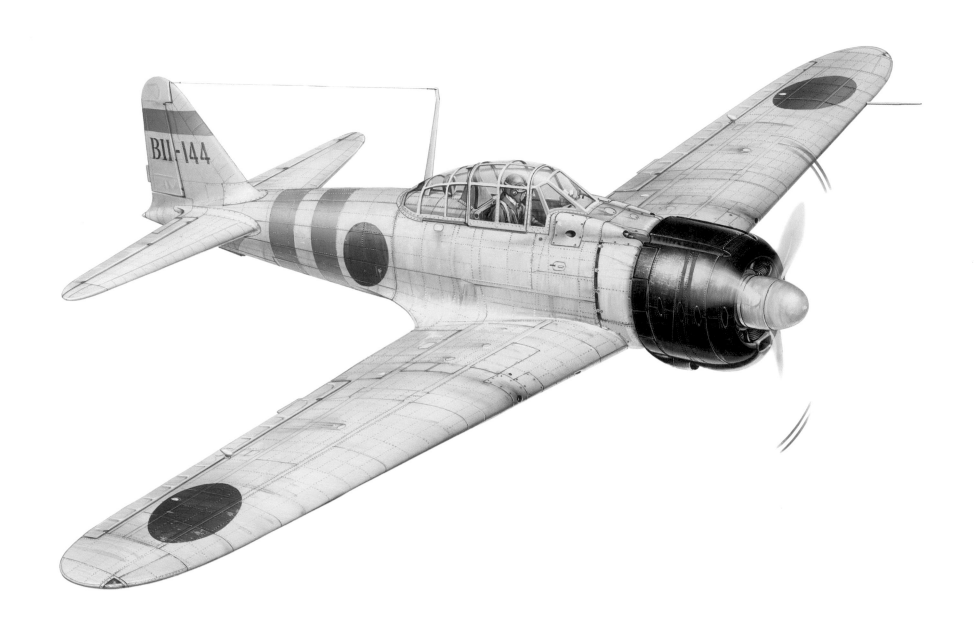

NORTH AMERICAN B-25H MITCHELL

United States Army Air Forces
North Africa, 1943

NORTH AMERICAN B-25H MITCHELL

Specification
- **Type** medium bomber
- **Crew** 5
- **Powerplant** two 1268kW (1700hp) Wright R-2600-13 18-cylinder two-row radial engines
- **Performance** max speed 457km/h (284mph); service ceiling 6460m (21,200ft); range 2454km (1525 miles)
- **Dimensions** wing span 20.60m (67ft 7in); length 16.12m (67ft 7in); height 4.82m (15ft 10in)
- **Weight** 18,960kg (41,800lb) loaded
- **Armament** six 12.7mm (0.50in) machine guns; internal and external bomb/torpedo load of 1361kg (3000lb)

One of the most important US tactical warplanes of World War II, the North American B-25 Mitchell flew for the first time in January 1939. US Army Air Forces (USAAF) B-25B Mitchells operated effectively against Japanese forces in New Guinea, carrying out low-level strafing attacks in the wake of Allied bombing operations. The B-25B was followed into service by the virtually identical B-25C and B-25D. The dedicated anti-shipping version of the Mitchell was the B-25G, 405 of which were produced.

Developed for use in the Pacific theatre, the B-25G had a four-man crew and was fitted with a 75mm (2.95in) M4 gun in the nose, adding to its already powerful nose armament of four 12.7mm (0.50in) guns. The follow-on variant, the B-25H (1000 built), had a lighter 75mm (2.95in) gun. The 4318 examples of the next variant, the B-25J, featured either a glazed B-25D nose or, in later aircraft, a 'solid' nose with eight 12.7mm (0.50in) machine guns. The Royal Air Force (RAF) took delivery of 869 Mitchells, and 458 B-25Js were transferred to the US Navy from 1943, these aircraft being designated PBJ-1H. The Soviet Union also took delivery of 862 Mitchells under Lend-Lease, and surplus B-25s were widely exported after World War II.

On 16 April 1942, the Mitchell leapt into the headlines when the aircraft carrier USS *Hornet*, from a position at sea 1075km (668 miles) from Tokyo, launched 16 B-25Bs of the 17th AAF Air Group, led by Lieutenant Colonel J.H. Doolittle, for the first attack on the Japanese homeland. The example of a B-25H Mitchell illustrated here bore the serial number 41-29896.

NORTH AMERICAN P-51D MUSTANG

47th Fighter Squadron, 15th Fighter Group, US Seventh Air Force, United States Army Air Forces, Iwo Jima, 1945

NORTH AMERICAN P-51D MUSTANG

Specification
- **Type** long-range fighter
- **Crew** 1
- **Powerplant** one 1111kW (1490hp) Packard Rolls-Royce Merlin V-1650-7 V-type engine
- **Performance** Max speed 704km/h (437mph); service ceiling 12,770m (41,900ft); range 3347km (2080 miles)
- **Dimensions** wing span 11.28m (37ft); length 9.85m (32ft 3in); height 3.71m (12ft 2in)
- **Weight** 5493kg (12,100lb) loaded
- **Armament** six 12.7mm (0.50in) machine guns, plus provision for up to two 454kg (1000lb) bombs or six 127mm (5in) rockets

The North American P-51 Mustang was initially produced in response to a 1940 Royal Air Force (RAF) requirement for a fast, heavily armed fighter able to operate effectively at altitudes in excess of 6100m (20,000ft), the prototype flying on 26 October 1940. The first of 320 production Mustang Is for the RAF flew on 1 May 1941, powered by an 820kW (1100hp) Allison V-1710-39 engine. RAF test pilots soon found that with this powerplant the aircraft did not perform well at high altitude, but that its low-level performace was excellent. It was therefore decided to use the type as a high-speed ground attack and tactical reconnaissance fighter.

The RAF suggested that the aircraft would perform better at high altitude if it were fitted with the Rolls-Royce Merlin engine, and this arrangement produced the P-51B Mustang, along with a dramatic improvement in performance. The P-51B/C Mustang was followed by the P-51D, which featured a one-piece sliding canopy. In this guise, the aircraft became the P-51D.

The first production P-51Ds began to arrive in England in the late spring of 1944 and quickly became the standard equipment of the US Army Air Forces (USAAF) Eighth Fighter Command. There is no doubt at all that the Mustang, with its ability to escort bombers all the way to their targets and back, won the daylight battle over Germany.

P-51D Mustangs, like the 47th Fighter Squadron aircraft seen here, given the name 'Li'l Butch', arrived in the Pacific theatre early in 1945. Operating from Iwo Jima, they were able to rove over southern Japan, achieving complete air superiority for the Allies.

NORTHROP P-61 BLACK WIDOW

548th Night Fighter Squadron, US Seventh Air Force, United States Army Air Forces, Ie Shima, June 1945

NORTHROP P-61 BLACK WIDOW

Specification
- **Type** night fighter
- **Crew** 3
- **Powerplant** two 1491kW (2000hp) Pratt & Whitney R-2800-65 18-cylinder radial engines
- **Performance** max speed 589km/h (366mph); service ceiling 10,090m (33,100ft); range 4506km (2800 miles)
- **Dimensions** wing span 20.12m (66ft); length 15.11m (49ft 7in); height 4.46m (14ft 8in)
- **Weight** 13,472kg (29,700lb) loaded
- **Armament** four 20mm (0.79in) cannon and (on some aircraft) four 12.7mm (0.50in) machine guns

Although the prototype XP-61 night fighter flew on 21 May 1942, but it was another 18 months before the first production P-61A Black Widow aircraft appeared. The 421st Night Fighter Squadron (NFS) of the 18th Fighter Group was the first to rearm with the new type, operating from Mokmer in New Guinea. The 421st NFS, which was joined in the theatre at later dates by the 418th and 547th NFSs, moved to Tacloban, Leyte, on 25 October 1944.

In the European theatre, P-61As were issued to the 422nd NFS at Scorton, Yorkshire, in May 1944, followed by the 425th at Charmy Down. Their task was to provide night protection for the American sectors of the Normandy invasion, which took place on 6 June 1944. Before departing for the continent, the two squadrons flew some sorties against V-1 flying bombs, shooting down nine of the pilotless aircraft. There were also two Black Widow squadrons, the 426th and 427th, in the China–Burma–India (CBI) theatre.

In the Central Pacific, the US Seventh Air Force had three Black Widow squadrons, the 6th, 548th and 549th. The last two arrived in the theatre on 7 and 24 March 1945, respectively, being based on Iwo Jima. The 548th NFS soon moved up to Ie Shima. The P-61B seen here, dubbed 'Midnite Madness II', was crewed by Captain James W. Bradford (pilot), First Lieutenant Lawrence K. Lunt (radar operator) and Master Sergeant Reno H. Sukow (gunner). This crew destroyed a Mitsubishi G4M Betty bomber on the night of 24 June 1945.

PETLYAKOV PE-2

12th Guards Dive Bomber Air Regiment, Baltic Fleet Air Arm, Gulf of Finland, 1944

PETLYAKOV PE-2

Specification
- **Type** dive bomber
- **Crew** 3
- **Powerplant** two 940kW (1260hp) Klimov VK-105PF 12-cylinder V-type engines
- **Performance** max speed 580km/h (360mph); service ceiling 8800m (28,870 ft); range 1315km (817 miles)
- **Dimensions** wing span 17.11m (56ft 1in); length 12.78m (41ft 11in); height 3.42m (11ft 2in)
- **Weight** 8520kg (18,783lb) loaded
- **Armament** two 7.62mm (0.3in) or one 7.62mm and one 12.7mm (0.50in) machine gun in nose, one 7.62mm machine gun in dorsal turret, one 7.62mm or 12.7mm machine gun in ventral position, and one 7.62mm or 12.7mm lateral-firing machine gun in window positions; 1600kg (3527lb) of bombs

Originally designated PB-100, the Pe-2 prototype flew for the first time in April 1940. In the early actions on the Russian front, the Pe-2's high speed and defensive armament proved their worth; in one action, when Pe-2s of the 39th Bomber Air Regiment were attacked by 10 Bf 109s, they shot down three of the German fighters and fought off the others.

Pe-2 operations received a setback in the spring of 1942, when the Messerschmitt Bf 109F appeared on the Russian front. This aircraft was some 50km/h (30mph) faster than the Pe-2 at 3000m (9840ft), the Russian bomber's preferred altitude for horizontal bombing. The Pe-2s were forced to push up their bombing altitude to 5000–7000m (16,400–22,960ft), which presented problems to the 109Fs and at the same time reduced bombing accuracy. The solution was to improve the Pe-2's armament and armour, so that it could return to medium-level bombing operations with a chance of survival, and late in 1942 the Pe-2FT appeared, this variant having two 940kW (1260hp) Klimov M-105PF engines and a 12.7mm (0.50in) UBT machine gun in a dorsal turret, replacing the flexible ShKAS machine gun at the rear of the cockpit. The FT suffix denoted '*Frontovoye Trebovanie*' ('Front Requirement').

The Pe-2FT pictured here was flown by Lieutenant Colonel Vasili I. Rakov, commander of the 12th Guards Dive Bomber Air regiment, who was twice awarded the Gold Star of a Hero of the Soviet Union.

POLIKARPOV I-16

4th Escuadrilla de Moscas, Spanish Republican Air Arm, 1938

POLIKARPOV I-16

Specification
- **Type** fighter
- **Crew** 1
- **Powerplant** one 820kW (1100hp) Shvetsov M-63 nine-cylinder radial engine
- **Performance** 489km/h (304mph); service ceiling: 9000m (29,530ft); range 700km (435 miles)
- **Dimensions** 9.00m (29ft 6in); length 6.13m (20ft 1in); height 2.57m (8ft 5in)
- **Weight** 2095kg (4619lb) loaded
- **Armament** four 7.62mm (0.3in) machine guns or two 7.62mm machine guns and two 20mm (0.79in) cannon; external bomb and rocket load of 500kg (1102lb)

The Polikarpov I-16, which first flew on 31 December 1933, was the first production monoplane in the world to feature a retractable undercarriage. The type saw considerable action during its career, starting with the Spanish Civil War. The first machines to arrive in Spain went into battle on 15 November 1936, providing air cover for a Republican offensive against Nationalist forces advancing on Valdemoro, Sesena and Equivias.

The I-16 – nicknamed '*Mosca*' ('Fly') by the Republicans and '*Rata*' ('Rat') by the Nationalists – proved markedly superior to the Heinkel He 51. It was also faster than its most numerous Nationalist opponent, the Fiat CR.32, although the Italian fighter was slightly more manoeuvrable and provided a better gun platform.

In 1937–39 the I-16 also saw action during the Sino-Japanese conflict and over the disputed Khalkhin-Gol area on the Soviet-Manchurian border. I-16s also took part in the Russo-Finnish 'Winter War' of 1939–40, specializing mainly in low-level attacks on Finnish airfields by flights of three or four aircraft.

The I-16 still equipped the majority of the Red Air Force's first-line fighter units at the time of the German invasion in June 1941. The I-16 continued to operate as a first-line combat aircraft on the Leningrad front and in the Crimea until 1942. Altogether, 6555 examples of the I-16 were built before production ended in 1940.

The distinctive 'Popeye' marking on the tail of this I-16 signifies that it is an aircraft of the 4th Escuadrilla. This particular aircraft, coded CM-125, was lost on 13 September 1938.

REPUBLIC P-47D THUNDERBOLT

56th Fighter Group,
United States Eighth Fighter Command,
United States Army Air Forces,
Boxted, England, 1944

REPUBLIC P-47D THUNDERBOLT

Specification
- **Type** fighter
- **Crew** 1
- **Powerplant** one 1715kW (2300hp) Pratt & Whitney R-2800-59 radial engine
- **Performance** max speed 689km/h (428mph); service ceiling 12,800m (42,000ft); range 2028km (1260 miles)
- **Dimensions** wing span 12.43m (40ft 9in); length 11.01m (36ft 1in); height 4.32m (14ft 2in)
- **Weight** 8800kg (19,400lb) loaded
- **Armament** six or eight 12.7mm (0.5in) machine guns; two 454kg (1000lb) bombs or ten rocket projectiles

One of the truly great fighters of World War II, the Republic XP-47B Thunderbolt prototype flew for the first time on 6 May 1941, with the first production P-47B coming off the assembly line in March 1942 after many teething troubles had been rectified.

In June 1942, the 56th Fighter Group began to rearm with the P-47, and in December 1942 – January 1943 it deployed to England, flying its first combat mission on 13 April 1943. During the next two years, it was to destroy more enemy aircraft than any other fighter group of the US Army Air Force (USAAF) Eighth Fighter Command. From that first operational sortie over Europe until the end of the fighting in the Pacific in August 1945, Thunderbolts flew 546,000 combat sorties. By the time the 56th Fighter Wing flew its first operational sortie in the spring of 1943, huge orders had been placed for the P-47D, the most numerous Thunderbolt variant. Considerable numbers of Thunderbolts were used by the Royal Air Force (RAF) in Burma. Overall P-47 production was 15,660 aircraft, many of which found their way into foreign air forces post-war. During World War II, the Soviet Union received 195 P-47s out of the 203 allocated, some having been lost en route.

The P-47D illustrated here was the personal mount of Colonel David C. Schilling, who took over as commander of the 56th Fighter Group from Colonel Hubert 'Hub' Zemke in August 1944. Schilling flew 132 combat missions with the 56th Fighter Group, recording 22.5 victories. He died in 1956, and Schilling Air Force Base, Kansas, is named in his honour.

SAVOIA-MARCHETTI SM-79 SPARVIERO

283rd Squadriglia, 130th Gruppo,
Autonomo Aerosiluranti,
Regia Aeronautica, Gerbini, Sicily, 1942

SAVOIA-MARCHETTI SM-79 SPARVIERO

Specification
- **Type** torpedo bomber
- **Crew** 5
- **Powerplant** three 746kW (1000hp) Piaggio P.XI RC 40 radial engines
- **Performance** max speed 435km/h (270mph); service ceiling 6500m (21,325ft); range 1900km (1181 miles)
- **Dimensions** wing span 21.20m (69ft 2in); length 15.62m (51ft 3in); height 4.40m (14ft 5in)
- **Weight** 11,300kg (24,912lb) loaded
- **Armament** three 12.7mm (0.5in) and one 7.7mm (0.303in) machine guns; two 450mm (17.7in) torpedoes or 1250kg (2756lb) of bombs

The prototype SM.79 was a fast eight-seater airliner which flew for the first time in October 1934. Production of the military SM.79 Sparviero (Sparrowhawk) began in October 1936 and was to have an uninterrupted run until June 1943, by which time 1217 aircraft had been built.

The *Regia Aeronautica* lost no time in testing the SM.79 operationally in Spain, where the type was used with considerable success. When Italy entered World War II in June 1940, SM.79s accounted for well over half the Italian air force's total bomber strength. From June 1940 onwards, SM.79s saw continual action in the air campaign against Malta and in North Africa, becoming renowned for their high-level precision bombing, while the torpedo-bomber version was active against British shipping.

After the Italian surrender in September 1943, SM.79s continued to fly with both sides. The SM.79B, first flown in 1936, was a twin-engined export model, the middle engine being replaced by an extensively glazed nose.

The 130th *Gruppo Autonomo Aerosiluranti* (Specialist Torpedo-Bomber Group), comprising the 280th and 283rd *Squadriglie*, concentrated on attacking convoys to the besieged island of Malta, inflicting heavy damage on the convoy code-named 'Harpoon' which sailed from Gibraltar in June 1942.

The SM.79 seen here features the standard 'sand-and-spinach' camouflage scheme, consisting of a sand-coloured base with mottles of two tones of green applied on top. In common with *Luftwaffe* aircraft operating in the Mediterranean, white theatre bands were worn around the rear fuselage and engine cowlings.

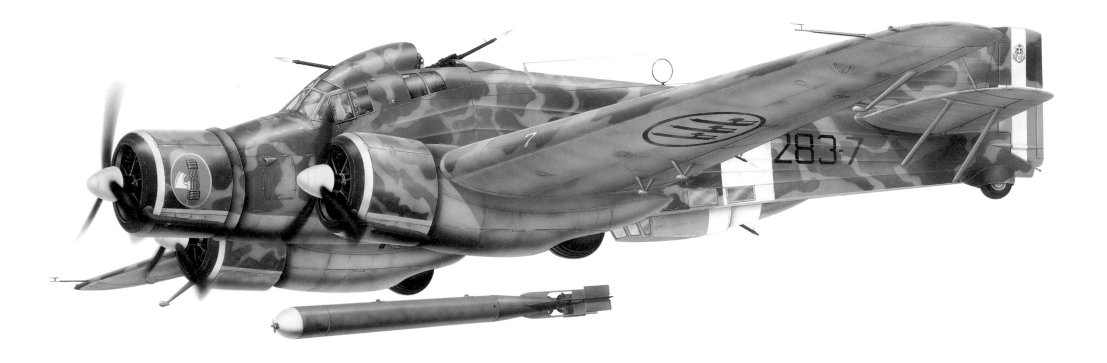

SHORT SUNDERLAND MK II

*No. 201 Squadron,
RAF Coastal Command,
Royal Air Force, Lough Erne,
Northern Ireland, 1942*

SHORT SUNDERLAND MK II

Specification
- **Type** patrol flying boat
- **Crew** 10
- **Powerplant** four 820kW (1100hp) Bristol Pegasus XVIII nine-cylinder air-cooled radial engines
- **Performance** max speed 330km/h (205mph); service ceiling 5445m (17,900m); range 4023km (2500 miles)
- **Dimensions** wing span 34.36m (112ft 9in); length 26.00m (85ft 3in); height 10.52m (34ft 6in)
- **Weight** 26,350kg (58,000lb) loaded
- **Armament** 10 7.7mm (0.303in) machine guns, plus a war load of up to 2250kg (4960lb) of bombs, mines or depth charges on retractable racks in hull sides

The design of the Short Sunderland, which eventually was to become one of the Royal Air Force's (RAF's) longest-serving operational aircraft, was based on that of the stately Short C Class 'Empire' flying boats, operated by Imperial Airways in the 1930s. The prototype first flew on 16 October 1937, and the first production Sunderland Mk Is were delivered to No. 230 Squadron in Singapore early in June 1938.

The Sunderland Mk.II was fitted with Pegasus XVIII engines with two-stage superchargers, a twin-gun dorsal turret, an improved rear turret and ASV Mk II radar. Production of the Sunderland Mk II reached 55 aircraft, these equipping Nos 119, 201, 202, 204, 228 and 230 Squadrons. The fitting of extra equipment meant that the Mk II had a much higher operating weight than the Mk I, and a new planing hull bottom was designed, with a less pronounced forward step that gave better unstick characteristics.

The hull was tested on a Mk II, which in effect became the prototype of the next variant, the Mk III, which was to be the major production model of the Sunderland. The Sunderland III equipped 11 RAF squadrons (including one Polish and one Free French). The last operational Sunderland was the Mk V. At the end of World War II, Sunderlands equipped no fewer than 28 RAF squadrons at home and overseas.

The Sunderland Mk II illustrated here was one of 20 of its type built by Blackburn Aircraft, Dumbarton. It carries No. 201 Squadron's ZM code letters and has the typical 'early war' Coastal Command camouflage scheme.

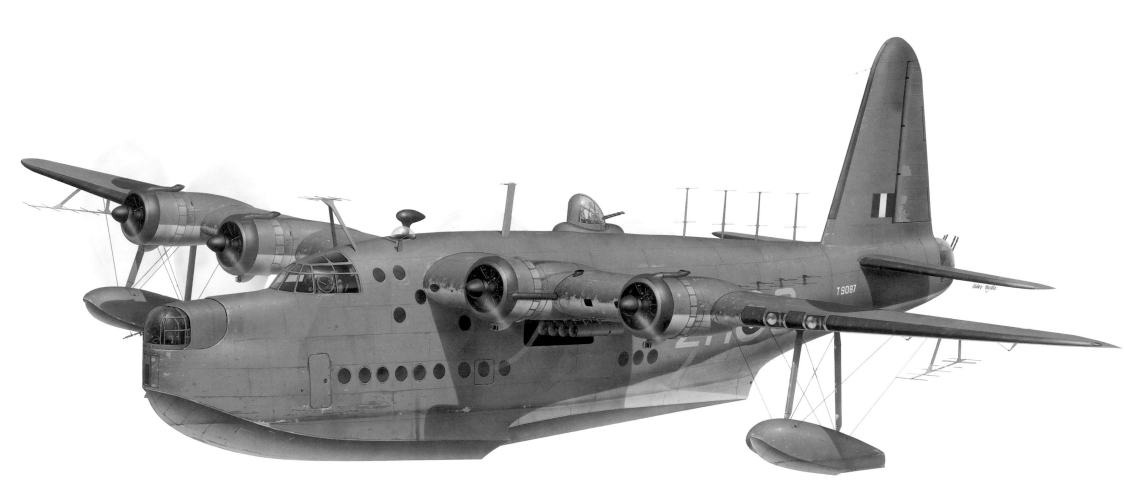

SUPERMARINE SPITFIRE V

No. 2 Squadron,
South African Air Force, Sicily, 1943

SUPERMARINE SPITFIRE V

Specification
- **Type** fighter/fighter-bomber
- **Crew** 1
- **Powerplant** one 1074kW (1440hp) Rolls-Royce Merlin 45/46/50 V-12 engine
- **Performance** max speed 602km/h (374mph); service ceiling 11,280m (37,000ft); range 756km (470 miles)
- **Dimensions** wing span 11.23m (36ft 10in); length 9.11m (29ft 11in); height 3.48m (11ft 5in)
- **Weight** 3078kg (6785lb) loaded
- **Armament** two 20mm (0.79in) cannon and four 7.7mm (0.303in) machine guns

Converted from Mk I airframes, the Spitfire Mk V was the major Spitfire production version, with 6479 examples completed. The first examples entered service with Royal Air Force (RAF) Fighter Command in March 1941.

The majority of Spitfire Vs were armed with two 20mm (0.79in) cannon and four machine guns, affording a greater chance of success against armour plating. The Mk V was powered by a Rolls-Royce Merlin 45 engine, developing 1055kW (1415hp) at 5000m (19,000ft) against the 858kW (1150hp) of the Merlin XII fitted in the Mk II. Nevertheless, the Mk V was essentially a compromise aircraft, rushed into service to meet an urgent Air Staff requirement for a fighter with a performance superior to that of the latest model of Messerschmitt.

The debut of the Spitfire V came just in time, for in May 1941 the *Luftwaffe* fighter units began to receive the Messerschmitt Bf 109F; it had suffered from technical problems in its development phase, but these had now been resolved. The Spitfire V, however, failed to provide the overall superiority Fighter Command needed so badly. At high altitude, where many combats took place, it was found to be inferior to the Bf 109F on most counts, and several squadrons equipped with the Mk V took a severe mauling during that summer. The type gave good service, however, in North Africa, Sicily and Italy.

No. 2 Squadron of the South African Air Force (SAAF), which was part of the Desert Air Force's No. 7 Wing, became operational in Sicily on 23 August 1943, subsequently moving to new bases on the Italian mainland.

TUPOLEV TU-2S

Soviet Air Force, August 1945

TUPOLEV Tu-2S

Specification
- **Type** light bomber
- **Crew** 4
- **Powerplant** two 1380kW (1850hp) Shvetsov Ash-82FN radial engines
- **Performance** max speed 547km/h (340mph); service ceiling 9500m (31,170ft); range 2000km (1243 miles)
- **Dimensions** wing span 18.86m (61ft 10in); length 13.80m 945ft 3in); height 4.56m (14ft 11in)
- **Weight** 12,800kg (28,219lb) loaded
- **Armament** two 20mm (0.79in) cannon and three 12.7mm (0.50in) machine guns

The prototype Tu-2 light bomber flew for the first time on 29 January 1941, and subsequent flight testing showed that the aircraft had an outstanding performance. Delays in engine availability, however, meant that limited production did not get under way until the beginning of 1942, and deliveries were slow because of the need to relocate many Soviet aircraft factories ahead of the rapid German advance into Russia. Pilots were particularly enthusiastic about the bomber, their reports stressing its substantial bomb load and excellent combat radius, good defensive armament, its ability to fly on one engine, and the ease with which crews were able to convert to the new type.

Series production of the Tu-2 did not start until 1943 because of the earlier problems, and combat units did not begin to rearm with the bomber until the spring of 1944, the initial major production model being the Tu-2S. The Tu-2 first saw action on a large scale in June 1944 on the Karelian (Finnish) front. In its primary bombing role, the Tu-2 carried out some extremely effective missions in the closing months of the war, particularly against fortified enemy towns.

In October 1944, a long-range variant, the Tu-2D (ANT-62), made its appearance. A torpedo-bomber variant, the Tu-2T (ANT-62T), was tested between January and March 1945, and issued to units of the Soviet Naval Aviation. The Tu-2R, also designated Tu-6, carried a battery of cameras in the bomb bay.

Seen here is a Tupolev Tu-2S wearing a similar camouflage scheme as those aircraft which participated in the Soviet Aviation day parade over Moscow on 18 August 1945.

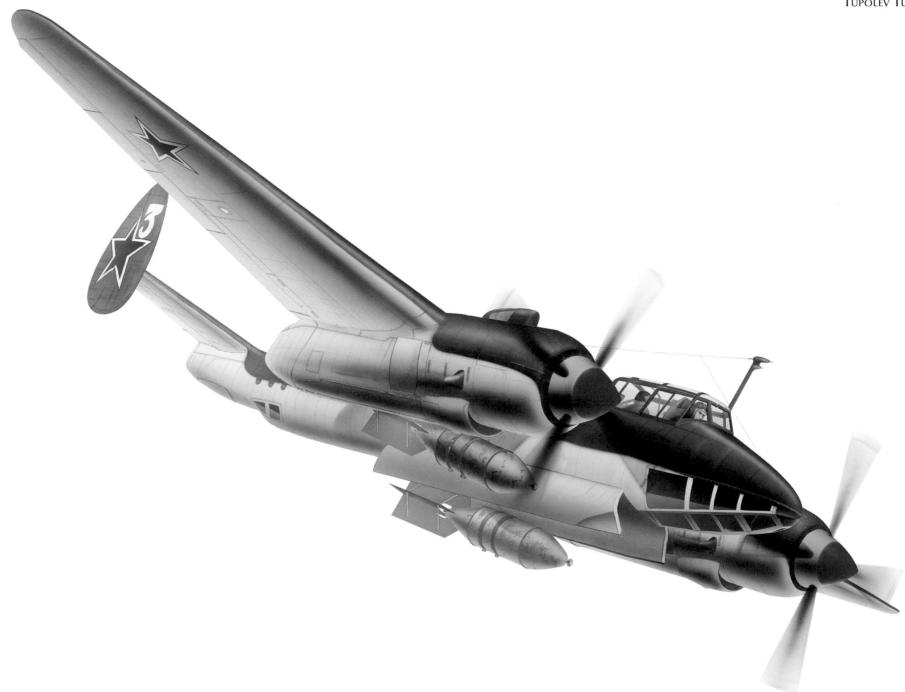

VICKERS WELLINGTON

No. 115 Squadron,
Royal Air Force, RAF Marham,
Norfolk, 1942

VICKERS WELLINGTON

Specification
- **Type** bomber
- **Crew** 6
- **Powerplant** two 1119kW (1500hp) Bristol Hercules XI radial engines
- **Performance** max speed 411km/h (255mph); service ceiling 5790m (19,000ft); range 2478km (1540 miles)
- **Dimensions** wing span 26.26m (86ft 2in); length 19.68m (64ft 7in); height 5.0m (17ft 5in)
- **Weight** 15,422kg (34,000lb) loaded
- **Armament** eight 7.7mm (0.303) machine guns; up to 2041kg (4500lb) of bombs

The Vickers Wellington was designed by Barnes Wallis, who was later to conceive the mines that destroyed the Ruhr Dams. The prototype flew on 15 June 1936 and was lost on 19 April 1937, when it broke up during an involuntary high-speed dive, the cause being determined as elevator imbalance. As a result, the production Wellington Mk I and subsequent aircraft were fitted with a revised fin, rudder and elevator. The first Mk I, L4212, flew on 23 December 1937, and the first Bomber Command squadron to rearm, No. 9, began receiving its aircraft in December 1938.

The most numerous early model was the Mk IC, but the principal version in service with Bomber Command was the Mk III (1519 built), with two 1119kW (1500hp) Bristol Hercules engines replacing the much less reliable Pegasus. The Wellington III entered service with the experienced No. 9 Squadron on 22 June 1941, and was to be the backbone of Bomber Command's night offensive against Germany until such time as the Command's four-engined heavy bombers became available in numbers. The last bomber version of the Wellington was the Mk X, of which 3803 were built, accounting for more than 30 per cent of all Wellington production. The Wellington was also used extensively by Royal Air Force (RAF) Coastal Command.

No. 115 Squadron received its first Wellington Mk Is in April 1939 and was the first RAF unit to attack a mainland target in World War II, bombing the German-occupied airfield of Stavanger-Sola in Norway in April 1940. It used Wellington Mk IIIs from November 1941 until March 1943, when it received Lancasters.

YAKOVLEV YAK-1/9

303rd Fighter Air Division, First Soviet Air Army, 3rd Ukrainian Front, 1944

YAKOVLEV YAK-1/9

Specification refers to the Yak-9
- **Crew** 1
- **Powerplant** one 1230kW (1650hp) Klimov VK-107A Vee-type engine
- **Performance** max speed 700km/h (435mph); service ceiling 11,900m (39,040ft); range 870km (540 miles)
- **Dimensions** wing span 9.77m (32ft); length 8.55m (28ft); height 2.44m (8ft)
- **Weight** 3068kg (6760lb) loaded
- **Armament** one 23mm (0.90in) cannon and two 12.7mm (0.50in) machine guns

It was not until 1939–40 that the prototypes of Soviet fighters that could really be classed as modern made their appearance. One was the Yak-1 Krasavyets (Beauty), which made its first public appearance during an air display on 7 November 1940. It was Aleksandr S. Yakovlev's first fighter design. The slow production rate of the Yak-1 in some areas following the relocation of factories led to the decision to convert a trainer variant of the Yak-1, the Yak-7V, into a single-seat fighter. In this new guise, the aircraft was designated Yak-7A. Its development proceeded through a line of variants with heavier armament and longer range, culminating in the Yak-9, a superb fighter aircraft that did much to win air superiority over the eastern battlefront.

The Yakovlev Yak-9 was used by the Soviet and satellite air arms for some years after the war, and saw combat over Korea. A further development of the basic Yak-1 airframe was the Yak-3, which reached the front line during the early summer months of 1943 and which was probably the most manoeuvrable fighter aircraft of World War II.

The Yak-3 illustrated here was flown by Major General Georgii Nefedovich, who ended the war with a total of 23 victories. Nefedovich commanded the 303rd Fighter Air Division, one of the units of which was the Regiment Normandie, composed of Free French pilots and ground crews who had arrived in Russia from the Middle East in 1942. The air regiment was given the title 'Normandie-Niemen' in honour of its exploits.

THE EARLY COLD WAR: 1946–1969

In the years immediately after World War II, as tensions grew between the Communist bloc and the West, the power and the menace of the strategic bomber – with its terrifying nuclear payload – led to the development of dedicated interceptors and integrated weapons systems, which saw action in the proxy wars between the superpowers in Korea and Vietnam.

USAF Convair F-106A Delta Dart interceptors on a training mission. The F-106A was a development of the F-102, and proved to be a capable dogfighter.

ARMSTRONG WHITWORTH METEOR NF.MK.12

No. 153 Squadron, No. 11 Group,
RAF Fighter Command,
Royal Air Force, West Malling, 1957

ARMSTRONG WHITWORTH METEOR NF.MK.12

Specification
- **Type** twin-engined, two-seat night-fighter
- **Crew** 2
- **Powerplant** two 17.48kN (3800lb thrust) Derwent 9 turbojet engines
- **Performance** max speed 940km/h (584mph); service ceiling 12,200m (40,028ft); range 1610km (2590 miles)
- **Dimensions** wing span 13.11m (43ft); length 14.80m (48ft 6in); height 4.24m (13ft 9in)
- **Weight** 9456kg (20,830lb) loaded
- **Armament** four 20mm (0.79in) Hispano cannons with 195 rounds each

Gloster's first fighter aircraft since the biplane Gladiator, the Meteor first flew in March 1942 and was the first operational jet fighter. It saw limited service in its initial day-fighter form in the last months of World War II. Many improved models followed and, by the mid-1950s, Meteors were the mainstay of Royal Air Force (RAF) Fighter Command and were sold to several foreign air forces including Israel, Argentina and Australia.

The Armstrong Whitworth Company built many Meteors under licence and developed the NF.11, NF.12, NF.13 and NF.14 radar-equipped night fighters. Armament remained four 20mm (0.79in) cannon, now mounted in the wings to leave room for the AI Mk.21 nose radar. None had ejection seats. These variants differed visually mainly in fuselage length and canopy detail. Different models of engine and radar were the main internal differences.

Egypt, Syria and Israel received a few Armstrong Whitworth NF.13s. One of the few actual combats for the NF Meteors saw an Israeli aircraft shoot down an Egyptian Il-14 transport in 1956.

No. 153 Squadron flew Defiant, Blenheim and Beaufighter night fighters from 1941–44. From October that year, it flew Lancaster bombers until it was disbanded in September 1945. Nearly a decade later, in February 1955, it was reformed at West Malling, Kent, as a night-fighter squadron, although its Meteor night fighters were not delivered until September.

This particular NF.12 was delivered from the factory in July 1953 and operated by Nos 125 and 25 Squadrons, as well as No. 153, between then and July 1958, when the latter unit disbanded. Stored with No. 60 Maintenance Unit, Rufforth, it was sold for scrap in April 1959.

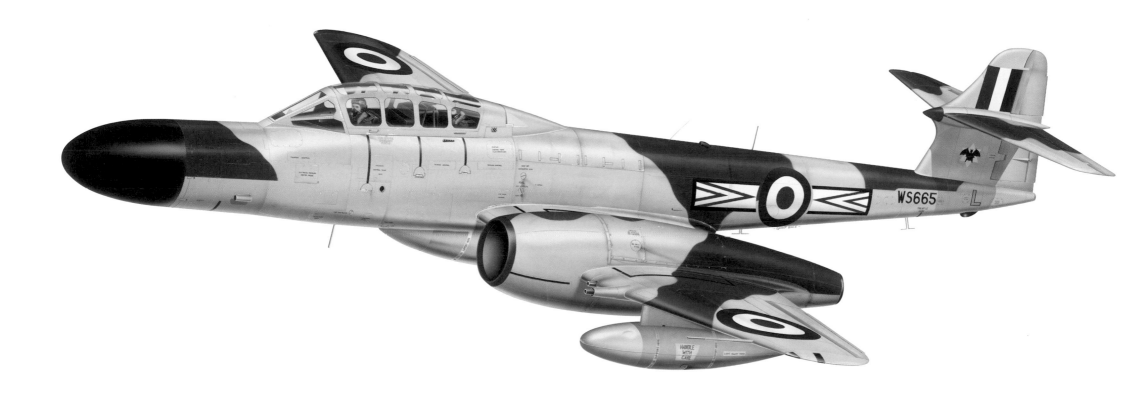

AVRO SHACKLETON MR. MK 2

No. 205 Squadron, Far East Air Force, Royal Air Force, RAF Changi, Singapore Late 1960s

AVRO SHACKLETON MR. MK 2

Specification
- **Type** long-range maritime patrol aircraft
- **Crew** 8–10
- **Powerplant** four 1831kW (2455hp) Rolls-Royce Griffon 57A V-12 piston engines
- **Performance** max speed 500km/h (311mph); service ceiling 6400m (21,000ft); range 5440km (3380 miles)
- **Dimensions** wing span 36.58m (120ft); length 26.59m (87ft 3in); height 5.1m (16ft 9in)
- **Weight** 39010kg (86,000lb) loaded
- **Armament** two Hispano No. 1 Mk 5 20mm (0.79in) cannon in nose turret; up to 4536kg (10,000lb)

Often said to have been derived from the Avro Lancaster, the Shackleton patrol aircraft in fact owed more to the Lincoln, with which it shared wings, engines, tail surfaces and landing gear. The fuselage of the Shackleton Mk 1 was shorter and more capacious, with a more oval cross-section compared to that of the Lincoln. The first Mk 1 flew in March 1949 and deliveries began in April 1951. The MR (maritime reconnaissance) Mk 2 had a redesigned, longer fuselage with the radar moved from the nose to a ventral 'dustbin' position, and a turret with two 20mm (0.79in) cannon in the nose, rather than tail guns. The bomb bay could carry up to three torpedoes or a variety of bombs and depth charges. Two fixed cameras were usually mounted in the tail.

Following conversion of an MR Mk 1 in June 1952, the first new production MR. Mk 2 was WG530, seen here. It was delivered to the Aircraft and Armaments Experimental Establishment (A&AEE) in September 1952 and later served with Nos. 120, 224 and 42 Squadrons. No. 205 was its last unit before it was sold for scrap in September 1968.

No. 205 Squadron was the first RAF unit to based in the Far East, being formed in Singapore in 1928. It remained in the region as a maritime patrol squadron for its whole existence, operating Southampton, Singapore, Catalina and Sunderland flying boats.

The Sunderlands were used in the Korean War and were the last examples in the RAF when the squadron transitioned to the Shackleton in 1958-9. No. 208 flew the Mk 1A, then the Mk 2, until the squadron disbanded and the RAF withdrew from a permanent presence in the Far East in October 1971.

BOEING B-47H STRATOJET

*338th Strategic Reconnaissance Squadron,
55th Strategic Reconnaissance Wing,
Strategic Air Command, United States
Air Force, Forbes Air Force Base,
Kansas, 1962*

BOEING B-47H STRATOJET

Specification
- **Type** strategic reconnaissance aircraft
- **Crew** 6
- **Powerplant** six 33.4 kN (7200lb thrust) General Electric J47-GE-25 turbojets
- **Performance** max speed 975km/h (605mph); service ceiling 12,345m (40,500ft); range 6437km (4000 miles)
- **Dimensions** wing span 35.36m (116ft); length 33.48m (109ft 10in); height 8.50m (17ft 11in)
- **Weight** 36,630kg (80,756lb) empty
- **Armament** two 20mm (0.79in) cannon with 350 rounds

Like the F-86 Sabre, the B-47 Stratojet design benefited from captured German wartime research into swept wings. Previous work by Boeing on what effectively was a jet B-29 was abandoned, and a new design with 35-degree swept wings and podded engines was accepted for production in late 1946.

The XB-47 prototype first flew in December 1947 and was unlike any previous bomber. The three crew sat one behind the other under a fighter-style bubble canopy, while the swept wings were so thin that they flexed greatly in flight. This was to cause some control problems at high speeds. Small outrigger wheels were fitted under the outer engines to prevent the wingtips touching the ground.

More than 1300 of the main production B-47E were built out of 2032 of all versions. They never saw combat as bombers, but specialized reconnaissance and Elint (electronic intelligence) versions were active around the periphery of the Soviet Union and several were shot down by Soviet fighters.

The RB-47H was an electronic reconnaissance and countermeasures version of the B-47E. A specialist crew of three 'crows', or electronics operators, was carried in a pressurized compartment in the bomb bay, and its job was to locate and analyse radar signals. Equipment was also carried to jam and spoof radar transmitters during wartime. The RB-47 had no bombing capability, but retained a pair of 20mm (0.79in) cannon in a remotely operated tail turret for self-defence.

The first RB-47H of 35 built entered service with the 55th Strategic Reconnaissance Wing in August 1955. The 338th Strategic Reconnaissance Squadron, one of whose RB-47Hs is illustrated here, was particularly active during the Cuban Missile Crisis in 1962. The 338th survives today as the crew training squadron for the 55th Wing, now based at Offutt Air Force Base, Nebraska.

CANADAIR CF-86E SABRE 5

434 (Fighter) Squadron, 3 (Fighter) Wing,
1 Air Division, Royal Canadian Air Force,
Zweibrücken, West Germany
1954–1957

CANADAIR CF-86E SABRE 5

Specification
- **Type** single-seat fighter
- **Crew** 1
- **Powerplant** one 32.36kN (7275lb thrust) Avro Orenda 14 turbojet engine
- **Performance** max speed 1080km/h (671mph); service ceiling 16490m (54,100ft); range 2391km (1486 miles)
- **Dimensions** wing span 11.30m (37ft 1in); length 11.40m (37ft 5in); height 4.45m (14ft 7in)
- **Weight** 7965kg (17,560lb) loaded
- **Armament** six 0.50-in (12.7-mm) machine-guns; up to two 1,000-lb (454-kg) bombs or 16 rockets

North American Aviation's F-86 Sabre was one of the post-war era's true classics, benefiting from captured German research to produce the first Western swept-wing jet fighter, which first flew in October 1947. The Sabre was widely exported and produced under licence in Australia, Italy, Japan and Canada. In the latter country, 1815 Sabres were built by Canadair, including 370 Sabre 5s with the Avro Canada Orenda 10 engine and 655 Sabre 6s with the more powerful Orenda 14. The Sabre 5's airframe was essentially that of the US-built F-86F-30, but the new engine gave greatly improved speed, acceleration and climb rate. Armament and dimensions were the same as the equivalent models of F-86.

The foreground aircraft (RCAF 23187) was often flown by squadron member R.J. 'Chick' Childerhose, author of the 1978 memoir *Wild Blue*. It first flew in March 1954 and entered service the same month. After a relatively short Royal Canadian Air Force (RCAF), career it was given to the *Luftwaffe* in June 1957 and used by it as BB+171 and later BB+231. Again its career was brief, being struck off *Luftwaffe* charge in November 1959.

In July 1942, 434 (Fighter) Squadron was re-formed at RCAF Station Uplands and flew its Sabres en masse to Europe in March 1953. The squadron badge featured a schooner and was known as the 'Bluenose' Squadron, a term usually referring to residents of Nova Scotia and the Maritime Provinces of Canada. Based at Zweibrücken, Germany, until June 1962 as part of 3 (Fighter) Wing, the squadron then moved to Marville, France, and 1(F) Wing a few months before disbanding as a Sabre unit, having swapped the Sabre 5 for the Sabre 6 in 1957. From 1963 to 1967, it flew the CF-104 Starfighter and later the CF-116 (F-5) Freedom Fighter, before final disbandment in 1988.

CONVAIR B-58A HUSTLER

305th Bomb Wing,
2nd Air Force Strategic Air Command,
United States Air Force,
Bunker Hill Air Force Base, Indiana,
1960s

CONVAIR B-58A HUSTLER

Specification
- **Type** supersonic strategic bomber
- **Crew** 3
- **Powerplant** four 69.3kN (15,600lb thrust) General Electric J79-GE-5 turbojets
- **Performance** max speed 2205km/h (1370mph); service ceiling 19,324m (63,400ft); range 3219 km (2000 miles) with internal fuel
- **Dimensions** wing span 17.3m (56ft 9in); length 29.5m (96ft 9in); height 8.87m (29ft 11in)
- **Weight** 73935kg (163,000lb) max take-off
- **Armament** one 20mm (0.79in) T-171 rotary cannon; one nuclear weapon in underfuselage pod or up to four B43 or B61 bombs on underwing pylons

Even as the first jet bombers were entering service, the US Air Force (USAF) formulated a requirement for a much more advanced supersonic aircraft. The Convair proposal was a delta-winged aircraft similar to its F-102A fighter, but with its engines in underwing pods. Unlike the F-102 and F-106 fighters, the B-58 Hustler, which first flew in November 1956, had no internal weapons bay. The Hustler's warload of a W39 nuclear warhead was carried in a huge, droppable pod under the fuselage. Different versions of the huge MB-1 pod also carried various amounts of fuel, which was to be used before any internal fuel, and the whole unit dropped on the target.

The B-58 set 19 world speed and altitude records and won a number of aviation trophies. The USAF ordered 116 Hustlers, of which 86 which were operational with Strategic Air Command (SAC) between 1960 and 1970.

The Hustler's range was inadequate to reach Soviet targets from its bases in the central United States without multiple aerial refuellings. Two Bomb Wings, the 305th at Bunker Hill (later Grissom) Air Force Base and the 43rd at Carswell, Texas, and later Little Rock, Arkansas, operated the USAF's Hustlers. Consideration was given to using them in a conventional role in Vietnam, but, although weapons trials were conducted, no Hustler ever saw combat.

This particular Hustler was not one of the 25 per cent of B-58s which were lost in service. It was retired to storage at Davis-Monthan Air Force Base in January 1970 and, like most of its brethren, was later scrapped.

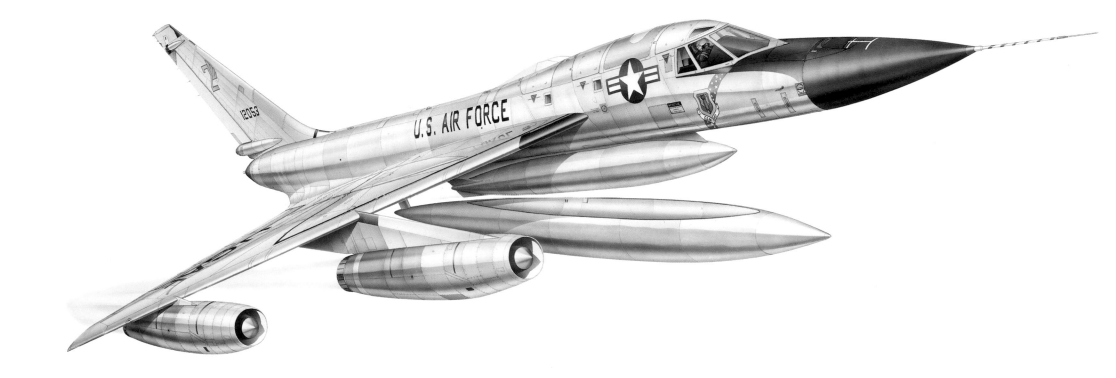

CONVAIR F-102A DELTA DAGGER

317th Fighter Interceptor Squadron, 21st Composite Wing, Alaskan Air Command, United States Air Force, Elmendorf, Alaska, 1968

CONVAIR F-102A DELTA DAGGER

Specification
- **Type** single-seat interceptor fighter
- **Crew** 1
- **Powerplant** one 77kN (17,200lb thrust) Pratt & Whitney J57-P-23 afterburning turbojet engine
- **Performance** max speed 1328km/h (825mph); service ceiling 16,460m (54,000ft); range 2173km (1350 miles)
- **Dimensions** wing span 11.60m (38ft 1.5in); length 20.82m (68ft 4.5in); height 6.45m (21ft 2.5in)
- **Weight** 12,565kg (28,150lb) loaded
- **Armament** four AIM-4 Falcon IR or radar-homing air-to-air missiles, or three and one AIM-26A Nuclear Falcon; early F-102As could also fire up to 24 folding-fin rockets

The Convair Delta Dagger was born of a 1950 United States Air Force (USAF) requirement for a missile-armed 'interim interceptor', although the company had been working on delta-wing designs based on German research for several years. The Delta Dagger was preceded by the smaller XF-92A, which flew in September 1948 and was the first pure delta-winged aircraft to fly. It was followed by the YF-102, designed around the MX-1179 missile system (later the AIM-4 Falcon) and which flew in October 1953, but refused to go supersonic in testing. The panic programme which resulted produced the YF-102A by December 1954.

Service began with the 327th Fighter Interceptor Squadron (FIS) of Air Defence Command in April 1956, and by 1960 Air National Guard (ANG) squadrons were also receiving 'Deuces'. The Delta Dagger was initially used for air defence of the Continental United States, Alaska and Hawaii, but were also based in Europe and on Okinawa. Deployments to Thailand led to involvement in Vietnam, where one unit defended US bases, flew B-52 escort and were used in a limited ground-attack role using rockets against buildings and watercraft. By 1977, the last F-102s were phased out of ANG service, and 213 of them became PQM-102 and QF-102 pilotless drones which were destroyed in missile tests and in exercises. In all, Exactly 1000 F-102s had been produced, 111 of them TF-102A two-seaters.

This F-102A was delivered in September 1957 and spent almost all its early years in Alaska with the 317th FIS at Elmendorf Air Force Base and various dispersed airfields. In 1969, it was transferred to the Air National Guard (ANG), serving with the 176th FIS in Wisconsin and the 102nd FIS in New York. In March 1975, it went to the 4950th Test Wing at Wright-Patterson Air Force Base, Ohio, and in January the following year was retired for good.

CONVAIR RB-36E PEACEMAKER

72nd Bombardment Squadron,
5th Bombardment Wing (Heavy),
13th Air Force Strategic Air Command,
United States Air Force, Travis Air Force
Base, California, 1951–1958

CONVAIR RB-36E PEACEMAKER

Specification
- **Type** long-range reconnaissance aircraft
- **Crew** 22
- **Powerplant** Six 2611kW (3500hp) Pratt & Whitney R-4360-41 radial piston engines and four 23.1kN (5200lb thrust) General Electric J47-GE-19 turbojets
- **Performance** max speed 657km/h (408mph); service ceiling 15240m (50,000ft); range 16,094km (10,000 miles)
- **Dimensions** wing span 70.14m (230ft); length 49.39m (162ft 1in); height 14.20m (46ft 8in)
- **Weight** 162,198kg (357,500lb) max take-off
- **Armament** 16 20mm (0.79in) cannon

In 1941, the US Army Air Forces (USAAF) began studies into a bomber that could reach Europe from the United States in the event of Germany conquering Great Britain. A contract was issued to Convair in November that year, and 100 of the new intercontinental bombers were ordered even before the first flight of the XB-36 Peacemaker in September 1945; other projects had taken priority, delaying the B-36 until after the war's end.

Twenty-two of the original B-36A models were built, each having six piston engines driving pusher propellers. The defensive armament of multiple remotely operated gun turrets gave difficulties, and the B-36As were delivered without it and were not considered operational. The main production model was the B-36H, of which 83 were built.

This aircraft, serial number 44-92020, was built as a B-36A and later modified to the RB-36E configuration shown here. The YB-36 prototype and 21 of the B-36As were converted to RB-36Es. As with the conversion of the B-36B to the RB-36D, this involved the addition of four jet engines in pods (making 'four burning and six turning'), fitting large cameras and extra fuel in the bomb bays, and adding more electronic countermeasures equipment. Normal bombs were not carried, but 45kg (100lb) photoflash bombs were used for night photography.

The 5th Bombardment Wing (Heavy) operated Peacemakers from 1951–58. The B-36 was not used in Korea and saw no other combat as a bomber, although the various RB-36s were active in snooping around and sometimes over the borders of the Soviet Union. The last of the giant Peacemakers was retired in 1959 after a relatively short career.

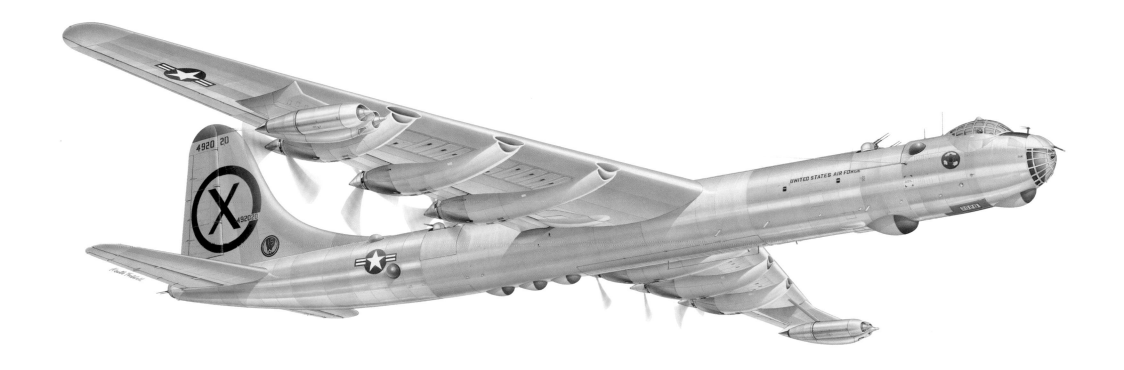

DASSAULT MYSTÈRE IVA

Escadron de Chasse 1/8,
Armée de l' Air, Orange, France, 1960s

DASSAULT MYSTÈRE IVA

Specification
- **Type** single-seat fighter-bomber
- **Crew** 1
- **Powerplant** one 34.3kN (7716lb thrust) Hispano-Suiza Verdon 350 turbojet engine
- **Performance** max speed 1120km/h (696mph); service ceiling 15000m (49,214ft); range 916km (569 miles)
- **Dimensions** wing span m (36ft 5in); length 12.8m (42ft 2in); height 4.6m (15ft 1in)
- **Weight** 9499kg (20,941lb) loaded
- **Armament** Two 30-mm (1.18in) DEFA cannon; optional 35-round SNEB rocket pack, rocket pods or up to 1000kg (2204lb) of bombs

The Mystère was France's first indigenous swept-wing fighter, and its later versions were the first quantity-built European aircraft capable of level supersonic flight. Following 150 Mystère IIs, production switched to the definitive Mystère IV, with a thinner wing with slightly more sweep and a new, oval section fuselage containing a Rolls-Royce Tay engine, or the Hispano Verdon, a licence-built version.

The prototype Mystère IV first flew in September 1952. The first production aircraft flew in May 1954 and the production Mystère IVA entered *Armée de l'Air* service in 1955, seeing action over Suez in 1956.

Under the Nato assistance programme, the United States paid for the first 225 Mystères, followed by 100 bought with French funds. *Escadron de Chasse* 1/8 'Maghreb' was based in Morocco when it replaced its Mistrals (licence-built Vampires) with Mystères in 1960. It saw some action with them against Algerian rebels before the 1961 cease-fire. The squadron returned to France and was renamed 'Saintonge', flying the Mystère (latterly in the operational training role) until the type was finally retired in 1981.

Israeli Mystère IV fighters also saw combat in 1956, claiming a number of Egyptian MiG-15s, MiG-17s and Vampires, and again in 1967 mainly in a ground support role. India's 110 Mystères were in action against Pakistan in 1965.

As an interceptor, the Mystère IV was replaced by the Mirage III in the early 1960s, but carried on in the ground-attack role until 1975 when replaced by the Jaguar. The Super Mystère B2 with afterburner and guided missiles was the first supersonic version. The career of the 180 French examples spanned 1957–77, and Israeli versions with American engines saw much action.

DE HAVILLAND MOSQUITO PR.34A

No. 81 Squadron,
Far East Air Force, Royal Air Force,
RAF Seletar, Singapore, 1955

DE HAVILLAND MOSQUITO PR.34A

Specification
- **Type** twin-engined reconnaissance aircraft
- **Crew** 2
- **Powerplant** two 1261kW (1690hp) Rolls-Royce Merlin 113/114 V-12 piston engines
- **Performance** max speed 684km/h (425mph); service ceiling 12,120m (40,000ft); range 5630km (3500 miles)
- **Dimensions** wing span 16.5m (54ft 2in); length 12.7m (41ft 9in); height 4.66m (15ft 3.5in)
- **Weight** 11,340kg (25,000lb) loaded
- **Armament** none

Although designed as an unarmed, high-speed day bomber, the de Havilland Mosquito branched into two distinct paths of development, including a very successful series of night-fighters and fighter-bombers. The glazed-nosed bombers spawned a series of photo-reconnaissance models, which used their speed and high-altitude capability to avoid interception. They were largely built of wood, which reduced weight and the need for strategic materials. Subassemblies were constructed by such enterprises as furniture makers and piano factories.

The later reconnaissance Mosquitoes featured pressurized cockpits, lightened airframes and longer wings for high-altitude performance. The P.R.34 was built from late 1944 for use in the Far East, with a range of over 5633km (3500 miles), helped by its 1818-litre (400-gallon) slipper tanks, which were usually carried on the wings. The PR.34 was fitted with four F.52 vertical cameras and one F.24 oblique camera. The vertical camera was sighted by the observer lying in the nose, but the oblique cameras were aimed by lining up markings on the wing with the subject. The PR.34A differed in detail, mainly in having different marks of Merlin engine.

The Royal Air Force's No. 81 Squadron flew a mix of photo-reconnaissance Spitfires and Mosquitoes from Seletar, Singapore, into the 1950s. The squadron flew the last operational flight by an RAF Spitfire in 1954. No. 81 Squadron played an important role in the Malayan campaign, mapping the jungle in a search for terrorist camps. Large surveys were also done of Java and Thailand.

A sister aircraft to this one flew the last operational flight of the Mosquito in RAF service in December 1955. The squadron converted to Meteors and then Canberras in 1958, which were flown until disbandment in January 1970.

DE HAVILLAND
SEA VIXEN FAW. MK 1

No. 893 Squadron, Fleet Air Arm,
Royal Navy, 1963

DE HAVILLAND SEA VIXEN FAW. MK 1

Specification
- **Type** two-seat twin-engined carrier-based fighter
- **Crew** 2
- **Powerplant** two 49.96kN (11,230lb thrust) Rolls-Royce Avon 203 turbojets
- **Performance** max speed 1110km/h (690mph); service ceiling 14640m (48,000ft); range 1287km (800 miles)
- **Dimensions** wing span 15.54m (51ft); length 16.94m (55ft 7in); height 3.28m (10ft 9in)
- **Weight** 16,793kg (37,700lb) loaded
- **Armament** four Red Top IR-guided air-to-air missiles and two retractable pods for 28 51mm (2in) rockets; up to 908 kg (2000lb) of bombs or rockets

The De Havilland Sea Vixen naval fighter began as the DH.110, a design built to a Royal Air Force (RAF) requirement for a twin-engined all-weather fighter. The DH.110 prototype first flew in September 1951 and was powered by two Rolls-Royce Avon RA.7 turbojets and armed with four 20mm (0.79in) cannon. The Gloster GA.5 (Javelin) was selected for production by the RAF, but de Havilland carried on private development.

The design was strengthened and revised after a crash at Farnborough in 1952, and the Royal Navy ordered a version in 1955 as the Sea Vixen FAW 1, with FAW standing for 'fighter all weather'. The Sea Vixen was the first British fighter to dispense with guns and have an air-to-air weapons load consisting only of missiles and rockets. The Sea Vixen FAW 2 had increased fuel capacity and ECM gear in enlarged forward sections of the tailbooms. Armament was four Red Top air-to-air missiles, an improved version of the Firestreak. Rocket pods and bombs could be carried for surface attack. Twenty-nine new FAW 2s were built and 79 converted from Mk 1s.

This FAW 1 was delivered to the Royal Navy in November 1961. In 1963, as part of No. 893 Squadron, it took part in a cruise to the Far East aboard HMS *Victorious*, during which its regular pilot was Lieutenant Mark Thompson. This squadron had a relatively short career, operating Sea Vixens from September 1960 to July 1965. XN694 was later converted to FAW 2 standard and went to No. 892 Squadron, where in 1968 it was part of an squadron aerobatic team named 'Simon's Circus'. After a career of less than a decade, it was scrapped at Sydenham, Belfast, in 1970.

DE HAVILLAND VAMPIRE FB.9

*No. 607 (County of Durham) Squadron,
Royal Auxiliary Air Force,
RAF Ouston, Yorkshire, 1950s*

DE HAVILLAND VAMPIRE FB.9

Specification
- **Type** single-seat day fighter
- **Crew** 1
- **Powerplant** one 19.57kN (4400lb thrust) Rolls-Royce Goblin 2/2 turbojet
- **Performance** max speed 853km/h (530mph); service ceiling 12,500m (41,000ft); range 1842km (1145 miles)
- **Dimensions** wing span 11.58m (38ft); length 11.58 m (30ft 9in); height 1.91m (6ft 3in)
- **Weight** 5606kg (12,360lb) loaded
- **Armament** four 20mm (0.79in) Hispano cannon, eight 27kg (60lb) rockets and two 227kg (500lb) bombs or two 454kg (1000lb) bombs

The de Havilland DH.100 Vampire was Britain's second jet fighter after the Gloster Meteor. The Meteor received priority for engines and did not enter service until after the war, despite having first flown in September 1943. Sharing many components with the Mosquito, the Vampire's fuselage pod was of plywood and balsa construction with armour plate bulkheads. The wings, control surfaces, tailplane and tailbooms were metal. Production examples had a quartet of 20mm (0.79in) Hispano cannon under the forward fuselage, as on the Mosquito.

The most important version was the FB 5, of which 888 were built from 1948. Strengthened for the ground-attack role, the FB 5 and related FB 50-series were exported to New Zealand, South Africa, France, Italy, India, Finland, Iraq and other countries. A number of countries licence-built Vampires. Australian production was undertaken by de Havilland Australia at Bankstown, Sydney, and Swiss aircraft were built by F+W at Emmen. The French Mistral was built by SNCASE, and HAL produced nearly 300 Vampires at Bangalore.

The Royal Auxiliary Air Force (RAuxAF) was integrated into the regular Royal Air Force (RAF) during the war, but was reformed in 1946. In May that year, No. 607 Squadron was re-established at Ouston in Yorkshire as a day-fighter squadron with Mk 14 and Mk 22 Spitfires. In June 1951, Vampire FB 5s were received and these were supplemented by FB 9s from April 1956. In February 1957, along with all the other flying units of the RAuxAF, it was disbanded.

Vampire FB 9 WR266 was first issued to No. 203 Advanced Flying School, then to No. 607 Squadron, with which it served from 1956–57. After that it was used by training units No. 233 OCU (Operational Conversion Unit) and Nos. 5 and 7 FTS (Flying Training Schools) before being struck off charge in 1960.

DOUGLAS SKYRAIDER AEW.MK 1

No. 849 Squadron C. Flight,
Fleet Air Arm, Royal Navy,
HMS Albion, 1956

DOUGLAS SKYRAIDER AEW.MK 1

Specification
- **Type** carrier-based airborne early warning aircraft
- **Crew** 3
- **Powerplant** one 2014kW (2700hp) Wright R-3350-26WA Duplex Cyclone 18-cylinder air-cooled radial engine
- **Performance** max speed 564km/h (350mph); service ceiling 7925m (26,000ft); range 2036km (1265 miles)
- **Dimensions** wing span 15.24m (50ft); length m (38ft 2in); height 3.66m (12ft)
- **Weight** 10,889kg (24,000lb) max take-off
- **Armament** Two 20mm (0.79in) cannon in the wing

The AD or A-1 Skyraider was one of many successful naval combat aircraft designed by Ed Heinemann at Douglas Aircraft. The Skyraider arose as a replacement for the TBM Avenger and SB2C Helldiver able to conduct torpedo-bombing and dive-bombing missions from aircraft carriers. The prototype, then known as the the XBT2D Destroyer II, was flown in March 1945. Renamed the AD-1 Skyraider, it entered service in December 1946.

There were many specialized versions, including the AD-4W, which replaced the TBM-3W Avenger as an airborne early warning (AEW) aircraft which extended the radar horizon of a carrier group to warn against approaching air attacks. In 1951, the Royal Navy ordered 50 versions of the AD-4W as the AEW.Mk 1; 20 of them were newly built and the remainder refurbished.

Built as an AD-4W with the US Navy Bureau Number 124768, this Skyraider first flew in May 1951 and was delivered to the Royal Navy in September 1953 after refurbishment and modification to British standard. The bulbous radome contained APS-20 search radar, and the tailplane needed additional fins to correct lateral instability caused by the extra keel area. The Skyraiders were operated by the Fleet Air Arm's No. 849 Squadron, which had been a wartime Avenger torpedo-bomber squadron that saw action at Normandy and in the Far East and Japan.

With flights on two carriers, HMS *Eagle* and *Albion*, No. 849 provided airborne radar coverage for attacks by British and French aircraft against Egypt during the Suez Crisis of October 1956. WT968 was struck off charge at Fleetlands, Hampshire, in February 1959 and later scrapped. No. 849 Squadron still carries out much the same role as it did with the Avenger, but is now equipped with the Sea King Mk.7 ASaC (Airborne Surveillance and Control) helicopter.

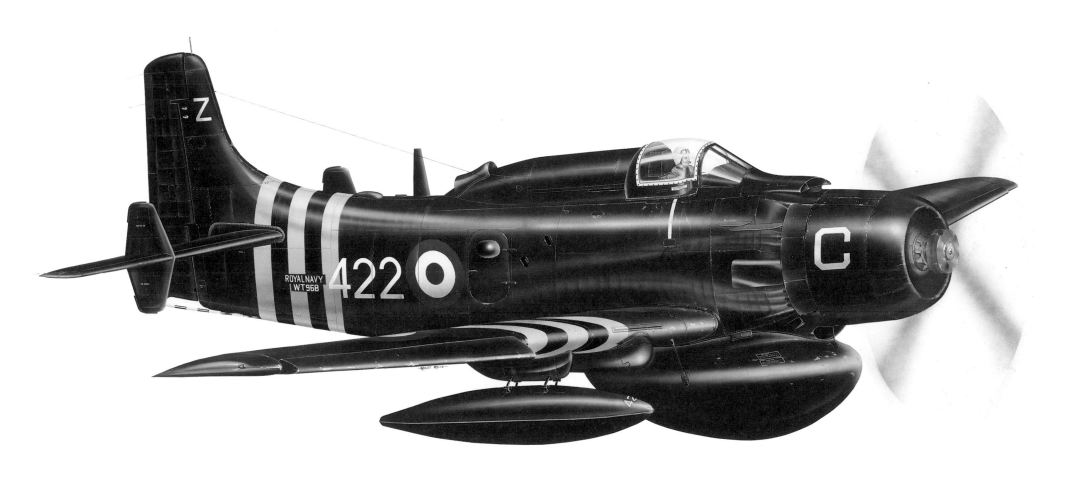

ENGLISH ELECTRIC (BAC) CANBERRA B(I).MK 8

No. 16 Squadron, Royal Air Force,
RAF Laarbruch, Germany
1960s

ENGLISH ELECTRIC (BAC) CANBERRA B(I).MK 8

Specification
- **Type** jet bomber/interdictor
- **Crew** 2
- **Powerplant** two 32.92kN (7400lb thrust) Rolls-Royce Avon RA.7 Mk 109 turbojets
- **Performance** max speed 541km/h (871mph); service ceiling 14,630m (48,000ft); range 4860km (3000 miles)
- **Dimensions** wing span 19.50m (63ft 11in); length 19.96m (65ft 6in); height 4.77m (15ft 8in)
- **Weight** 19,505kg (43,000lb) loaded
- **Armament** four 20mm (0.79in) Hispano cannon with 525 rounds per gun; up to eight 454kg (1000lb) bombs in bomb bay and external pylons; one B61 nuclear weapon in bomb bay

The Canberra was the first important aircraft designed by the English Electric company, previously known as a domestic appliance manufacturer and aircraft subcontractor. It was the result of the first British specification for a jet bomber, issued in 1945. The prototype flew in May 1949, and the B. Mk1 model entered service two years later.

Several specialized versions were created, the B(I)8 being a dedicated interdictor (or intruder) model and the first to have an offset teardrop canopy, previous Canberras having side-by-side seating under a bubble canopy. Variations of the interdictor models were exported to South Africa, New Zealand and India, and saw action with all of these nations.

The aircraft in the foreground, WT346, was built in 1955 and issued to No. 88 Squadron, Royal Air Force (RAF), at Wildenrath, Germany. Apart from a period of trials use in the United Kingdom, its career was entirely with RAF Germany, serving with Nos. 3 and 88 Squadrons before transfer to No. 14 Squadron, known as the 'Saints'. The squadron's primary role was to thwart a Soviet attack on Germany by nuclear strike against their lines of communication and supply bases. Eight No. 14 Squadron aircraft were detached to Borneo in 1965 and may been in action against Indonesian troops during the 'Confrontation' with Indonesia.

In 1972, WT346 was delivered to the RAF Museum outstation at Colerne and later displayed at Cosford. Deemed surplus to museum requirements in the early 1990s, it was obtained by the Royal New Zealand Air Force (RZNAF) Museum at Wigram and shipped to New Zealand in 1993. It remains in storage awaiting reassembly for eventual display.

ENGLISH ELECTRIC (BAC) LIGHTNING F.MK 3

No. 111 Squadron, Fighter Command, Royal Air Force, Wattisham, Suffolk late 1960s

ENGLISH ELECTRIC (BAC) LIGTHNING F.MK3

Specification

- **Type** single-seat interceptor fighter
- **Crew** 1
- **Powerplant** two 72.8kN (16,360lb thrust) Rolls-Royce Avon 301R afterburning turbojet engines
- **Performance** max speed 2414km/h (1500mph); service ceiling 18,300m (60,000ft); range 1287km (800 miles)
- **Dimensions** wing span 10.62m (34ft 10in); length 16.84m (55ft 3in); height 5.97m (19ft 7in)
- **Weight** 18,915kg (41,700lb) loaded
- **Armament** two Red Top or Firestreak IR-guided air-to-air missiles or up to 44 50mm (2in) unguided rockets; two 30-mm (1.18in) Aden cannon in a ventral pack

In 1948, the team behind the Canberra bomber won the contract for a supersonic research aircraft with its English Electric P.1 design. The English Electric P.1A flew with two Sapphire Sa.5 turbojets on 4 August 1951. Subsequent aircraft had twin Rolls-Royce Avon engines in an under-and-over configuration. The intake was in the nose, with the AI 23 Airpass radar fitted in the intake shock cone. The radar could fly the aircraft to within range of the target and fire the missiles, although the system was not as sophisticated as on contemporary US fighters.

The F 1 was followed by the F 1A with optional refuelling probe, the F 2 with fully variable reheat (afterburner), and the two-seat T 4 with side-by-side seating. The first 'second generation' Lightning was the F 3, with improved radar, Red Top air-to-air missiles and provision for fuel tanks in overwing mounts. The F 3A had an enlarged ventral fuel tank and led to the definitive F 6. The Lightning intercepted many Soviet bombers and patrol aircraft in the airspace around the British Isles, and served for years in Germany in the low-level role.

'Treble One' is one of the most famous fighter squadrons of the Royal Air Force (RAF). Formed in Palestine in 1917, it became the first Hurricane squadron in 1938 and flew Spitfires during World War II. Disbanding in 1947, it re-formed in 1953 with Meteors, exchanging them for Hunters in 1955 and Lightnings in 1961.

Lightning F.3 XP762 served with No. 111 Squadron almost all of its career. It was delivered in January 1965 and, apart from a period in 1969 spent at No. 60 Maintenance Unit, remained there until August 1974, when it was transferred to No. 29 Squadron. It was struck off charge at No. 60 MU in June 1975 and scrapped during the 1980s. No. 111 Squadron disbanded and re-formed with Phantom FG.1s in September 1974. Today, it flies the Tornado F.3 from Leuchars, Scotland.

GLOSTER JAVELIN FAW.MK 9R

No. 60 Squadron, Royal Air Force,
Tengah, Singapore, 1968

GLOSTER JAVELIN FAW.MK 9R

Specification
- **Type** all-weather interceptor fighter
- **Crew** 2
- **Powerplant** two 48.93kN (11,000lb thrust) Armstrong Siddely Sapphire Sa7R turbojets
- **Performance** max speed 1141km/h (709mph); service ceiling 16,000m (52,500ft); range 1530km (950 miles)
- **Dimensions** wing span 15.85m (52ft); length 17.3m (56ft 9in); height 4.88m (16ft)
- **Weight** 19,597kg (43,165 lb) loaded
- **Armament** two 30mm (1.18in) Aden cannon; four Firestreak air-to-air missiles

---

The Gloster Javelin was conceived in 1947 as a high-altitude night fighter for the Royal Air Force (RAF) and seen as a counterpart to the Hunter day fighter. The Gloster GA.5 prototype flew in November 1951 and was selected over de Havilland's DH.110 in 1952. The Javelin was the first twin-engined delta-winged fighter, but due to its thick wing was not supersonic. The FAW.1 entered service in 1956, and the Javelin soon became known as the 'Flatiron' and the 'Dragmaster'.

The lengthened FAW 7 was the first missile-armed version with four Firestreak IR-guided air-to-air missiles and two cannon, rather than four, and entered service in 1958. Many were later converted to FAW 8 standard with a refuelling probe and limited afterburners. Seventy-six Mk 7s were converted to definitive FAW 9 standard in 1959. Those with probes became FAW 9Rs.

No. 60 Squadron exchanged its Meteor night fighters for Javelins in July 1961 and was equipped with over 30 aircraft at a time. During the Indonesian Confrontation, they intercepted Tu-16 'Badgers' on numerous occasions and one reputedly shot down a C-130 Hercules in 1964. This FAW 9R was delivered in June 1960 and wears the customized code letters signifying the initials of No. 60 Squadron's commanding officer, Wing Commander Michael H. Miller.

In April 1968, the squadron became the last frontline unit to operate the Javelin before being disbanded at Tengah. XH872 was donated to the Republic of Singapore Air Force for technical training in December 1968. The squadron was re-formed at Wildenrath, Germany, as a communications unit with Percival Pembroke transports. In 1992, it switched to Wessex helicopters at Benson. Its identity currently resides with the RAF element of the Defence Helicopter Flying School at RAF Shawbury, which flies the Squirrel HT.1 and Griffin HT.1.

GRUMMAN TAF-9J COUGAR

*Training Squadron 23, 'Professionals',
Naval Advanced Training Command,
Naval Air Station Kingsville, Texas, 1963*

GRUMMAN TAF-9J COUGAR

Specification
- **Type** single-seat jet trainer
- **Crew** 1
- **Powerplant** one 27.80kN (6250lb thrust) Pratt & Whitney J48-P-8A turbojet engine
- **Performance** max speed 1041km/h (647mph); service ceiling 12,802m (42,000ft); range 1944km (1208 miles)
- **Dimensions** wing span 10.52m (34ft 6in); length 12.85m (42ft 2in); height 3.73m (12ft 3in)
- **Weight** 9116kg (20,098lb) loaded
- **Armament** four 20mm (0.79in) cannon; Zuni rockets in the training role

Following on from the successful F9F Panther carrier-based fighter, Grumman developed a swept-wing version to equal the performance of the MiG-15, which appeared in Korea in late 1950. In a rapid development programme, the Panther fuselage was lengthened and a new wing with 35-degree sweepback and no tip tanks was installed. A prototype of the F9F-6 was flown in September 1951. Despite its differences, the new fighter was designated as a variant of the Panther, although it was renamed the Cougar. The first squadron was equipped in late 1952, but not in time to participate in the Korean War.

The F9F-8 was the last production fighter version of the Cougar. The fuselage was again lengthened and the wing was thinner, with a broader chord and cambered leading edges, which gave better stalling characteristics. Just over 600 F9F-8s were built from 1954 onwards. During that year, the 'Blue Angels' flight demonstration flew F9F-8s from 1955–57.

Under the 1962 redesignation system, the F9F-8B fighter-bomber became the AF-9J. By this time they were only serving with Naval Reserve units, having left fleet service in 1959. The two-seat F9F-9T (TF-9J) became the first high-performance dual control jet trainer in US Navy service. Some single-seaters were used as TAF-9J trainers, as was Bureau No. 131076 seen here. Previously Advanced Training Unit 222 (ATU-222), the unit to which this Cougar belonged was redesignated Training Squadron 23 (VT-23) in 1960 and flew the F11F Tiger. TF-9 and TAF-9 Cougars arrived in 1965, and carrier qualification and air-to-ground rocketry training were added to the syllabus. In April 1970, the TA-4J Skyhawk began to replace the Cougar, but was itself replaced in these in 1972 by the T-2 Buckeye when the advanced part of the syllabus was allocated to VT-22.

HAWKER SEA FURY FB.11

No. 802 Squadron, Fleet Air Arm, HMS Ocean, Korea, 1952

HAWKER SEA FURY FB.11

Specification
- **Type** naval fighter-bomber
- **Crew** 1
- **Powerplant** one 1849kW (2480hp) Bristol Centaurus 18 18-cylinder radial engine
- **Performance** max speed 740km/h (460mph); service ceiling 10,970m (36,000ft); range 1130km (700 miles)
- **Dimensions** wing span 11.71m (38ft 5in); length 10.56m (34ft 8in); height 4.82m (15ft 10in)
- **Weight** 5670kg (12,500lb) loaded
- **Armament** four 20mm (0.79in) Hispano cannon; 907kg (2000lb) of bombs or rocket projectiles

The Hawker Sea Fury came too late to see action in World War II, the prototype making its first flight on 21 February 1945. Deliveries to the Fleet Air Arm began in July 1947.

The type performed very effectively in the Korean War, in which it was operated by six Fleet Air Arm squadrons from British and Australian light fleet carriers. It carried out many attacks on North Korean lines of communication and claimed the destruction of at least two MiG-15s.

The first encounter between the piston-engined Sea Furies and Russian-built MiG-15 jet fighters occurred on August 1952, when eight MiGs attacked a flight of Sea Furies led by Lieutenant Peter 'Hoagey' Carmichael, of No. 802 Squadron. (Pictured at right is the Hawker Sea Fury 114/O, flown by Carmichael.) During the ensuing air battle, Lieutenant Carmichael shot down a MiG, becoming the first pilot of a piston-engined aircraft to destroy an enemy jet fighter in the Korean War. There was another skirmish between Sea Furies and MiGs on the following day, resulting in the destruction of a second MiG-15. The Fleet Air Arm pilots also claimed three MiG-15s damaged. It was a formidable testimony to the ruggedness of the Sea Fury and its excellent dog-fighter characteristics.

Twenty-five FB.11s were operated by the Royal Canadian Navy. Sea Furies were exported to the Netherlands, Burma, Cuba and Federal Germany. Total Sea Fury production was 565 aircraft. Some of the Cuban Sea Furies saw action in the abortive CIA-sponsored 'Bay of Pigs' landing by Cuban exiles in 1961.

HAWKER TEMPEST F.MK.II

No. 16 Squadron, Second Tactical Air Force, Royal Air Force, Fassberg, Germany, 1947

HAWKER TEMPEST F.MK.II

Specification
- **Type** fighter-bomber
- **Crew** 1
- **Powerplant** one 1931kW (2590hp) Bristol Centaurus V 18-cylinder two-row radial engine
- **Performance** max speed 708km/h (440mph); service ceiling 10,975m (36,000ft); range 2736km (1700 miles)
- **Dimensions** wing span 12.49m (41ft); length 10.49m (34ft 5in); height 4.42m (14ft 6in)
- **Weight** 6305kg (13,900lb) loaded
- **Armament** four 20mm (0.79in) cannon; external bomb or rocket load of up to 907kg (2000lb)

The origins of the Tempest Mk II can be traced to a proposal by Hawker Aircraft for a Typhoon Mk II with a radial engine, but the prototype of the Centaurus-Typhoon Mk II was abandoned without being flown because sufficient experience had already been amassed through flight trials with the Centaurus-engined Hawker Tornado.

First flown in September 1943, the radial-engined Tempest II was intended primarily for operations in the Far East, but the war ended before the type made its operational debut. The Tempest II entered service with No. 54 Squadron at Chilbolton, Hampshire, in November 1945, and the type subsequently equipped eight squadrons, serving in India, Malaya and with 2nd Tactical Air Force (TAF) in Germany.

Development of the Tempest II was delayed by problems with the powerplant, and in the event it was the Napier-engined Mk V which was the first Tempest model to enter production, seeing action in the last year of World War II. However, the fast and powerful Mk II peformed a useful ground-attack function in Germany during the dangerous early years of the Cold War, and No. 33 Squadron used the type successfully against communist insurgents in Malaya from 1949–51. India and Pakistan took delivery of 89 and 24 Tempest IIs, respectively, in 1947–48.

The Tempest II was the last of the Royal Air Force's single-engined piston fighters, the squadrons that used it mostly converting to de Havilland Vampire FB.5 jet fighter-bombers in 1948. Total production of the Tempest II reached 472 examples, the first of which was completed in October 1944.

ILYUSHIN IL-28R BEAGLE

7 Brygada Lotnictwa Bombowego
Bombowo-Rozpoznawcezgo,
Ludowe Lotnictwo Polskie
(Polish People's Aviation)
Powidz, Poland, 1960s

ILYUSHIN IL-28R BEAGLE

Specification
- **Type** twin-engined jet reconnaissance aircraft
- **Crew** 3
- **Powerplant** two 26.48kN (5952lb thrust) Klimov VK-1A turbojet engines
- **Performance** max speed 902km/h (560mph); service ceiling 12,300m (40,350ft); range 2400km (1491 miles)
- **Dimensions** wing span 21.45m (70ft 4.5in); length 17.65m (57ft 11in); height 6.7m (21ft 11.75in)
- **Weight** 18,400kg (40,564lb) loaded
- **Armament** two 23mm (0.91mm) NR-23 cannon in tail and two in nose; bomber versions can carry up to 3000kg (6614lb) of bombs

The Il-28 was the Soviet Union's first jet bomber, and regarded as the Eastern Bloc's equivalent of the English Electric Canberra, which it preceded into flight by nearly a year. First flown in July 1948, using British Nene engines, the Il-28 entered service with Soviet bomber squadrons in 1950 and remained in production for many years. NATO gave it the reporting name 'Beagle'. Over 6000 were built by the Soviet Union and (without a licence) in China, where it was designated the Harbin H-5. The basic bomber was modified for a variety of roles, including reconnaissance, torpedo bombing, anti-submarine warfare, training, transport, target tug and even as an unpiloted target drone. The 'Beagle' was exported to more than 20 countries.

The IL-28 was introduced into Polish service in 1953 and the *Ludowe Lotnictwo Polskie* (air force) and *Lotnictwo Marynarki Wojennej* (naval aviation) operated the Il-28 bomber, Il-28R reconnaissance aircraft and the Il-28U 'Mascot' trainer with a raised rear cockpit. The Il-28R variant was a three-seat tactical reconnaissance version containing four or five cameras. The tail of the 'Beagle' contains the rear gunner/radio operator and two 23mm (0.91in) NR-23 cannon. The pilot had a fighter-type cockpit and an ejection seat. The Il-28R introduced wingtip fuel tanks, which were also used on electronic intelligence versions, which were based on the R and the Il-28T target tug.

The Polish Air Force's Il-28Rs served with 7 BLB (*Brygada Lotnictwa Bombowego* (Bomber Brigade) at Powidz Air Base from 1953. The Navy also used the Il-28R with the 15 *selr* MW (*samodzielna eskadra rozpoznawcza Marynarki Wojennej* – Navy Aviation independent reconnaissance squadron). In 1979 the last target tug versions were retired from Polish service.

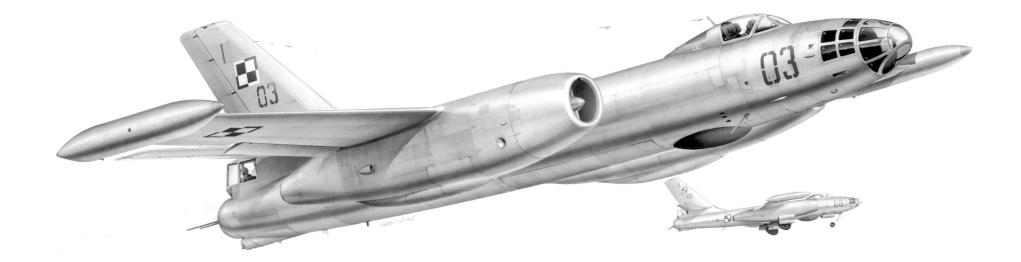

LOCKHEED AC-130H PAVE SPECTRE

16th Special Operations Squadron, United States Air Force, Ubon, Thailand, 1969

LOCKHEED AC-130H PAVE SPECTRE

Specification
- **Type** gunship
- **Crew** 15
- **Powerplant** four 3362kW (4508hp) Allison T56-A-15 turboprop engines
- **Performance** max speed 583km/h (362mph); service ceiling 5485m (18,000ft); range 3600km (2238 miles)
- **Dimensions** wing span 40.41m (132ft 7in); length 29.79m (97ft 9in); height 11.68m (38ft 4in)
- **Weight** 70,308kg (155,000lb) loaded
- **Armament** one 105mm (4.13in) Howitzer; one Bofors L60 40mm (1.47in) cannon; two M61A1 20mm (0.79in) Vulcan cannon

The Lockheed C-130H, known as the Pave Spectre, was the final incarnation in the various stages of Hercules gunship development that began with the AC-130E. The formidable AC-130 gunships have an impressive combat history.

During the Vietnam War, they destroyed more than 10,000 trucks and were credited with many life-saving close air support missions. Following the end of the Vietnam War, they saw action during the attempted rescue of the crew of the USS *Mayaguez* (1975), Operation Urgent Fury in Grenada (1983), Operation Just Cause in Panama (1989), Operation Desert Storm in Iraq (1991), Operation Restore Hope in Somalia (1993–94), and Operation Deliberate Force in Bosnia (1995).

On 31 January 1991, the first AC-130H was lost in combat while supporting coalition forces engaged in ground combat during the battle of Khafji during Operation Desert Storm. A second aircraft supporting operations in Somalia was lost on 15 March 1994 when the 105mm (4.13in) cannon exploded while the aircraft was airborne.

The eight remaining AC-130H 'Spectre' gunships were still flying in 2004 with the 16th Special Operations Squadron (SOS), part of the 16th Special Operations Wing (SOW), at Hurlburt Field, Florida. In all, 43 C-130E Hercules aircraft were converted to gunship configuration.

Although the AC-130 Hercules gunships could lay down formidable firepower, they were also vulnerable to enemy ground fire. As well as the losses detailed above, six AC-130s were lost on operations over Vietnam.

Illustrated here is a Lockheed AC-130H Pave Spectre demonstrating its formidable firepower of M61A1 Vulcan cannon, 40mm (1.47in) Bofors L2A1 and 105mm M102 Howitzer guns.

LOCKHEED C-130E HERCULES

United States Air Force
Vietnam, 1966

LOCKHEED C-130E HERCULES

Specification
- **Type** transport aircraft
- **Crew** 4
- **Powerplant** four 3020kW (4050hp) Allison T56-A-7 turboprop engines
- **Performance** max speed 547km/h (340mph); service ceiling 10,060m (33,000ft); range 6145km (3820 miles)
- **Dimensions** wing span 40.41m (132ft 7in); length 29.79m (97ft 9in); height 11.68m (38ft 4in)
- **Weight** 70,308kg (155,000lb) loaded
- **Payload** 19,051kg (42,000lb)

Without doubt the most versatile tactical transport aircraft ever built, the Lockheed C-130 Hercules flew for the first time on 23 August 1954, and many different variants were produced over the next half-century. The initial production versions were the C-130A and C130-B, of which 461 were built. These were followed by the major production variant, the C-130E, 510 examples of which were produced.

The first C-130E flew on 15 August 1961, deliveries to the 4442nd Combat Crew Training Group, Tactical Air Command, began in April 1962, and the first export C-130E went to the Royal Canadian Air Force (RCAF) in December 1964. The C-130E can carry a maximum of 92 troops, 64 paratroops or 70 stretchers with six attendants. Other versions include the AC-130E gunship, the WC-130E weather reconnaissance aircraft, the KC-130F assault transport for the US Marine Corps (USMC), the HC-130H for aerospace rescue and recovery, the C-130K for the Royal Air Force (RAF), and the LC-130R, which has wheel/ski landing gear.

Total production of the Hercules, all variants, was some 2000 aircraft. As well as the US forces and the RAF, the Hercules was supplied to no fewer than 61 air forces around the world. The RAF is the second-largest Hercules user, operating 80 aircraft (C.1s, C.3s, C.4s and C.5s).

The Low-Altitude Parachute Exctraction System (LAPES) seen on the aircraft illustrated here was devised for delivering bulky or heavy cargo in situations where landing the Hercules was not possible or desirable. Parachutes pull the cargo pallet from the hold while the aircraft flies a few feet above the ground.

LOCKHEED F-80 SHOOTING STAR

36th Fighter-Bomber Squadron,
Eighth Fighter-Bomber Wing,
United States Air Force,
Itazuke, Japan, June 1950

LOCKHEED F-80 SHOOTING STAR

Specification
- **Type** fighter-bomber
- **Crew** 1
- **Powerplant** one 2449kg (5400lb thrust) Allison J33-A-35 turbojet
- **Performance** max speed 966km/h (594mph); service ceiling 14,265m (46,800ft); range 1328km (825 miles)
- **Dimensions** wing span 11.81m (38ft 9in); length 10.49m (34ft 5in); height 3.43m (11ft 3in); wing area 22.07m² (237.6sq ft)
- **Weight** 7646kg (16,856lb) loaded
- **Armament** six 12.7mm (0.50in) machine guns, plus two 454kg (1000lb) bombs and eight rockets

The prototype Lockheed XP-80 Shooting Star first flew on 9 January 1944, with early production P-80As entering US Army Air Forces (USAAF) service late in 1945 with the 412th Fighter Group, which became the 1st Fighter Group in July 1946 and comprised the 27th, 71st and 94th Fighter Squadrons.

The P-80A was followed by the P-80B; the major production version was the F-80C (the P for 'pursuit' prefix having changed to the much more logical F for 'fighter' in the meantime). The F-80C was the fighter-bomber workhorse of the Korean War, flying 15,000 sorties in the first four months alone.

On 28 June 1950, the third day of the Korean War, the 35th Fighter Squadron, nicknamed the 'Panthers' and operating out of Itazuke in Japan, became the first American jet squadron to destroy an enemy aircraft. The engagement took place while the F-80s were protecting a flight of North American Twin Mustangs. Captain Raymond E. Schillereff led four aircraft into the Seoul area and caught a quartet of Ilyushin Il-10s which were attempting to interfere with US transport aircraft embarking civilians at Seoul's Kimpo airfield; all four Il-10s were shot down.

The Shooting Star was assured of its place in history when First Lieutenant Russell Brown of the 51st Fighter Wing shot down a MiG-15 jet fighter on 8 November 1950, during history's jet-versus-jet battle. The F-80 held the line in Korea until the arrival of the first North American F-86 Sabres.

LOCKHEED F-94C STARFIRE

96th Fighter Squadron, United States Air Force, New Castle County Airport, Delaware, 1952

The Lockheed F-94 Starfire all-weather fighter was developed from the T-33A trainer, two production T-33 airframes being converted as YF-94s. The first of these flew on 16 April 1949. The F-94A went into production in 1949; 200 examples were built, the first entering service in June 1950 with the 319th All-Weather Fighter Squadron.

The next variant, the F-94B, was followed by the F-94C, which differed so extensively from its predecessors that it was originally known as the YF-97A. Total production of the F-94C came to 387 aircraft before the series was completed in 1954.

F-94Cs saw limited service during the Korean War with the 68th and 319th Fighter Interceptor Squadrons, when they were mainly used to combat North Korean Po-2 'intruder' biplanes. One F-94 pilot did manage to shoot down a Po-2 by throttling right back and lowering undercarriage and flaps to reduce speed, but the fighter stalled immediately afterwards and spun into the ground, killing its crew. Another F-94 was lost when it collided with a Po-2.

Towards the end of the Korean War, F-94s began to operate over enemy territory to provide a protective screen for B-29 night bombers and reconnaissance aircraft and had some success against communist aircraft, shooting down a number of Lavochkin La-9 piston-engined fighter and at least one MiG-15 jet.

The 96th Fighter Squadron was variously assigned to the 4710th Air Defense Wing, 525th Air Defense Group and, finally, the 82nd Fighter Group. It was equipped with F-84Cs until 1957, when it was deactivated.

LOCKHEED F-94C STARFIRE

Specification
- **Type** night and all-weather fighter
- **Crew** 2
- **Powerplant** one 2742kg (6000lb thrust) Allison J33-A-33 turbojet
- **Performance** max speed 933km/h (580mph); service ceiling 14,630m (48,000ft); range 1850km (1150 miles)
- **Dimensions** wing span 11.85m (38ft 10in) not including tip tanks; length 12.20m (40ft 1in); height 3.99m (12ft 8in)
- **Weight** 7125kg (15,710lb)
- **Armament** four 12.7mm (0.50in) machine guns or 24 unguided folding-fin aircraft rockets

LOCKHEED (CANADAIR) CF-104 STARFIGHTER

No. 434 'Bluenose' Squadron, Royal Canadian Air Force, Zweibrücken, Federal Republic of Germany, 1966

LOCKHEED (CANADAIR) CF-104 STARFIGHTER

Specification
- **Type** strike aircraft
- **Crew** 1
- **Powerplant** one 7076kg (15,600lb) thrust Orenda-built General Electric J79-GE-11A turbojet
- **Performance** max speed 1845km/h (1146mph); service ceiling 15,240m (50,000ft); range 1740km (1081 miles)
- **Dimensions** wing span 6.36m (21ft 9in); length 16.66m (54ft 8in); height 4.09m (13ft 5in)
- **Weight** 13,170kg (29,035lb) loaded
- **Armament** Sidewinder air-to-air missiles on wing or fuselage stations; up to 1814kg (4000lb) of ordnance, including tactical nuclear weapons

Canada was a major user of the Starfighter, with 200 aircraft being built by Canadair as the CF-104. The type was powered by an Orenda-built J79 engine and was intended only for the nuclear strike role, the 20mm (0.79in) cannon of the F-104G being replaced by an extra 454kg (1000lb) of fuel.

By early 1964, eight former Royal Canadian Air Force (RCAF) Sabre units in Europe had converted to the CF-104. The organization comprised No. 1 Fighter Wing (439 and 441 Squadrons) at Marville, France; No. 2 Fighter Wing (421 and 430 Squadrons) at Gros Tenquin, France; No. 3 Fighter Wing (427 and 434 Squadrons) at Zweibrücken, Germany; and No. 4 Fighter Wing (421 Squadron at Lahr, Germany. When Marville closed following France's withdrawal from Nato in 1966, Nos 439 and 441 Squadrons also moved to Lahr.

The German-based CF-104 force was progressively reduced in the late 1960s, and, by 1972, the three remaining CF-104 squadrons (Nos 421, 439 and 441) were concentrated on Baden-Söllingen, the rest having disbanded. The Baden Wing was redesignated the 1st Canadian Air Group, which began to rearm with the CF-188 Hornet in 1985. The last Canadian Starfighter unit was No. 439 Squadron, which relinquished its aircraft in 1987.

No. 434 'Bluenose' Squadron, formed at Tholthorpe in Yorkshire in 1943, took its title from the common nickname for Nova Scotians. Operating Halifaxes and then Lancasters, it flew from another Yorkshire base, Croft, until June 1945, when it returned to Canada. It re-formed in 1952 and returned to Europe with Canadair Sabre Mk 2 aircraft.

LOCKHEED F-104G STARFIGHTER

Jagdbombergeschwader 33, Luftwaffe, Büchel, Federal Republic of Germany 1960s

LOCKHEED F-104G STARFIGHTER

Specification
- **Type** supersonic multi-role fighter
- **Crew** 1
- **Powerplant** One 70.3kN (15,800lb thrust) General Electric J79-GE-11A afterburning turbojet engine
- **Performance** max speed 2338km/h (1453mph); service ceiling 17,678m (58,000ft); range 3500km (2175 miles)
- **Dimensions** wing span 6.68m (21ft 11in); length 16.69m (54ft 9in); height 4.11m (13ft 6in)
- **Weight** 13054kg (28,779lb) loaded
- **Armament** one M61A1 Vulcan 20mm (0.79in) cannon with 750 rounds, plus up to 1955kg (4310lb) of ordnance, including conventional and nuclear bombs and AIM-9 air-to-air missiles

In the so-called fighter sale of the century, the F-104 Starfighter was supplied to Nato air forces from Norway to Spain, and factories in four European countries produced many hundreds of F-104s, as did facilities in the United States and Canada. All of these factories built Starfighters for their own forces and for Germany, which was by far the biggest user.

The *Luftwaffe*'s first Starfighter (a two-seat F-104F) was received in 1960, and eventually 917 entered service – a mixture of F-104F and TF-104G trainers, reconnaissance RF-104Gs and F-104G fighter-bombers. The F-104G was better equipped than US Air Force (USAF) Starfighters, having its weapons system based on that of the F-105 Thunderchief. In *Luftwaffe* service, the Starfighter was used largely as a low-level strike aircraft, and pilots found it hard to adjust European weather and airspace restrictions after training in sunny Arizona.

Starfighters suffered a very high accident rate; about 270 F-104s were lost by the *Luftwaffe* and *Marineflieger* (naval air arm) in air and ground mishaps. Over 100 pilots were killed, and there was great controversy about the F-104's purchase and operation. The fatality rate was reduced when the Lockheed C-2 ejection seats were modified, then replaced with the Martin-Baker Mk 7 zero-zero seat in 1966. The F-104G depicted has the original seat and also the alpha-numeric codes used until 1968, when a wholly numeric system was introduced – DC+244 became 21+91.

Jagdbombergeschwader 33 (JMB 33) flew the Starfighter at Büchel from August 1962 to May 1985 and now flies the Tornado IDS at Büchel. Its main role was nuclear strike and during the Cold War kept six F-104s on alert at all times armed with the one-megaton B43 nuclear bomb. Secondary roles included conventional strike with bombs, rockets and cannon.

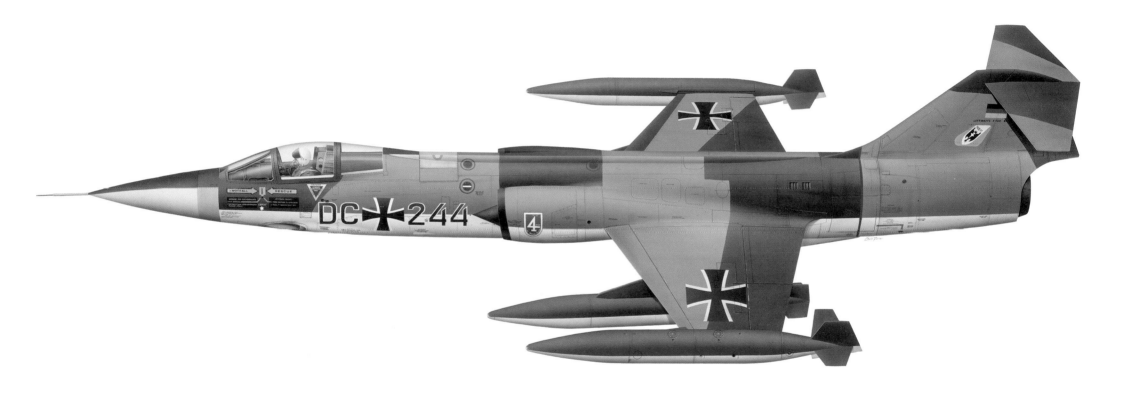

LOCKHEED F-104J STARFIGHTER

204th Hikotai (Squadron), 5th Kokudan (Wing), Japanese Air Self-Defence Force 1966

LOCKHEED F-104J STARFIGHTER

Specification
- **Crew** interceptor
- **Crew** 1
- **Powerplant** one 7076kg (15,600lb thrust) General Electric J79-GE-11A turbojet
- **Performance** max speed 1845km/h (1146mph); service ceiling 15,240m (50,000ft); range 1740km (1081 miles)
- **Dimensions** wing span 6.36m (21ft 9in); length 16.66m (54ft 8in); height 4.09m (13ft 5in)
- **Weight** 13,170kg (29,035lb) loaded
- **Armament** one 20mm (0.79in) General Electric M61A1 cannon; Sidewinder air-to-air missiles on wing or fuselage stations; up to 1814kg (4000lb) of ordnance, including Bullpup air-to-surface missiles

Development of the F-104 began in 1951, when the lessons of the Korean air war were starting to bring about profound changes in combat aircraft design. A contract for two XF-104 prototypes was placed in 1953, and the first of these flew on 7 February 1954, only 11 months later.

The aircraft was ordered into production as the F-104A, with deliveries to the US Air Force (USAF) Air Defense Command beginning in January 1958. F104As were also supplied to Nationalist China and Pakistan, and saw combat during the Indo-Pakistan conflict of 1969. The F104B was a two-seat version, and the F-104C was a tactical fighter-bomber, the first of 77 examples being delivered to the 479th Tactical Fighter Wing (the only unit to use it) in October 1958.

Two more two-seat Starfighters, the F-104D and F-104F, were followed by the F-104G, which was numerically the most important variant. The basically similar CF-104 was a strike-reconnaissance aircraft, 200 of which were built by Canadair for the Royal Canadian Air Force (RCAF). Also similar to the F-104G was the F-104J for the Japan Air Self-Defence Force; the first one flew on 30 June 1961 and 207 were produced by Mitsubishi. The F-104S was an interceptor development of the F-104G, with provision for external stores, and was capable of Mach 2.4; 165 examples were licence-built in Italy.

The Lockheed F-104J was first-line equipment in the Japanese Air Self-Defence Force (JSDAF) from October 1962 to December 1967, when it was replaced by the F-4 Phantom.

LOCKHEED P-3C ORION

US Navy Patrol Squadron 19 (VP-19), United States Navy, Naval Air Station Moffett Field, California, 1963

LOCKHEED P-3C ORION

Specification
- **Type** maritime patrol aircraft
- **Crew** 10
- **Powerplant** four 3661kW (4910hp) Allison T56-A-14 turboprop engines
- **Performance** max speed 761km/h (473mph); service ceiling 8625m (28,300ft); range 3835km (2383 miles)
- **Dimensions** wing span 30.37m (99ft 8in); length 35.61m (116ft 10in); height 10.29m (33ft 8in)
- **Weight** 61,235kg (135,000lb) loaded
- **Armament** up to 8735g (19,250lb) of ASW stores

A development of the Lockheed Electra airliner, the P-3 (formerly P3V-1) Orion was Lockheed's winning submission in a 1958 US Navy contest for a new off-the-shelf ASW aircraft which could be brought into service very rapidly by modifying an existing type. The first of two YP3V-1 prototypes flew on 19 August 1958, and deliveries of production P-3As began in August 1962.

The WP-3A was a weather reconnaissance version, the next patrol variant being the P-3A. Total P-3A/B production ran to 286 aircraft for the US Navy, plus five for the Royal New Zealand Air Force (RNZAF), 10 for the Royal Australian Air Force (RAAF) and five for Norway. The definitive P-3C variant appeared in 1969; in addition to the 132 P-3Cs delivered to the US Navy, 10 aircraft were ordered by the RAAF.

Further variants of the Orion include the EP-3A electronic intelligence aircraft, the P-3F, six of which were delivered to the Imperial Iranian Air Force in 1975, and the CP-140 Aurora for the Canadian Armed Forces. The Orion was built under licence in Japan, and also serves with the RAAF, the RNZAF, the Republic of Korea, the Netherlands, Pakistan, Portugal and Spain. Foreign-operated Orions have all undergone upgrades over the years.

The Lockheed Orion shown here, 159511, is an early production P-3C. The type replaced the P2V Neptune in service with US Navy Patrol Squadron 19 (VP-19). One of the squadron's Neptunes was shot down by Soviet MiG-17s off the Siberian coast in September 1954.

MCDONNELL F2H-2N BANSHEE

Composite Squadron VC-4,
USS Coral Sea, *United States Navy,*
Mediterranean, 1952

MCDONNELL F2H-2N BANSHEE

Specification
- **Type** carrier-based night fighter
- **Crew** 1
- **Powerplant** one 1474kg (3205lb thrust) Westinghouse J34-E-34 turbojet
- **Performance** max speed 933km/h (580mph); service ceiling 14,205m (46,600ft); range 1883km (1170 miles)
- **Dimensions** wing span 12.73m (41ft 9in); length 14.68m (48ft 2in); height 4.42m (14ft 6in)
- **Weight** 11,437kg (25,214lb) loaded
- **Armament** four 20mm (0.79in) cannon; underwing racks with provision for two 227kg (500lb) or four 113kg (250lb) bombs

The F2H Banshee, which stemmed from a 1945 contract for a jet fighter-bomber for the US Navy, was the direct successor to the US Navy's first jet fighter, the McDonnell FH-1 Phantom. The prototype, designated XF2D-1, flew for the first time on 11 January 1947, powered by two Westinghouse J34 turbojets, and the first series production F2H-1s were delivered to Navy Fighter Squadron VF-171 in March 1949.

The Banshee went into combat in Korea for the first time on 23 August 1951, when F2H-2s of VF-172 (USS *Essex*) struck at targets in northwest Korea. The F2H-2N was a night-fighter version. The F2H-2P was a photo-reconnaissance variant, 89 of which were built. The F2H-3 (redesignated F2-C in 1962) was a long-range limited all-weather development; 250 were built, and the type equipped two squadrons of the Royal Canadian Navy, operating from the carrier HMCS *Bonaventure*. The F2H-4 (F2-D) was a variant equipped for flight refuelling.

Composite Squadron VC-4 was a specialist night-fighter unit. In 1952, while embarked on the USS *Coral Sea* in the Mediterranean, it comprised four Vought F4U-5N Corsairs and four F2H-2N Banshees. Also attached to the squadron at this time were some F2H-2B Banshees, configured to carry two small nuclear weapons.

During the Korean War, VC-4 provided Banshee night-fighter detachments to the carrier *Bonne Homme Richard*, operating in that theatre. The squadron was based on the East Coast of the United States, and its principal deployments were to the carriers *Roosevelt*, *Tarawa*, *Midway*, *Siboney*, *Leyte*, *Saipan*, *Wright*, *Mindoro*, *Salerno Bay*, *Coral Sea* and *Wasp*.

MCDONNELL F-101 VOODOO

60th Fighter Interceptor Squadron, Air Defense Command, United States Air Force, Hanscom Air Force Base, Massachusetts, 1957

MCDONNELL F-101B VOODOO

Specification
- **Type** all-weather fighter
- **Crew** 2
- **Powerplant** two 7672kg (16,900lb thrust) Pratt & Whitney J57-P-55 turbojets
- **Performance** max speed 1965km/h (1221mph); service ceiling 16,705m (54,800ft); range 2494km (1550 miles)
- **Dimensions** wing span 12.09m (39ft 8in); length 20.54m (67ft 4in); height 5.49m (18ft)
- **Weight** 23,768kg (52,400lb) loaded
- **Armament** two Mb-2 Genie nuclear-tipped air-to-air missiles and four AIM-4C, AIM-4D or AIM-4G Falcon missiles, or six Falcons

In 1946, the US Air Force (USAF) Strategic Air Command issued a requirement for a so-called 'penetration fighter', intended primarily to escort the Convair B-36, or rather to sweep ahead of the bomber force and tear gaps in the enemy's fighter defences. One of the contenders was the McDonnell XF-88, which was flown in prototype form, but later abandoned.

In 1951, McDonnell used the design of the XF-88 as the basis for a completely new aircraft, lengthening the fuselage to accommodate two Pratt & Whitney J57-P-13 engines, giving it a top speed of over 1600km/h (1000 mph) and a ceiling of 15,850m (52,000ft), and increased fuel tankage. In its new guise, the aircraft became the F-101A Voodoo, which first flew on 29 December 1954.

The next Voodoo variant, the two-seat F-101B, equipped 16 squadrons of Air Defense Command. This version also equipped three Canadian air defence squadrons as the CF-101B, and formed a very important component of Canada's air defences. The F-101C was a single-seat fighter-bomber version for Tactical Air Command (TAC), entering service with the 523rd Tactical Fighter Squadron of the 27th Fighter-Bomber Wing in May 1957. It equipped nine squadrons, but its operational career was relatively short-lived, as it was replaced by more modern combat types in the early 1960s. F-101Cs served with the 81st Tactical Fighter Wing at Bentwaters, Suffolk, England.

This 60th Fighter Intercept Squadron F-101B Voodoo is pictured here in the so-called 'ADC Grey' scheme of light gloss grey with white undersides. Most units applied colourful insignia, such as the 60th Fighter Intercept Squadron's stylized bird of the fuselage.

MIKOYAN-GUREVICH MIG-25P FOXBAT-A

Sakhalovka Interceptor Wing, Soviet Air Defence Forces, Vladivostok, Russia 1967

The prototype MiG-25 was flown as early as 1964 and was apparently designed to counter the projected North American B-70 bomber, with its Mach 3.0 speed and ceiling of 21,350m (70,000ft). The cancellation of the B-70 left the Foxbat in search of a role; it entered service as an interceptor in 1970 with the designation MiG-25P (Foxbat-A), its role now redefined as being capable of countering all air targets in all weather conditions, day or night, and in dense hostile electronic warfare environments.

The MiG-25P continues to serve in substantial numbers and constitutes part of the Russian S-155P missile interceptor system. Variants of the MiG-25 are also in service in the Ukraine, Kazakhstan, Azerbaijan, India, Iraq, Algeria, Syria and Libya. The MiG-25R, MiG-25RB and MiG-25BM are derivatives of the MiG-25P. The MiG-25R, as its suffix implies, is a reconnaissance variant, while the MiG-25RB has a high-level bombing capability against area targets.

This version is fitted with a reconnaissance station, aerial camera, topographic aerial camera, the Peteng sighting and navigation system for bombing programmed targets, and electronic countermeasures (ECM) equipment, which includes active jamming and electronic reconnaissance systems. The MiG-25BM variant has the capability to launch guided missiles against ground targets, and to destroy area targets, targets with known coordinates, and enemy radars.

The MiG-25P's enormous main radar, code-named 'Fox Fire' by Nato, is a typical 1959 technology set. It uses thermionic valves (vacuum tubes) and puts out 600kW (805hp) of power to burn through enemy jamming.

MIKOYAN-GUREVICH MIG-25P FOXBAT-A

Specification
- **Type** interceptor
- **Crew** 1
- **Powerplant** two 10,200kg (22,487lb) thrust Tumanskii R-15B-300 turbojets
- **Performance** max speed 2974km/h (1848mph); service ceiling 24,383m (80,000ft); combat radius 1130km (702 miles)
- **Dimensions** wing span 14.02m (45ft 11in); length 23.82m (78ft 1in); height 6.10m (20ft)
- **Weight** 37,425kg (82,508lb) loaded
- **Armament** four underwing pylons for various combinations of air-to-air missile

NORTH AMERICAN F-86D SABRE

498th Fighter Interceptor Squadron, 84th Fighter Group, United States Air Force, Geiger Field, Washington, 1955

NORTH AMERICAN F-86D SABRE

Specification
- **Type** night and all-weather interceptor (F-86D)
- **Crew** 1
- **Powerplant** one 3402kg (7500lb thrust) General Electric J47-GE-17B turbojet
- **Performance** max speed 1138km/h (707mph); service ceiling 16,640m (54,600ft); range 1344km (835 miles)
- **Dimensions** wing span 11.30m (37ft 1in); length 12.29m (40ft 4in); height 4.57m (15ft)
- **Weight** 7756kg (17,100lb) loaded
- **Armament** 24 70mm (2.75in) 'Mighty Mouse' air-to-air unguided rocket projectiles

The most famous of the early generation of jet fighters, the F-86 Sabre flew for the first time on 1 October 1947, powered by a General Electric J35 turbojet. The first operational F-86As were delivered to the 1st Fighter Group early in 1949. During the Korean War, Sabres claimed the destruction of 810 enemy aircraft, 792 of them MiG-15s.

The next Sabre variants were the F-86C penetration fighter (which was redesignated YF-93A and which flew only as a prototype) and the F-86D all-weather fighter, which had a complex fire control system and a ventral rocket pack; 2201 were built, the F-86L being an updated version. The F-86E was basically an F-86A with power-operated controls and an all-flying tail; it was replaced by the F-86F, the major production version, with 2247 examples being delivered. The F-86H was a specialized fighter-bomber capable of carrying a tactical nuclear weapon; the F-86K was essentially a simplified F-86D; and the designation F-86J was applied to the Canadair-built Sabre Mk.3. Most of the Sabres built by Canadair were destined for Nato air forces; the Royal Air Force, for example, received 427. The Sabre was also built under licence in Australia as the Sabre Mk.30/32, powered by a Rolls-Royce Avon turbojet.

Known as the 'Geiger Tigers', the 498th Fighter Interceptor Squadron was activated on 18 August 1955 August, equipped with F-86Ds inherited from the 520th Fighter Interceptor Squadron. Its Sabres were replaced by F-102 Delta daggers in 1956.

NORTH AMERICAN F-100D SUPER SABRE

416th Tactical Fighter Squadron,
31st Tactical Fighter Wing,
United States Air Force,
Tuy Hoa Air Base, Vietnam, 1965

NORTH AMERICAN F-100D SUPER SABRE

Specification
- **Type** fighter-bomber
- **Crew** 1
- **Powerplant** one 7711kg (17,000lb) thrust Pratt & Whitney J57-P-21A turbojet
- **Performance** max speed 1390km/h (864mph); service ceiling 14,020m (46,000ft); range 966km (600 miles)
- **Dimensions** wing span 11.82m (38ft 9in); length 14.36m (47ft 1in); height 4.95m (16ft 3in)
- **Weight** 15,800kg (34,832lb) loaded
- **Armament** four 20mm (0.79in) cannon; eight external hardpoints with provision for up to 3402kg (7500lb) of stores

---

The North American F-100 Super Sabre was the first combat aircraft in the world capable of sustained level flight above Mach 1. The first prototype F-100 flew on 25 May 1953 and exceeded Mach 1 on its maiden flight. The type was grounded in November 1954 following a series of unexplained crashes, which turned out to be caused by structural failure of the wing centre box, but after various modifications the F-100A began flying operationally again in February 1955, and 22 examples were built.

The next series production variant was the F-100C, which was capable of carrying out both ground-attack and interception missions. First deliveries to the US Air Force (USAF) were made in July 1955, and total production was 451, of which 260 went to the Turkish Air Force. The F-100D differed from the F-100C in having an automatic pilot, jettisonable underwing pylons and modified vertical tail surfaces; it was supplied to the USAF Tactical Air Command, Denmark, France and Greece. The TF-100C was a two-seat trainer variant and served as the prototype of the TF-100F, which flew in July 1957. Total production of all Super Sabre variants was 2294, with many aircraft serving in Vietnam.

The F-100D illustrated here is seen in natural metal finish, which changed to tactical camouflage late in 1965. The blue chevrons on the tail identify the aircraft as belonging to the 416th Fighter Squadron. Many F-100Ds were later converted to the unmanned target drone role as QF-100Ds by Tracor/Flight Systems.

NORTH AMERICAN FJ FURY

Navy Fighter Squadron VF-21,
USS Forrestal, *United States Navy, 1956*

NORTH AMERICAN FJ FURY

Specification
- **Type** carrier-based jet fighter
- **Crew** 1
- **Powerplant** one 3648kg (7800lb) thrust Wright J65-W-2 turbojet
- **Performance** max speed 1091km/h (678mph); service ceiling 16,640m (54,600ft); range 1344km (835 miles)
- **Dimensions** wing span 11.30m (37ft 1in); length 11.43m (37ft 6in); height 4.47m (14ft 8in)
- **Weight** 9350kg (20,611lb) loaded
- **Armament** six 12.7mm (0.50in) Colt-Browning M-3 machine guns; up to 907kg (2000lb) of underwing stores

In 1951, the US Navy Bureau of Aeronautics asked North American Aviaion to 'navalize' two F-86E Sabre airframes for carrier trials, as the Korean War was proving that existing fighters were inferior to the MiG-15. Designated XFJ-2, the first navalized aircraft flew on 19 February 1952, and the second aircraft carried an armament of four 20mm (0.79in) cannon in place of the F-86's six 12.7mm (0.50in) machine guns.

Carrier trials aboard the USS *Midway* were completed in August 1952, and the type entered full production for the US Navy as the FJ-2 Fury. The FJ-2 gave way on the production line to the FJ-3, with a Wright J65-W-3 turbojet, and the last variant was the FJ-4, which incorporated so many new design features that it was virtually a new aircraft. The FJ-4B was developed specifically for low-level attack, featuring a good deal of structural strengthening and a low-altitude bombing system for the delivery of a tactical nuclear weapon.

The FJ-3M Fury shown here was the personal aircraft of Lieutenant Commander Donald Engen, Executive Officer of VF-21. Engen had been awarded the Navy Cross as a Curtiss Helldiver pilot in World War II, and led VF-21's Fury-equipped aerobatic team, the 'Gray Ghosts'. He reached the rank of vice admiral before leaving the US Navy.

At the time of VF-21's deployment on the USS *Forrestal* in January 1956, the carrier was brand new. On returning to the *Forrestal*'s home port at Norfolk, Virginia, the squadron transferred to USS *Bennington*.

NORTH AMERICAN X-15

NASA

Edwards Air Force Base, 1962

NORTH AMERICAN X-15

Specification
- **Type** hypersonic research aircraft
- **Crew** 1
- **Powerplant** one 31,751kg (70,000lb) thrust Thiokol (Reaction Motors) XLR99-RM-2 rocket unit
- **Performance** max speed 6693km/h (4159mph); maximum ceiling 107,960m (354,200ft)
- **Dimensions** wing span 6.7m (22ft); length 15.24m (50ft); height 4.1m (13ft 6in)
- **Weight** 14,186kg (31,276lb)
- **Armament** none

The North American X-15 rocket-powered research aircraft bridged the gap between manned flight within the atmosphere and manned flight beyond the atmosphere into space. Its weight and size precluded the launch of the aircraft by existing B-29 and B-50 mother aircraft; after briefly considering the modification of a Convair B-36 for this role, the contractor and government selected the Boeing B-52 as the X-15 launch aircraft.

Accordingly, a B-52A and a B-52B were delivered to North American to be modified as an NB-52A and NB-52B, respectively, by the installation of a launch pylon below the starboard wing, rocket fuel top-up tanks in the bomb bays, and observation and recording blisters on the right fuselage side. After completing its initial test flights in 1959, the X-15 became the first winged aircraft to attain velocities of Mach 4, 5 and 6. Three X-15s were built, the aircraft being air-launched at altitude from a B-29. The second X-15A was rebuilt after a landing accident to become the X-15A-2, and was the fastest aircraft ever flown. The third X-15 was destroyed during a test flight.

The aircraft illustrated here, X-15 56-6671, was the first to complete a powered flight – with the XLR99 rocket motor. It was damaged in a forced landing at Mud Lake, Nevada, on 9 November 1962, in the hands of NASA test pilot John McKay. It was subsequently rebuilt as the X-15A-2 with provision for large external fuel tanks.

NORTH AMERICAN XB-70 VALKYRIE

NASA
Edwards Air Force Base, 1964–1969

NORTH AMERICAN XB-70 VALKYRIE

Specification
- **Type** supersonic strategic bomber/research aircraft
- **Crew** 2
- **Powerplant** six 14,060kg (31,000lb) thrust General Electric YN93-GE-3 turbojets
- **Performance** max speed Mach 3; service ceiling (est) 18,300m (60,000ft); range (est) 12,230km (7600 miles)
- **Dimensions** wing span 32m (105ft); length 59.64m (196ft); height 9.14m (30ft)
- **Weight** 249,480kg (550,104lb)
- **Armament** up to 14 nuclear weapons (projected)

Originally designed as a supersonic bomber to replace the Boeing B-52, the large, delta-wing B-70 was in fact produced only as a research aircraft, the first of two prototypes flying on 21 September 1964. The second XB-70A made its maiden flight on 17 July 1965 and flew at Mach 3 for more than 30 minutes in January 1966. On 3 June that year, it was lost when an F-104 chase aircraft collided with it. The first XB-70A continued to serve as a high-speed aerodynamic research vehicle in connection with the US supesonic transport programme un til the latter was abandoned.

Test flying continued until 4 February 1969, when the surviving XB-70A made its last flight. Most NASA XB-70 flights were made during the morning hours, in order to take advantage of the cooler ambient air temperatures, which resulted in improved propulsion efficiency. The three-position folding wingtips of the XB-70, which were extended to give maximum lift, pivoted in flight, and were folded down for supersonic cruise. This reduced directional stability problems, and reduced trim drag at high speed.

The XB-70 recorded its greatest speed on 12 April 1966, when North American's chief test pilot Al White and Colonel Joe Cotton of the US Air Force (USAF) attained Mach 3.8 at 22,189m (72,000ft). The highest altitude was achieved by White and Van Shepard on 19 March 1966, when the aircraft reached 22,555m (74,000ft).

The surviving XB-70 is on display at the North Modern Flight Gallery of the USAF Museum, Dayton, Ohio.

NORTHROP F-89D SCORPION

66th Fighter Interceptor Squadron,
Elmendorf Air Force Base, Alaska, 1956

The most potent all-weather interceptor in the world at the time of its service debut with the US Air Force (USAF), the Northrop F-89 Scorpion was one of two contenders for a USAF contract in May 1946, the other being the Curtiss XF-87 Nighthawk. The first of two Northrop XF-89 prototypes flew on 16 August 1948, and after USAF evaluation Northrop received an order for an initial batch of 48 production aircraft, the first of these flying late in 1950.

The first production model of the Scorpion, the F-89A, was powered by two Allison J35-A-21 turbojets with reheat and carried a nose armament of six 20mm (0.79in) cannon. The F-89B and F-89C were progressive developments with uprated Allison engines, while the F-89D had its cannon deleted and carried an armament of 42 folding-fin aircraft rockets in wingtip pods. Additional fuel tanks under the wings gave an 11 per cent range increase over the F-89C, and the aircraft was fitted with an automatic fire control system.

The F-89D was followed into production by the F-89H, which could carry Falcon missiles as well as the MB-1 Genie nuclear air-to-air missile. Three hundred and fifty F-89Ds were converted to F-89J standard, which became the Air Defense Command's first fighter-interceptor to carry nuclear armament. The Scorpion was retired from first-line service in 1961–62, being replaced by the Convair F-102 and F-106; however, it remained in operational service for some years more with the Air National Guard.

The Northrop F-89D Scorpion of the USAF Air Defense Command seen here is firing a salvo of folding-fin aircraft rockets.

NORTHROP F-89D SCORPION

Specification
- **Type** night and all-weather interceptor
- **Crew** 2
- **Powerplant** two 3266kg (7200lb) thrust Allison J35-A-35 turbojets
- **Performance** Max speed 1023km/h (636mph); service ceiling 14,995m (49,200ft); range 2200km (1370 miles)
- **Dimensions** Wing span 18.18m (59ft 8in); length 16.40m (53ft 10in); height 5.36m (17ft 7in)
- **Weight** 19,160kg (42,241lb) loaded
- **Armament** 48 2.75in folding-fin aircraft rockets (FFAR) in wingtip pods

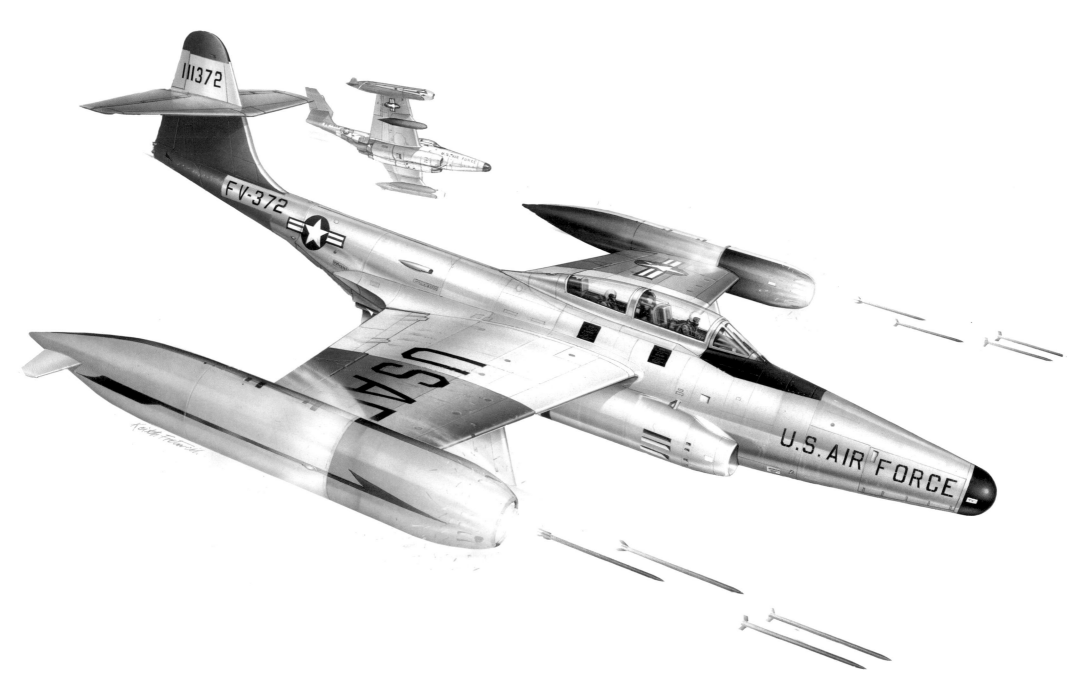

REPUBLIC F-84G THUNDERJET

69th Fighter-Bomber Squadron, 58th Fighter-Bomber Wing, United States Air Force, Taegu, Korea, 1953

REPUBLIC F-84G THUNDERJET

Specification
- **Type** fighter-bomber
- **Crew** 1
- **Powerplant** one 2542kg (5600lb) thrust Wright J65-A-29 turbojet
- **Performance** max speed 973km/h (605mph); service ceiling 12,353m (40,500ft); range 1609km (1000 miles)
- **Dimensions** wing span 11.05m (36ft 4in); length 11.71m (38ft 5in); height 3.90m (12ft 10in)
- **Weight** 12,701kg (28,000lb) loaded
- **Armament** six 12.7mm (0.50in) Browning M3 machine guns; provision for up to 1814kg (4000lb) of external stores

The Republic F-84 Thunderjet, which was to provide many of Nato's air forces with their initial jet experience, began life in the summer of 1944, when Republic Aviation's design team investigated the possibility of adapting the airframe of the P-47 Thunderbolt to take an axial-flow turbojet. This proved impractical, and in November 1944 the design of an entirely new airframe was begun around the General Electric J35 engine.

The first of three XP-84 prototypes was completed in December 1945 and made its first flight on 28 February 1946. The F-84B was the first production model, featuring an ejection seat, six 12.7mm (0.50in) M3 machine guns and underwing rocket racks. Deliveries of the F-84B began in the summer of 1947 to the 14th Fighter Group, and 226 were built.

The F-84G, which appeared in 1952, was the first Thunderjet variant to be equipped for flight refuelling from the outset. It was also the first US Air Force (USAF) fighter to have a tactical nuclear capability. The F-84G made its appearance in Korea in 1952, and in the closing months of the war Thunderjets of the 49th and 58th Fighter-Bomber Wings carried out a series of heavy attacks on North Korea's irrigation dams, vital to that country's economy. The Thunderjet's final missions in Korea were flown on 27 July, the very last day of hostilities.

F-84G Thunderject 51-111 'Five Aces', so named because of its unusual serial number, was mostly flown by Lieutenant Jim 'Suitcase' Simpson, who completed 56 combat missions over Korea.

REPUBLIC F-84F THUNDERSTREAK

Jagdbombergeschwader 34, Luftwaffe, Memmingen, Federal Republic of Germany, 1960

The swept-wing Republic XF-84F Thunderstreak, which used about 60 per cent of the F-84's components, flew for the first time on 3 June 1950, only 167 days after it was ordered. The first production F-84F flew on 22 November 1952, and the type was officially accepted by the US Air Force (USAF) in the following month. The first USAF unit to arm with the F-84F, in 1954, was the 407th Tactical Fighter Wing.

The F-84F replaced the Thunderjet in several Nato air forces, giving many European pilots their first experience of modern, swept-wing jet aircraft. Widespread use of the F-84F was made by Nato, with the air forces of Germany, France, Italy, Belgium, the Netherlands, Greece and Turkey operating the type. In French Air Force service, it saw action during the 1956 Anglo-French operation to secure the Suez Canal, flying from a base in Israel to destroy a number of Egyptian Il-28 jet bombers that had been evacuated to Luxor. The RF-84F Thunderflash was a low-level tactical reconnaissance variant.

Jagdbombergeschwader 34 (JBG 34) was activated at Fassberg in 1958, taking its Thunderstreaks to Memmingen in the following year. It used the type until 1964, when it rearmed with the F-104G Starfighter. After being phased out of *Luftwaffe* service, a number of German F-84Fs were refurbished and used by the Hellenic and Turkish air forces. *Luftwaffe* F-84Fs assumed a nuclear alert role in the early 1960s, the weapons remaining under American control. For political reasons, this fact was never publicized.

REPUBLIC F-84F THUNDERSTREAK

Specification
- **Type** fighter-bomber
- **Crew** 1
- **Powerplant** one 3278kg (7220lb) thrust Wright J65-W-3 turbojet
- **Performance** max speed 1118km/h (695mph); service ceiling 14,020m (46,000ft); combat radius 1304km (810 miles)
- **Dimensions** wing span 10.24m (33ft 7in); length 13.23m (43ft 4in); height 4.39m (14ft 4in)
- **Weight** 12,701kg (28,000lb) loaded
- **Armament** six 12.7mm (0.50in) Browning M3 machine guns; provision for up to 2722kg (6000lb) of external stores

SUPERMARINE SPITFIRE FR.MK.18

No. 28 Squadron, Royal Air Force, Kai Tak, Hong Kong, 1950

SUPERMARINE SPITFIRE FR.MK.18

Specification
- **Type** fighter-reconnaissance aircraft
- **Crew** 1
- **Powerplant** one 1529kW (2050hp) Rolls-Royce Griffon 65 12-cylinder Vee-type engine
- **Performance** max speed 721km/h (448mph); service ceiling 13,565m (44,500ft); range 1368km (850 miles)
- **Dimensions** wing span 11.23m (36ft 10in); length 10.14m (33ft 3.25in); height 3.86m (12ft 7.75in)
- **Weight** 4990kg (11,000lb) loaded
- **Armament** two 20mm (0.79in) cannon and two 12.7mm (0.50in) machine guns; external bomb and rocket load of 227kg (500lb)

The first Spitfire to be fitted with the powerful Rolls-Royce Griffon engine was the Mk XII, which was developed specifically to counter low-level attacks on the English south coast by German fighter-bombers, which were becoming increasingly troublesome in the first half of 1942. The type equipped only two squadrons, Nos 41 and 91.

The next Griffon-engined Spitfire variant was Mk XIV. Based on a Mk VIII airframe, it was the first Griffon-engined Spitfire variant to go into large-scale production, a total of 957 being built, and the first examples were issued to No. 322 (Netherlands) and No. 610 Squadrons in March and April 1944. The Mk XIV was based on a Mk VIII airframe, and its most distinguishing feature was a five-blade Rotol propeller, driven by a 1517kW (2035hp) Griffon 65.

The Mks XII and XIV both performed well against the V-1; in No. 91 Squadron, 14 pilots flying the Mk XII destroyed five or more flying bombs, including five with scores of over 10. Both 41 and 91 Squadrons exchanged their Mk XIIs for Mk XIVs before the V-1 offensive was over.

The Spitfire XIV's speed gave it a good chance of catching Me 262 jet fighters, several of which were destroyed by the Spitfires of No. 127 Wing, which was based in Belgium, in 1944–45. The Spitfire Mk 18 was the last Griffon-engined development of the original Spitfire airframe.

No. 28 Squadron's Spitfire FR.18s formed the Royal Air Force's fighter-reconnaissance element at Hong Kong from February 1949 to March 1951, when the squadron rearmed with Vampire FB.5s.

TUPOLEV TU-16 BADGER

967th Long-Range Air Reconnaissance Regiment, Northern Fleet, Murmansk late 1960s

TUPOLEV TU-16 BADGER

Specification
- **Type** strategic bomber/maritime warfare aircraft
- **Crew** 7
- **Powerplant** two 9500kg (20,944lb) thrust Mikulin RD-3M turbojets
- **Performance** max speed 960km/h (597mph); service ceiling 15,000m (49,200ft); range 4800km (2983 miles)
- **Dimensions** wing span 32.99m (108ft 3in); length 34.80m (114ft 2in); height 10.36m (34ft 2in)
- **Weight** 75,800kg (167,110lb) loaded
- **Armament** two 23mm (0.91in) cannon in radar-controlled barbettes in lower ventral fuselage and tail positions

The Tupolev Tu-16 jet bomber flew for the first time in 1952, and production of the type, which was allocated the Nato reporting name 'Badger', began in 1953. The principal subvariant of the Badger-A was the Tu-16A, configured to carry the Soviet Union's air-deliverable nuclear weapons.

The next major variant, the Tu-16KS-1 Badger-B, was similar to Badger-A, but was equipped initially to carry the KS 1 Komet III (AS 1 Kennel) anti-shipping missile, with retractable dustbin radome aft of bomb bay. The Tu-16K-10 Badger-C was an anti-shipping version armed with the K-10 (AS-2 Kipper) air-to-surface missile beneath the fuselage. The Tu-16K-26 Badger-C Mod was a conversion of the Tu-16K-10 with provision for the smaller K-26 (AS-6 Kingfish) air-to-surface missile under the wings instead of, or in addition to, the centreline-mounted K-10.

The Tu-16R Badger-D was a conversion of the Badger C for maritime reconnaissance, while the Badger-E was basically a Badger-A with a battery of cameras in the bomb bay. The Badger-G was armed with two AS-5 Kelt or AS-6 Kingfish air-to-surface missiles and was a dedicated anti-shipping version, while the Badger-J was equipped for barrage jamming in the A- to I-bands. The Badger-L was one of the last variants in a long line of electronic intelligence gatherers.

Some Badgers were converted to flight refuelling tankers, and still served in that role in the 1990s. The Tu-16, more than 2000 examples of which are thought to have been produced, was also licence-built in China as the Xian H-6. Illustrated here is a Tupolev Tu-16 Badger-C Mod of the Soviet Union's 967th Long-Range Air Reconnaissance Regiment.

VICKERS VALIANT B(K)1

No. 214 Squadron, Royal Air Force,
RAF Marham, Norfolk
early 1960s

VICKERS VALIANT B(K)1

Specification
- **Type** strategic bomber/flight refuelling tanker
- **Crew** 5
- **Powerplant** four 4559kg (10,050lb) thrust Rolls-Royce Avon 204 turbojets
- **Performance** max speed 912km/h (567mph); service ceiling 16,460m (54,000ft); range 7424km (4500 miles)
- **Dimensions** wing span 34.85m (114ft 4in); length 33.0m (108ft 3in); height 9.8m (32ft 2in)
- **Weight** 79,378kg (175,000lb) loaded
- **Armament** one 4530kg (10,000lb) MC Mk 1 Blue Danube nuclear bomb; four 906kg (2000lb) Red Beard tactical nuclear bombs; one 2722kg (6000lb) Mk 5 (US) nuclear bomb; four Mk 28 or Mk 43 (US) thermonuclear bombs; or 21 453kg (1000lb) conventional bombs

Designed to meet the requirements of Specification B.9/48, the Vickers Valiant was the first of the Royal Air Force's (RAF's) trio of 'V-Bombers', and played a vital part in building up Britain's strategic nuclear deterrent. The first Vickers Type 660 Valiant flew on 18 May 1951 and production Valiant B.Mk.Is were delivered to No 232 OCU at Gaydon, Warwickshire, in January 1955.

The Valiant subsequently armed 10 RAF squadrons, including one (No. 543) tasked with strategic reconnaissance. No. 138 Squadron was the first to equip with the type, and No. 49 Squadron was the nuclear weapons trials unit, its aircraft participating in nuclear weapons tests in Australia (1956) and Christmas Island (1957–58). Valiants saw action in the Anglo-French Suez operation of October–November 1956, attacking Egyptian airfields with conventional bombs.

In 1963, the Valiant force was assigned to SACEUR in the tactical bombing role, but was withdrawn prematurely because of fatigue cracks in the main spar. The Valiant B(K)1 was a flight refuelling tanker conversion, equipping Nos 90 and 214 Squadrons to form the RAF Marham Tanker Wing, and the Valiant B.Mk.2 was a one-off prototype stressed for low-level, high-speed penetration.

This Vickers Valiant B.Mk.1 of No. 214 Squadron is seen flight refuelling a Gloster Javelin FAW.9 of No. 23 Squadron, RAF Coltishall. No. 214 Squadron, which assumed the flight refuelling tanker role in April 1962, provided tanker support for the RAF's Vulcan and Victor nuclear bombers until February 1965, when it disbanded following the discovery of fatigue cracks in the main wing spars of the Valiant. It re-formed in 1966 with Handley Page Victor tankers.

VOUGHT F4U CORSAIR

Marine Night Fighter Squadron VMF(N)-513, United States Marine Corps, Itazuke, Japan, 1950

VOUGHT F4U-5N CORSAIR

Specification
- **Type** night fighter
- **Crew** 1
- **Powerplant** one 1678kW (2250hp) Pratt & Whitney R-2800-18W radial engine
- **Performance** max speed 718km/h (446mph); service ceiling 12,650m (41,500ft); range 2511km (1560 miles)
- **Dimensions** wing span 12.50m (41ft); length 10.27m (33ft 8.25in) height 4.50m (14ft 9in)
- **Weight** 6350kg (14,000lb) loaded
- **Armament** : six 12.7mm (0.50in) machine guns; bomb and rocket load of 907kg (2000lb)

T he prototype XF4U-1 flew for the first time on 29 May 1940 and the first production F4U-1 was delivered to the US Navy on 31 July 1942. Carrier trials began in September 1942, and the first Corsair unit, Marine Fighting Squadron VMF-214, was declared combat-ready in December, deploying to Guadalcanal in February 1943. After trials with VF-12, the Corsair became operational with Navy Fighting Squadron VF-17 in April 1943, deploying to a land base in New Georgia in September. As pilots became experienced in flying their powerful new fighter-bombers, they became formidable opponents.

Of the 12,681 Corsairs built during World War II, 2012 were supplied to the Royal Navy, equipping 19 squadrons of the Fleet Air Arm; some of these aircraft were diverted to equip three squadrons of the Royal New Zealand Air Force, operating in the Solomons.

Variants of the Corsair included the F4U-1C cannon-armed fighter, F4U-1D fighter-bomber, F4U-2 night fighter, F4U-3 high-altitude research version and F4U-4 fighter. Post-war developments included the F4U-5 fighter-bomber, F4U-5N night fighter and F4U-5P photo-reconnaissance aircraft – all of which gave tremendous service during the Korean War of 1950–53 – the F4U-6 (later A-1) attack aircraft and the F4U-7, also supplied to the French Navy. French Corsairs saw combat during the Anglo-French Suez operation of 1956.

The Corsairs of VMF(N)-513 played a very important part in the Korean War, attacking enemy troops moving under the cover of darkness. At first, they operated from Itazuke, Japan, but later moved up to airfields in Korea itself.

VOUGHT F-8E CRUSADER

Fighter Squadron 191, United States Navy,
USS Bon Homme Richard,
South China Sea, 1965

VOUGHT F-8E CRUSADER

Specification
- **Type** naval tactical fighter-bomber
- **Crew** 1
- **Powerplant** one 8165kg (18,000lb) thrust Pratt & Whitney J57 P-20 turbojet
- **Performance** max speed 1800km/h (1120mph); service ceiling 17,983m (40,000ft); combat radius 966km (600 miles)
- **Dimensions** wing span 10.72m (35ft 2in); length 16.61m (54ft 6in); height 4.80m (15ft 9in)
- **Weight** 15,422kg (34,000lb) loaded
- **Armament** four 20mm (0.79in) cannon; various underwing combinations of rockets, bombs and air-to-surface missiles

---

The first carrier-borne fighter capable of supersonic speed in level flight, the prototype Vought XF8U-1 Crusader flew on 25 March 1955 and exceeded Mach 1.0 on its maiden flight. The first production F8U-1 flew on 30 September 1955, and it completed carrier trials for the US Navy in April 1956. Production of the F8U-1 (later F-8A) ended in 1958, by which time 218 had been built.

The F8U-1 was followed in September 1958 by the F8U-1E (F-8B), 130 examples of which were built and which had an all-weather capability. The F8U-1P (RF-8A), flown in December 1956, was capable of both day and night reconnaissance and was used extensively for surveillance during the Cuban crisis of 1962 and its aftermath. Of the 144 built, 53 were modernized in 1965–66 and redesignated RF-8G; these were used for fast low-level reconnaissance over Vietnam.

The F8U-2N (F-8D) Crusader, which first flew in February 1960, was powered by a J57-P20 turbojet with reheat, giving it a maximum speed approaching Mach 2.0. Of the 152 built, 89 were later refurbished, given an attack capability and designated F-8H. The F-8E was the first Crusader to be developed for the strike role; more than 250 F-8Es were built, and 136 were refurbished under the designation F-8J. The F-8E(FN) was a version for the French Navy.

The F-8E seen here was flown by Commander Billy Phillips, Officer Commanding Fight Squadron 191 (VF-191) 'Satan's Kittens', which made eight deployments to the Vietnam war zone aboard the US Navy carriers *Bon Homme Richard* and *Ticonderoga*.

THE LATER COLD WAR: 1970–1989

As the Cold War continued, massive research funding and military spending by the superpowers led to the development and deployment of some of the most expensive and complex fighting machines ever designed. Upgraded and combat-proven, many of these aircraft are still in use today around the world.

A Boeing B-52G pictured in flight carrying a load of air-launched cruise missiles. The B-52 has been a powerful symbol of US military might for more than 40 years.

AEROSPATIALE (EUROCOPTER) SA.321G SUPER FRELON

Flotille 32F, Aéronavale,
Lanvéoc-Poulmic, France, 1970

AEROSPATIALE (EUROCOPTER) SA.321G SUPER FRELON

Specification
- **Type** multi-role helicopter
- **Crew** 5
- **Powerplant** three Turboméca 3C III turbines each rated at 895kW (1200hp)
- **Performance** max speed 248km/h (154mph); service ceiling 3100m (10,170ft); range 1010km (633 miles)
- **Dimensions** rotor diameter 18.9m (62ft); length 23m (75ft 7in); height 6.76m (22ft 2.25in)
- **Weight** 13,000kg (28,660lb) loaded
- **Armament** two AM39 Exocet missiles or four Mk 46 homing torpedoes

The story of the SA.321 Super Frelon began with the Frelon (Hornet), built by Sud-Est and designated SE. 3200. Only two Frelons were built, the first making its maiden flight on 10 June 1959. The information amassed from flight testing these two machines enabled what had then become Sud-Aviation to develop a more advanced version, the SA.321 Super Frelon. Two prototype and four pre-series Super Frelons were flown from 7 December 1962 onwards.

The Super Frelon had little success in the civil market and the *Armée de l'Air* was not interested, but in December 1963 the *Aéronavale* ordered an initial batch of 14 as the SA.321G, these being earmarked for for tactical transport and long-range search and rescue missions. In the anti-submarine role with *Flotille* 32F at Lanvéoc-Poulmic, which was equipped in 1970, the type's duties included support of the Redoutable-class nuclear missile submarines based at l'Ile Longue, Brest.

Super Frelons were supplied to Israel, Libya, Iraq and South Africa, and the type was built under licence in the Chinese People's Republic as Changhe Z-8. Iraqi Super Frelons were used to launch Exocet missiles against Iranian shipping in the 1980s war between the two countries, and Israeli aircraft saw action in the air assult role during the Six-Day War of 1967.

The SA.321's spacious, soundproofed and ventilated cabin can accommodate 27 troops or 5000kg (11,023lb) of cargo. Alternatively, up to 15 stretchers, with two attendants, can be carried in the air ambulance role. In all, 110 Super Frelons were built, the last being an aircraft for Libya in 1981.

AERMACCHI (EMBRAER) EMB-326GB/AT-26 XAVANTE

2° Esquadrão, 5° Grupo de Aviaçio,
Gav Comando, Aéreo de Treinamento
Força Aérea Brasileira, Base Aérea de
Natal, Brazil, late 1980s

AERMACCHI (EMBRAER) EMB-326GB/AT-26 XAVANTE

Specification
- **Type** two-seat jet trainer/light attack aircraft
- **Crew** 2
- **Powerplant** one 15.17kN (3410lb thrust) Rolls-Royce Viper 20 Mk 540 turbojet engine
- **Performance** max speed 867km/h (539mph); service ceiling 11,890m (39,000ft); range with external fuel 2446km (1520 miles)
- **Dimensions** wing span 10.85m (35ft 7.25in); length 10.67m (35ft 0.25in); height 3.72m (12ft 2in)
- **Weight** 4211kg (9285lb) loaded
- **Armament** up to 1962kg (4352lb) of bombs or rockets; 12.7mm (0.50in) gun pods

Still in service in many countries, the design of the MB-326 jet trainer dates back nearly half a century, with the prototype flying in December 1957. The first production examples were delivered to the Italian Air Force in early 1962, but it was in the export market where the 'Macchi' had its greatest success, being supplied to Argentina, Australia, Brazil, Dubai, Ghana, Paraguay, South Africa, Tunisia, Zaire and Zambia.

In all, about 800 MB-326s have been built, and the basic design formed the basis of the successful MB-339, which has also been widely exported. A single-seat attack version of the MB.326 was built as the MB.326K and known as the Impala in South Africa, where many were built under licence by Atlas.

Embraer of Brazil acquired a licence to build the MB-326 as the T-26 Xavante (the name of a Brazilian Indian tribe) and constructed 166 for its own air force, 10 for Paraguay and six for Togo. The Brazilian aircraft are usually known as the AT-26 to signify their secondary attack role. Some have reconnaissance cameras and refuelling probes and are known as the RT-26.

This Xavante belongs to the 2nd Squadron of the 5th Air Group (2° Esquadrão, 5°Grupo de Aviaçio, or 2°/5° GAv) at Natal, on the furthest eastern point of Brazil. The squadron uses the call sign 'Joker' and is one of two units at Natal which train pilots for the operational AT-26 units and other combat aircraft. For the weapons training role, the Xavante often carries Avbras SBAT-70 rocket launchers, as seen here. Other options include up to six 118kg (260lb) bombs or 12.7mm (0.50in) gun pods. It is planned that 2°/5°GAv will receive the AT-29 Super Tucano to replace the AT-26 in the coming years.

AGUSTA BELL AB 212ASW

5° Gruppo Elicotteri, Maristaeli Luni,
Marina Militare Italiana, Sarzana,
La Spezia, Italy
late 1980s

AGUSTA BELL AB 212ASW

Specification
- **Type** anti-submarine/anti-ship helicopter
- **Crew** 3
- **Powerplant** one 1398kW (1875hp) Pratt & Whitney Canada PT-6T-6 Turbo Twin Pac turboshaft engine
- **Performance** max speed 240km/h (150mph); service ceiling 3200m (10,500ft); range 667km (414 miles)
- **Dimensions** rotor diameter 14.63m (48ft 0in); fuselage length 12.92m (42ft 4.75in); height 3.91m (12ft 10in)
- **Weight** 4973kg (19,961lb) loaded
- **Armament** two Mk.46 torpedoes or two Marte 2 or two Sea Skua anti-ship missiles

Experience with the Bell 206 UH-1 'Huey' in Vietnam showed the benefits a twin-engined variant would bring to 'hot and high' operating conditions. Pratt & Whitney Canada teamed up with Bell to offer the Model 212 powered by two PT6T-3 turbines, which was ordered by the Canadian military in 1968. The US Navy, US Marine Corps (USMC) and US Air Force (USAF) followed suit by procuring the new UH-1N for various roles including combat rescue, assault transport and as a VIP 'taxi'.

More than 40 air arms acquired the 'Twin Huey' in various forms. Further developments include the Bell 412 with a four-bladed rotor and the UH-1Y with an all-new powerplant for the USMC.

Agusta in Italy had long-standing licence agreement to produce Bell helicopters, including the Model 47 Sioux and the UH-1 Iroquois. It developed its own versions of the 212, most notably the anti-submarine AB 212ASW, which was sold to Greece, Iran, Saudi Arabia, Spain and Turkey. Iraq ordered aircraft, which were embargoed and not delivered.

The AB 212ASW mounts a search radar above the cockpit and can carry a dipping sonar with an operator in the rear cabin. Weapons options include torpedoes, Sea Skua anti-ship missiles and the Marte 2 anti-ship missile seen here.

Italy bought 68 AB 212s for its navy, the *Marina Militare Italiana*, from 1968, and more than 50 examples remain in service. Three squadrons are equipped, and this particular aircraft has served with the 5th *Gruppo Elicotteri* (helicopter group) since at least 1990. More recently, the AB 212s at Maristaeli Luna, near La Spezia, were transferred to the 1st *Gruppo* (*1° Grupelicot*), and the 5th Gruppo left with the Agusta 109E, EH-101ASW, and the SH-3D/H Sea Kings.

AERITALIA/FIAT (ALENIA) G222

*Regimento Aéreo del Ejercito Venezolana,
BAM Generalissimo Miranda, Venezuela
late 1980s*

AERITALIA/FIAT (ALENIA) G222

Specification
- **Type** twin-engined tactical transport
- **Crew** four and up to 24 paratroops
- **Powerplant** two 2535kW (3400hp) General Electric T64-GE-P4D turboprop engines
- **Performance** max speed 487km/h (303mph); service ceiling 7620m (25,000ft); range 4633km (2879 miles)
- **Dimensions** wing span 28.70m (94ft 2in); length 22.70m (74ft 5.5in); height 9.8m (32ft 2in)
- **Weight** 28,000kg (61,728lb) loaded
- **Armament** none

In 1962, Nato issued a requirement for a vertical/short take-off and landing tactical transport aircraft for service with many of its air forces. None of the many proposals was built, but Italy ordered development of the Fiat G222 design for its own military in 1968. The prototype flew in July 1970, and the first of 44 initial production aircraft, built by a consortium of Italian companies, entered service with the *Aeronautica Militare Italiana* in 1976.

Something of a 'mini-Hercules', the G222 offers a spacious cargo hold and extremely good short take-off and landing characteristics. Although it carries less, it is faster and better climbing than the contemporary C.160 Transall. Italy proved to be the only European customer, but sales have been made to Argentina, Dubai, Nigeria, Somalia, Thailand and Venezuela. The United States ordered a small number for use in Central America as the C-27A Spartan, and, in conjunction with Lockheed Martin, Alenia (which succeeded Aeritalia and Fiat Aerospace) is marketing the C-27J, a version with a new two-man 'glass' cockpit and the new-generation engines of the C-130J Hercules. Italy and Greece have become the initial customers for the C-27J.

The Venezuelan Army (*Regimento Aéreo del Ejercito Venezolana*) purchased two G222s in 1982, and the Venezuelan Air Force (*Fuerza Aérea Venezolana*, or FAV) received six more in 1984–85. One Army G222, believed to be EV8228 illustrated here, was lost in an accident in the early 1990s. G222 operations were later consolidated within the FAV, and the survivors now serve alongside the Shorts 330 and 360 with *Escuadrón* T2 of *Grupo Aéreo Transporte* 6 at El Liberatador Air Base.

ANTONOV AN-12PS CUB-B

Soviet Naval Aviation, 1980s

ANTONOV AN-12PS CUB-B

Specification
- **Type** four-engined Elint aircraft
- **Crew** five in cockpit, unknown number of operators in cabin
- **Powerplant** four 2983kW (4000hp) Ivchencko AI-20K turboprop engines
- **Performance** max speed 777km/h (482mph); service ceiling 10,200m (33,465ft); range 5700km (3542 miles)
- **Dimensions** wing span 38.10m (124 ft 8in); length 33.10m (108ft 7in); height 10.53m (34ft 6.5in)
- **Weight** 61,000kg (134,480lb) loaded
- **Payload** 20,000kg (44,092lb) cargo

The Antonov An-12 could be said to be the Soviet Union's equivalent of the C-130 Hercules, although it is slightly smaller and lighter than the basic Lockheed product. First flown in December 1957 in the Ukraine, around 1300 An-12s were built in the Soviet Union and a further 100 or so unlicenced copies in China as the Shaanxi Y-8. Versions of the Y-8 serve as transports, maritime patrol aircraft and drone launchers.

Soviet-built An-12s (Nato code name 'Cub') were exported to Algeria, Bulgaria, China, Cuba, Czechoslovakia, Egypt, Ghana, Guinea, India, Indonesia, Iraq, Poland, Yemen and Yugoslavia. Many specialist variants were delivered for roles including airborne command post, radiation and chemical sampling, ejection-seat testing, weather research and even (in China) for the seasonal movement of animals. Since the dissolution of the Soviet Union, many An-12s have entered the civil market.

Ostensibly used for the search and rescue (SAR) role, the An-12PS was in fact generally employed on electronic intelligence (Elint) duties. The radio locator equipment could home in not only on rescue beacons, but also on Nato transmitters. It was said that this variant carried a droppable rescue boat in the freight hold. The full Aeroflot markings and civil registrations were often seen on An-12s that on closer inspection had a definite military role. These aircraft were frequently intercepted by Western fighters over the Baltic Sea and other locations, particularly during Nato naval manoeuvres.

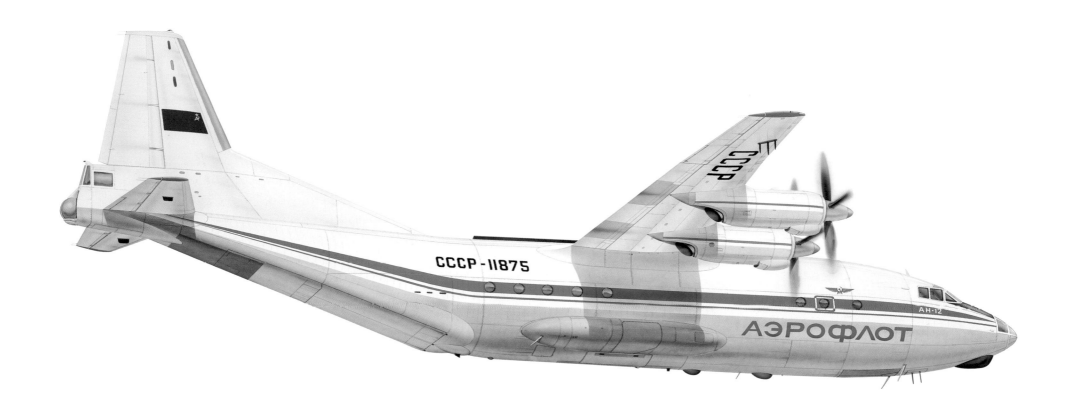

ANTONOV AN-26 CURL

Transportfliegerstaffel 24,
DDR Luftstreitkräfte, Dresden-Klotsche,
German Democratic Republic, 1980s

ANTONOV AN-26 CURL

Specification
- **Type** twin-engined transport aircraft
- **Crew** five-six
- **Powerplant** two 2103kW (2820hp) Ivchencko AI-24VT turboprop engines
- **Performance** max speed 540km/h (336mph); service ceiling 7400m (24,605ft); range 2550km (1585 miles)
- **Dimensions** wing span 29.20m (95ft 9.5in); length 23.80m (78ft 1in); height 8.58m (28ft 1.5in)
- **Weight** 24,400kg (53,790lb) loaded
- **Payload** 40 passengers or 5500kg (12,100lb) cargo

Originally designed as a civil transport to replace the piston-engined Ilyushin Il-12 and Il-14s in Aeroflot service, the Antonov An-24 of 1959 was soon adapted to become a military transport with a side freight door. The similar-looking An-26 (Nato code name 'Curl') was in fact an all-new design with a rear loading ramp, a pressurized cargo hold and more powerful engines. A small turbojet auxiliary power unit (APU) in the tail provides electrical power on the ground, but also can be used to supplement the main turboprop engines on take-off.

The aircraft was used by the Soviet Union and most of the Warsaw Pact nations and was exported to more than 20 foreign air forces. Many of these continue to fly the An-26 and/or its successor the An-32 'Cline', which remains in production in the Ukraine. A derivative is the An-30 'Clank', which is a purpose-built survey aircraft with a raised cockpit and glazed nose. The An-26 is still produced in China as the Xian Y-7H-500.

The aircraft illustrated is an early model An-26, delivered in 1980 to the *Luftstreitkräfte* (air force) of the German Democratic Republic, which had at least 12 'Curls'. As well as standard transports, the East Germans had special variants for electronic intelligence gathering and calibrating aeronautical navigation aids.

Some of the An-26s were retained by the *Luftwaffe* after the reunification of Germany, but they were soon put in museums or sold on to Russian airline Komi Avia. The new *Luftwaffe* used the C-160 Transall as its main tactical transport aircraft instead. In 1991, No. 371 became 52+01 with the *Luftwaffe*, then in 1993 RA-49264 with Komi Avia. It spent two years working with the United Nations as UN-488 before being returned to Russia.

AVRO VULCAN B.MK 2A

No. 101 Squadron, Royal Air Force, Wideawake Airfield, Ascension Island, 1982

AVRO VULCAN B.MK 2A

Specification
- **Type** strategic bomber
- **Crew** 5
- **Powerplant** four 78.8kN (17,000lb thrust) Bristol Olympus 201 turbo jets
- **Performance** max speed 1038km/h (645mph); service ceiling 19,812m (65,000ft); range 7400 km (4600 miles)
- **Dimensions** wing span 38.83m (111ft); length 32.15m (105ft 6in); height 7.94m (26ft 1in)
- **Weight** 92,534kg (204,000lb) max take-off
- **Armament** Blue Danube or Yellow Sun nuclear weapons, up to 21 454kg (1,000lb) bombs

The Avro Vulcan was the most distinctive of the three Royal Air Force (RAF) V-bombers and the one that served the longest in the bombing role. Built to a 1947 specification, the prototype flew in August 1952, but the first training unit was not equipped with the production Vulcan B.Mk 1 until 1957. The B.Mk 2 with a revised wing flew the following year, and after 1956 many were able to carry the Blue Steel stand-off missile. Otherwise the Vulcan could carry freefall nuclear weapons or up to 21 454kg (1000lb) bombs in its bomb bay. The delta wing gave a smooth ride at low level and was less prone to stress than the more conventional Vickers Valiant, which had to be withdrawn due to fatigue.

The Vulcan was approaching retirement in 1982 when the Falklands War saw it participate in its only combat missions. Flying from Ascension Island in the South Atlantic, the Vulcans flew five 'Black Buck' missions against Argentine forces in the Falklands, at the time the longest bombing raids in history.

Vulcan B.2 XM597 entered service in 1963 with No. 12 Squadron and went on to serve with Nos. 35, 50, 9, and 101 Squadrons. During the Falklands War, it was used on two missions to attack Argentine radars around Stanley Airfield, modified to carry four AGM-45A Shrike anti-radiation missiles on underwing pylons. On the night of 2/3 June 1982, the Vulcan destroyed a Skyguard radar with two Shrikes, but damaged its refuelling probe while connecting to the Victor tanker. Without enough fuel for a return to Ascension Island, XM597 diverted to Rio de Janeiro and landed with very little fuel and one missile which would not fire, causing something of a diplomatic incident. The pilot, Squadron Leader Neil McDougall, was awarded the Distinguished Flying Cross. After the war XM597 flew with 50 and 44 Squadrons before retirement in March 1984.

BAC STRIKEMASTER MK 88

No. 14 Squadron,
Royal New Zealand Air Force,
Ohakea, New Zealand, 1970s

BAC STRIKEMASTER MK 88

Specification
- **Type** advanced jet trainer/light attack aircraft
- **Crew** 2
- **Powerplant** one 15.17kN (3410lb thrust) Rolls-Royce Viper 20 Mk 525 turbojet engine
- **Performance** max speed 724km/h (450mph); service ceiling 12,190m (40,000ft); ferry range 2224km (1382 miles)
- **Dimensions** wing span 11.23m (36ft 10in); length 10.36m (34ft); height 3.10m (10ft 2in)
- **Weight** 5216kg (11,500lb) loaded
- **Armament** up to 1361kg (3000lb) of ordnance, including bombs, rockets or gun pods

The basic design of the British Aircraft Corporation (BAC) Strikemaster can be traced to the piston-engined Percival Provost trainer of 1950. Hunting Aviation took the wings and tail, and created a jet version with the Bristol-Siddeley (later Rolls-Royce) Viper engine in 1954. The Jet Provost became the Royal Air Force's most numerous advanced trainer and served in this role into the 1990s, the later versions being pressurized with wingtip fuel tanks.

In 1967, BAC flew a strengthened version of the 'JP' Mk 5 as the Strikemaster, intended for the export market as a light attack aircraft and weapons trainer. With a more powerful Viper and extra wing hardpoints, the Strikemaster could carry a useful weapons load and over 100 were sold, to Ecuador, Kenya, Kuwait, New Zealand, Oman, Saudi Arabia, Singapore, Sudan and South Yemen. Botswana later acquired some ex-Kuwaiti aircraft.

This is one of 16 Strikemaster Mk 88s acquired by the Royal New Zealand Air Force (RNZAF) in the 1970s to replace the two-seat Vampire in the advanced training, jet conversion and weapons training roles. During this time, all RNZAF trainee pilots flew the 'Blunty', as it was known, whether they were destined for the A-4, C-130, P-3, Andover, 727 or the UH-1. NZ6376 was delivered in June 1975 and served with No. 14 Squadron at Ohakea in the central North Island.

In the late 1980s, the Strikemasters suffered from fatigue problems and, despite getting new wings, were phased out in favour of the Aermacchi MB.339 by 1993. NZ6376 was in the final flypast of four Strikemasters on 17 December 1992 and later converted to an instructional airframe for use at No. 4 Technical Training School at Woodbourne. Several of the RNZAF's aircraft are now flying in civilian hands in Australia.

BELL AH-1F HUEYCOBRA

United States Army 13th Attack Helicopter Brigade, 3rd Infantry Division, United States Army, Giebelstadt, Germany, 1985

BELL AH-1F HUEYCOBRA

Specification
- **Type** attack helicopter
- **Crew** 2
- **Powerplant** one 1342kW (1800hp) Textron Lycoming T53-L-703 turboshaft engine
- **Performance** max speed 227km/h (141mph); service ceiling 3720m (12,200ft); combat radius 507km (315 miles)
- **Dimensions** main rotor diameter 13.41m (44ft); fuselage length 13.59m (44ft 7in); height 4.09m (13ft 5in)
- **Weight** 4536kg (10,000lb) loaded
- **Armament** one M197 triple-barrelled 20mm (0.79in) cannon; eight TOW missiles or pods for 70mm (2.75in) rockets

The Bell AH-1 was the first purpose-designed attack helicopter to enter service, arising from the need to escort troop-carrying helicopters in Vietnam with something more potent and manoeuvrable than armed UH-1 Hueys. The AH-1G first flew in September 1965 and entered combat in Vietnam with the US Army two years later.

The AH-1 had a new fuselage and weapons system, but shared the tail, engine and power system of the UH-1. As such it was known as the HueyCobra. A total of 93 of the original AH-1G model were modified to take TOW (tube-launched, optically aimed, wire-guided) missiles and redesignated AH-1Q. Further upgrades resulted in the more powerful AH-1S, which appeared in various standards. The AH-1F was an attempt to achieve commonality and could be distinguished by its flat plate canopy, which was less reflective than the original blown unit, and its sighting system in a new nose turret.

This Cobra was built as an AH-1G, later became an AH-1S and by the mid-1980s was serving with the 13th Attack Helicopter Brigade (AHB) in Germany. During the 1990s, it was converted to AH-1F standard. With the arrival of the AH-64A Apache, the Cobras were relegated to Army National Guard (ArNG) units, and its last known unit was the 1st Battalion of the 104th Cavalry, Pennsylvania ArNG at Fort Indiantown Gap (Muir Army Airfield). In May 2001 it was withdrawn from use and placed into storage. It is a possible candidate for sale to a foreign user.

A number of nations, particularly in the Middle East, use the 'first generation' Cobras, and the US Marine Corps is an enthusiastic user of the twin-engined, four-bladed AH-1W 'Whiskey' Cobra.

BOEING B-52G STRATOFORTRESS

*72nd Strategic Wing (Provisional),
Strategic Air Command, United States
Air Force, Andersen Air Force Base,
Guam, 1972*

BOEING B-52G STRATOFORTRESS

Specification
- **Type** strategic bomber
- **Crew** 5
- **Powerplant** eight 61.2kN (13,750lb thrust) Pratt & Whitney J57-P-43WB turbojet engines
- **Performance** max speed 1024km/h (636mph); service ceiling 14,326m (47,000ft); ferry range 12836km (7976 miles)
- **Dimensions** wing span 56.4m (185ft); length 48.0m (157ft 7in); height 12.4m (40ft 8in)
- **Weight** 137,275kg (302,634lb) loaded
- **Armament** four 12.7mm (0.50in) Browning M3 machine guns with 600 rounds each in tail turret; maximum ordnance 22,680kg (50,000 lb)

The B-52G version of the long-lived Stratofortress bomber was intended as a stopgap measure while troubles with the B-58 Hustler were worked out. Work began in 1956, and the first of 193 B-52Gs was completed at Wichita, Kansas, in October 1958. It had the same engines as the preceding B-52F, but a lighter structure and a shorter tailfin. The tail-gunner's position was moved from the rear fuselage to a seat in the main forward cabin, and he operated the guns using a video monitor or radar. Larger fuel tanks were installed and spoilers replaced ailerons for roll control. The capability to carry the AGM-28 Hound Dog missile was added during production, and later the AGM-69A short-range attack missile (SRAM).

Although intended as a nuclear bomber and missile launcher, the B-52 entered combat as a conventional 'dumb' bomber. In April 1972, 28 (of an eventual 98) B-52Gs were sent to Guam to support the B-52D and F in operations against North Vietnam. Most were equipped with a more sophisticated ECM suite, but the G could not carry bombs externally and was generally less effective as a conventional bomber.

On Guam, the B-52Gs were assigned to the 486th and 329th Bomb Squadrons (Provisional), part of the 72nd Wing (Provisional). In an effort to move stalled peace talks, the United States launched Operation Linebacker II in December 1972; the B-52s were used to attack targets around the heavily defended capital, Hanoi, in what was called the 'Eleven-Day War'. The B-52s dropped over 15,000 tons of bombs and flew nearly 730 sorties during these raids. Six B-52Gs were shot down by suface-to-air missiles and one was damaged out of a total of 15 'Buff' losses. Of the 92 crew members, 32 were killed or missing, 33 were captured and 26 were recovered. The raids were instrumental in getting the North Vietnamese to return to the negotiating table.

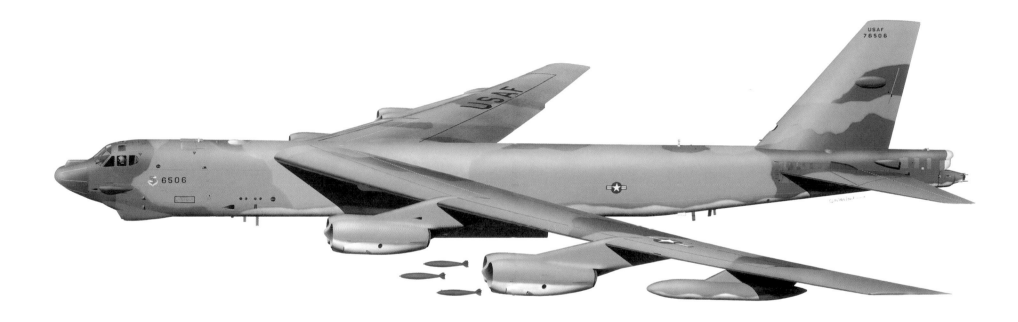

BOEING CHINOOK HC.1

No. 7 Squadron, Royal Air Force,
Odiham, Hampshire,
late 1980s

BOEING CHINOOK HC.1

Specification
- **Type** medium-lift transport helicopter
- **Crew** 3
- **Powerplant** two 2796kW (3750hp) Textron Lycoming T55-L-712 turboshaft engines
- **Performance** max speed 298km/h (185mph); service ceiling 6735m (22,100ft); range (ferry) 2026km (1259 miles)
- **Dimensions** main rotor diameter 18.29m (60ft); fuselage length 15.54 (51ft); height 5.77m (18ft 11in)
- **Weight** 22,679kg (50,000lb) loaded
- **Armament** one or two 7.62mm (0.30in) machine guns can be mounted in door hatch and/or on rear ramp for self-defence

First flown in September 1961, the Boeing Vertol (later Boeing) CH-47 Chinook entered service in August 1962 and has since been the US Army's standard medium-lift helicopter. With a similar configuration to the Piasecki H-21 and Vertol CH-46 Sea Knight, the Chinook is significantly larger with externally mounted turbine engines. The CH-47C had uprated engines and more fuel than the A and B models, and was exported to several nations including Australia, Argentina, Iran and the United Kingdom, where they were designated Chinook HC.1.

The first British Chinook unit, No. 18 Squadron, was formed in February 1982 and was soon involved in preparations for the Falklands War. Four HC.1s were loaded aboard the merchant vessel *Atlantic Conveyor* and joined the Task Force on 18 May. ZA718 was the first to be made airworthy and flew off on 25 May. Later that day, the ship was hit by an Exocet missile fired by an Argentine Navy Super Etendard. The three remaining Chinooks were destroyed and the *Atlantic Conveyor* was burnt out and abandoned, sinking two days later. This left only one Chinook, coded BN or 'Bravo November', to support the landings, with no spare parts or specialist tools. On one occasion Bravo November lifted 22 Marine commandos and three field guns at night onto Mt Kent. On the return flight. it flew so low that it struck the surface of a creek. Although water entered the main hold and soaked the loadmaster, the Chinook was able to climb away for a safe landing. Eventually carrying over 2100 troops and 550 tonnes of equipment, Bravo November continued to support British forces until the end of the conflict.

After the war, ZA718 was transferred to No. 7 Squadron and coded EQ as seen here. Later converted to HC.2 standard, it was last noted back in service with No. 18 Squadron, again coded 'Bravo November' with a small Falklands flag by the door.

BOEING E-3A SENTRY

Nato Airborne Early Warning Force,
Geilenkirchen, Germany
late 1980s

BOEING E-3A SENTRY

Specification
- **Type** airborne early warning and control aircraft
- **Crew** four flight deck and 13 in cabin
- **Powerplant** four 93.41kN (21,000lb thrust) Pratt & Whitney TF33-P-100A turbofan engines
- **Performance** max speed 853km/h (530mph); service ceiling 10,670m (35,000ft); range over 9266km (5758 miles)
- **Dimensions** wing span 44.45m (145ft 9in); length 46.68m (152ft 11in); height 12.70m (41ft 9in)
- **Weight** 147,429kg (325,000lb) loaded
- **Armament** none

The E-3 Sentry is just one part of the AWACS (airborne early warning and control system) used by the United States, France, Saudi Arabia, the United Kingdom and Nato. As early as 1963, the US Air Force (SAF) began studies to replace the EC-121 Warning Star. The solution was to mount a large rotating radar dome (rotodome) on a Boeing 707 airframe. The first two test aircraft flew in 1972 and the very expensive and controversial E-3A entered USAF service in 1978. Saudi Arabia was the first export customer and, like the United Kingdom and France, took aircraft powered by the CFM-56 high-bypass turbofan engine.

Using its powerful AN/APY-1 or AN/APY-2 radar, each E-3 can continuously scan more than 312,000 km^2 (120,464 square miles) of the earth's surface. The radar system can detect and track aircraft at low or high level and has a maritime mode for monitoring enemy shipping. The Nato Airborne Early Warning Force (NAEWF) received the first of 18 E-3As in 1982 (registered in Luxembourg). It has two operational elements, the NATO component at Geilenkirchen, Germany, operating the E-3As with crews from Belgium, Canada, Denmark, Germany, Greece, Italy, the Netherlands, Norway, Portugal, Spain, Turkey and the United States, and the British component with seven E-3Ds at RAF Waddington, England.

Only some of the E-3As are usually to be found at Geilenkirchen; others are always deployed to the forward operating bases in Greece, Italy and Turkey; or the forward operating location in Norway. After the attacks of 11 September 2001, Nato despatched two E-3As to help with the surveillance of US airspace.

This aircraft, delivered in 1982, has now been upgraded with large antennae under the nose for the 'Quick Look' electronic support measures (ESM) system. USAF E-3s are undergoing the same upgrades to become E-3Cs.

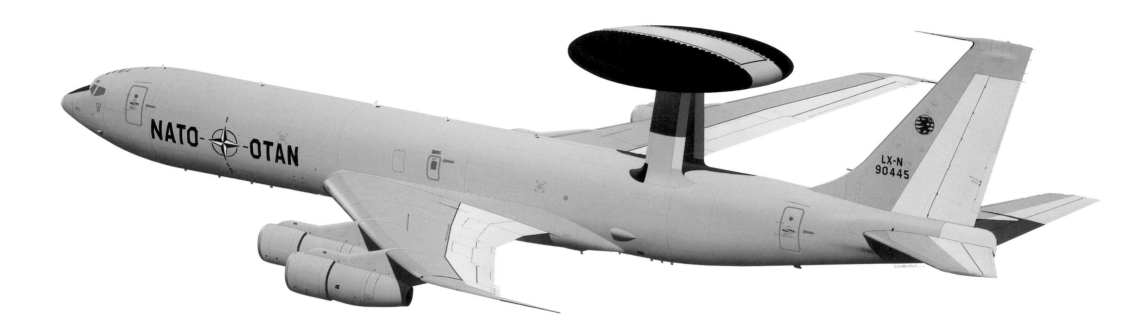

BOEING RC-135V RIVET JOINT

*33rd Strategic Reconnaissance Squadron,
55th Strategic Reconnaissance Wing,
Strategic Air Command, United States Air
Force, Offut Air Force Base, Nebraska
1980s*

BOEING RC-135V RIVET JOINT

Specification
- **Type** strategic reconnaissance aircraft
- **Crew** four on flight deck, up to 32 in cabin
- **Powerplant** four 80.1kN (18,000lb thrust) Pratt & Whitney TF-33-PW-9 turbofan engines
- **Performance** max speed 850km/h (530mph); service ceiling 12,725m (41,750ft); range 9100km (5650 miles)
- **Dimensions** wing span 39.88 m (130ft 10in); length 42.82m (140ft 6in); height12.7m (41ft 8in)
- **Weight** 141,522kg (298,997lb) loaded
- **Armament** none

The RC-135V is one of a variety of specialized electronic surveillance versions of the basic C-135 transport aircraft derived from the Boeing 367-80, which also served as the prototype for the 707 airliner family. These aircraft were originally designed to observe Soviet missile tests and launches from Alaskan bases, but developed a wide range of missions including signals intelligence (Sigint), imagery intelligence (Imint), electronic intelligence (Elint) and telemetry intelligence (Telint).

This aircraft, 64-14842, was delivered to the US Air Force (USAF) in October 1964 as an RC-135B and later became an RC-135C. It was the second of seven to be converted under project Big Safari to RC-135V standard. The conversion work was done by Ling-Temco-Vought (LTV) and took from November 1973 to January 1975. The main piece of new equipment was the Automatic Elint Emitter Locator System (AEELS), which was installed in huge cheek fairings. The new 'hog' nose contained a new signals intelligence antenna, as well as the usual radar found on standard C-135s. RC-135V 4842 took part in the El Dorado Canyon raids on Libya in 1986 and was at one time named 'Shot at and Missed' and later 'Fair Warning'.

Reorganization of the USAF in 1991 saw Strategic and Tactical Air Commands merge into Air Combat Command, and the 55th Strategic Reconnaissance Wing (SRW) became simply the 55th Wing. The RC-135s stayed where they were, but gained 'OF' tailcodes, signifying Offut as their home base. The present 55th Wing RC-135 fleet includes two RC-135S Cobra Balls, one RC-135X Cobra Eye, two RC-135U Combat Sents, 14 RC-135V/W Rivet Joints, and 2 RC-135 trainers. Many of these aircraft are receiving the CFM-56 high-bypass turbofan engines, the first being an RC-135W that was completed in 1999.

BLACKBURN (HAWKER SIDDELEY) BUCCANEER S.MK 2B

No. 12 Squadron, Strike Command, Royal Air Force, RAF Lossiemouth late 1980s

The Blackburn Buccaneer originated in the early 1950s as a design for a carrier-borne attack aircraft able to carry a nuclear bomb below radar coverage. As the NA.39, the prototype flew in April 1958 and was followed by an order for 50 Buccaneer S.Mk 1s for the Royal Navy. From 1962 until 1978, the S.1 and the improved S.Mk 2 flew from the Royal Navy's large-deck aircraft carriers. The Royal Air Force (RAF) took over some of the Royal Navy's 'Buccs' in 1969 and ordered more, most of them the S.Mk 2B version with a bulged bomb bay and Martel guided missile capability. The Buccaneer was famed for its smooth low-level ride and was one of the best strike aircraft of the 1960s and 1970s. The Navy gave its remaining aircraft to the RAF in 1978. South Africa was the only export user, purchasing 15 S.Mk 50s, which saw action over Angola.

This Buccaneer, XW530 was built for the RAF and was one of 12 that served in the 1991 Gulf War, where she was known as Guinness Girl and Pauline. The Buccaneers initially designated targets for the laser guided bombs (LGBs) of Tornadoes, but later in the war dropped LGBs themselves. Depicted here firing a TV-guided Martel anti-ship missile, this aircraft is in the markings of No. 12 Squadron, which was re-formed with Buccaneers in 1969 as a dedicated maritime attack unit. The fox badge originated when the squadron operated the Fairey Fox bomber in the 1930s.

With the imminent arrival of the maritime attack version of the Tornado, the GR.1B, No. 12 Squadron was disbanded in October 1993, marking the end of the Buccaneer in regular RAF service. XW530 is preserved at the Buccaneer Petrol Station in the town of Elgin, near Lossiemouth.

BLACKBURN (HAWKER SIDDELEY) BUCCANEER S.MK 2B

Specification
- **Type** maritime strike aircraft
- **Crew** 2
- **Powerplant** two 51.5kN (11,000lb thrust) Rolls-Royce RB.168-1A Spey turbofans
- **Performance** max speed 1112km/h (691mph); service ceiling 12,192m (40,000ft); range 3701km (2300 miles)
- **Dimensions** wing span 13.41m (44ft); length 19.33m (64ft 5in); height 4.95m (16ftft 3in)
- **Weight** 25,402kg (56,000lb) loaded
- **Armament** up to 7264kg (16,000lb) of bombs, or rocket pods or Martel or Sea Eagle air-to-surface missiles, or two WE.177 nuclear weapons

BRITISH AEROSPACE HARRIER GR.MK 3

No. 1 Squadron, No. 38 (Tactical) Group, Royal Air Force, RAF Wittering, Cambridgeshire, late 1980s

BRITISH AEROSPACE HARRIER GR.MK 3

Specification
- **Type** vertical take-off/landing attack aircraft
- **Crew** 1
- **Powerplant** one 85.8kN (19,289lb thrust) Rolls-Royce Pegasus Mk 103 vectored-thrust turbofan engine
- **Performance** max speed 1185km/h (735mph); service ceiling 15,545m (51,000ft); range 1000km (620 miles)
- **Dimensions** wing span 7.60m (25ft 3in); length 14.37m (47ft 2in); height 3.42m (11ft 3in)
- **Weight** 11,793kg (26,000lb) loaded
- **Armament** two 30-mm ADEN cannon pods with 150 rounds each; up to 3630kg (8000lb) of weapons including bombs, rockets and AIM-9 Sidewinder air-to-air missiles

The Harrier originated in the early 1960s as the Hawker P.1127, the most successful of many experimental vertical take-off and landing (V/TOL) aircraft of the era. The original Harrier GR.1 entered service with No. 1 Squadron of the Royal Air Force (RAF) in 1969. No. 1 Squadron was officially formed in 1912 from No. 1 Airship Company of the Royal Engineers at Farnborough, and thus lay claim to being the oldest military flying unit in the world.

Many of the RAF's GR.1s were redesignated as the GR.1A when they were refitted with the more powerful Pegasus 203 engine. They remained without much in the way of electronic sensors until the GR.3 upgrade, which saw the installation of a laser rangefinder and marked target seeker (LRMTS) in the nose. This unit allowed the use of laser-guided bombs by locating the laser 'spot' on the target as generated by an airborne or ground-based designator.

A number of Harrier GR.3s were deployed to the Falklands Islands aboard the Royal Navy's carriers in 1982. As well as flying strikes from the ships, they operated from a temporary airstrip ashore and flew close support missions for British army and marine forces.

XV740 was the third production Harrier GR.1, delivered to the Ministry of Defence (Procurement Executive) at Boscombe Down in July 1968. It served with the RAF's No. 1 and No. 4 Squadrons through the 1970s and 1980s, but was not deployed to the Falklands. It was modified to GR.1A standard by 1975 and later became a GR.3. By 1989 it was stored at RAF Abingdon as a battle damage repair training (BDRT) airframe. Increasing use of composite construction in aircraft such as the Harrier II reduced the need for metal repair training, and by June 1992 XV740 had been scrapped.

CASA C.101EB AVIOJET

Escuadrón 793, Escuelo de Vuelo Básico,
Academia General del Aire,
Ejército del Aire, San Javier,
Spain, 1980s

CASA C.101EB AVIOJET

Specification
- **Type** advanced jet trainer
- **Crew** 2
- **Powerplant** one 20.91kN (4700lb thrust) Garrett TFE-731-5-1J turbofan engine
- **Performance** max speed 769km/h (478mph); service ceiling 12,800m (42,000ft); range over 1038km (644 miles)
- **Dimensions** wing span 10.60m (34ft 9.5in); length 12.50m (41ft 5in); height 4.25m (13ft 11.25in)
- **Weight** 6300kg (13,889lb) loaded
- **Armament** one 30mm (1.18in) DEFA cannon pod or two 12.7mm (0.50in) machine guns; up to 1840kg (4056lb) of bombs or rockets

To replace the elderly Hispano Saeta trainer, Spanish aircraft maker CASA (Construcciones Aeronauticas SA) began work on the C.101 Aviojet in 1975. Germany's MBB and Northrop in the United States helped with the development, and the first of four prototypes flew in June 1977. The design followed that of other jet trainers such as the Hawk and Alpha Jet, but was less aerodynamically sophisticated, with an unswept wing, and it had limited weapons capability. The *Ejército del Aire* (Spanish Air Force designated the C.101 as the E-25 Mirlo (Blackbird) and purchased 88 in two batches. In 1990–92, all had their navigation/attack capability modernized.

Export sales have been limited. Four Aviojets were sold to Honduras, and Jordan bought 16 C.101CC-04 dedicated attack versions. Chile bought four similar aircraft and built a further 19 as the ENAER A-36CC Halcón. A more sophisticated C.101DD variant was developed which had provision for Maverick missiles, a new HUD, a radar warning system and chaff/flare dispensers. It has so far failed to receive any orders.

This E-25 is depicted when in service with the *Escuelo de Vuelo Básico* (Basic Flying School) of the *Academia General del Aire* (General Air Academy) at San Javier in southeast Spain. The Patrulla Aguila aerobatic team is also based here, and its C.101s are flown by the academy's instructors. This Aviojet was last noted in service with the team.

CESSNA A-37B DRAGONFLY

2 Brigada, Aérea Grupo Caza Y Bombardero, Fuerza Aérea Salvadoreña, Comalapa, El Salvador, 1980s

CESSNA A-37B DRAGONFLY

Specification
- **Type** two-seat light attack/counterinsurgency jet
- **Crew** 2
- **Powerplant** two 12.68kN (2850lb thrust) General Electric J85-GE-17A turbojet engines
- **Performance** max speed 816km/h (507mph); service ceiling 12,730m (41,765ft); range 1628km (1012 miles)
- **Dimensions** wing span 10.93m (35ft 10.5in); length excluding probe 8.93m (29ft 3.5in); height 2.70m (8ft 10.5in)
- **Weight** 6350kg (14,000lb) loaded
- **Armament** up to 1860kg (4100lb) of ordnance on eight underwing pylons

Derived from the T-37 'Tweety Bird' trainer, the A-37 Dragonfly (or 'Super Tweet') is a cheap, reliable and hard-hitting light attack platform that has seen action in numerous conflicts. The prototype, designated YAT-37D, flew in October 1963 and was followed by a batch of T-37Bs converted to A-37As, with an internal 20-mm minigun, wing pylons and tip tanks. The definitive A-37B was strengthened and weighed more than twice as much as a T-37.

US and South Vietnamese squadrons used the Dragonfly to great effect in Vietnam, where it proved a more accurate bomber than the much more sophisticated F-4 Phantom, as well as being easier and cheaper to maintain. After Vietnam, the United States continued to operate a small number of A-37s, some of them designated as OA-37s for the forward air control (FAC) role. The US Air Force (USAF) retired the A-37 in 1992. A-37s have been supplied to numerous nations for the counterinsurgency (CoIn) role, particularly in Latin America. Many of these have seen action against or on behalf of rebels in various conflicts, notably El Salvador and Nicaragua in the 1980s.

Depicted carrying Mk 81 bombs with 'daisy cutter' fuse extenders, this is one of 19 A-37Bs delivered to El Salvador from surplus USAF stocks from 1982 and used by the *Fuerza Aérea Salvadoreña* (El Salvador Air Force) against left-wing guerrillas in the civil war which lasted until 1990. During a battle at the town of Berlin in February 1983, strafing and bombing attacks by the Dragonflies were instrumental in allowing recapture of the town from rebel forces. In June 1983, they made many attacks on rebel positions around the capital, San Salvador. Only about six of the Dragonflies were serviceable by the mid-1990s.

CESSNA O-1E BIRD DOG

20th Tactical Air Support Squadron, PACAF, United States Air Force, Da Nang, Republic of Vietnam, circa 1970

CESSNA O-1E BIRD DOG

Specification
- **Type** light observation/forward air control aircraft
- **Crew** 2
- **Powerplant** one 157kW (210hp) Continental O-470-11 piston engine
- **Performance** max speed 184km/h (115mph); service ceiling 18,500ft (5640m); range 853km (530 miles)
- **Dimensions** wing span 10.97m (36ft); length 7.89m (25ft 10in); height 2.23m (7 ft 4in)
- **Weight** 1088kg (2400lb) loaded
- **Armament** four target marking rockets; sometimes one M60 machine gun for observer

Cessna's L-19 liaison aircraft was derived from the civilian model 170 and first flew in 1950. It performed many duties in Korea with the US Army and US Marine Corps (USMC), such as officer transport and artillery spotting. The L-19E entered production in 1957 with a more powerful engine and more modern avionics. The US Navy and USMC designated this version the OE-1, but in 1962 designations were rationalized and all services renamed it the O-1E, 'O' standing for 'observation'. In 1963, the Army gave the US Air Force (USAF) a number for use as forward air control (FAC) aircraft to mark targets for artillery or air strikes in Vietnam. Nearly 500 O-1Es were built, later models being modified during production for FAC duties with hardpoints for rockets and additional radios.

During the early phases of the war, when US involvement was ostensibly in an 'advisory' capacity, American pilots would fly with a South Vietnamese crewman to maintain the pretence that the United States was not directing the fighting. Later in the war, when US policy was to withdraw its own troops in favour of 'Vietnamization' of the conflict, experienced USAF FACs often controlled strikes by South Vietnamese Air Force (VNAF) A-1 Skyraiders and other aircraft with a Vietnamese observer/interpreter aboard. Generally the FAC pilots preferred to operate alone, flying the aircraft, talking on the radios and firing white phosphorous rockets to mark the targets for attack.

The USAF lost 178 Bird Dogs in Vietnam to enemy action, 25 of them belonging to the 20th Tactical Air Support Squadron (TASS). The 20th TASS was established at Da Nang in April 1965, and the squadron remained there (with many detachments at other bases and airstrips) until 1973. Later in the war, it flew O-2A Skymasters and OV-10A Broncos.

CONVAIR F-106A DELTA DART

49th Fighter Interceptor Squadron, Tactical Air Command, Griffiss Air Force Base, New York, 1983

CONVAIR F-102A DELTA DART

Specification
- **Type** supersonic interceptor fighter
- **Crew** 1
- **Powerplant** one Pratt & Whitney J75-P-17 turbojet rated at 76.50kN (17,200lb thrust) static and 108.98kN (24,500 lb thrust) with afterburner
- **Performance** max speed 2137km/h (1328mph); combat radius 925km (575 miles); service ceiling 17,374m (57,000ft)
- **Dimensions** wing span 11.67m (38ft 3.5in); length 21.56m (70ft 8.75in); height 6.18m (20ft 3.5in)
- **Weight** loaded 17,779 kg (39,195 lb)
- **Armament** one MB-1 Genie nuclear-tipped air-to-air missile and four AIM-4 Falcon radar or IR-guided air-to-air missiles; ;ater models also had one M61A1 Vulcan 20-mm (0.79in) cannon

Begun as the '1954 Ultimate Interceptor', and for a time known as the F-102B, the F-106 emerged as a much more capable and long-lived interceptor than its predecessor, and also proved to be a useful dogfighter in its later years. The prototype YF-106 flew in December 1956 and was similar in configuration and dimensions to the F-102A, but with refined aerodynamics, a square-topped fin, completely revised intakes and a more powerful Pratt & Whitney J75 engine.

The airframe was regarded as just one component of the MA-1 integrated weapons system. The MA-1 included an automated interception system that would fly the aircraft 'hands off' to the firing point. Weapons included the same Falcon missiles as the F-102A, but also the MB-1 Genie rocket with a nuclear warhead. Late in their careers, some aircraft such as this one had a Vulcan cannon fitted between the bomb bay doors and clear-topped canopy installed.

Mainly based in the United States, F-106 units were rotated to South Korea to bolster local air defence during the 1968–70 period of tension with North Korea over the capture of the intelligence ship USS *Pueblo*.

Delta Dart 58-0780 was the 140th of 330 F-106s to be built and was delivered in November 1959 to the 27th Fighter Interceptor Squadron (FIS) at Loring Air Force Base (AFB), Maine. It moved between units quite regularly, serving with the 94th, 71st, 319th 460th, 159th, 194th and the Air Development Weapons Center (AWDC). In 1983, it joined the 49th FIS at Griffiss AFB, New York, and served there until 1987 when the unit disbanded. After four years in storage it was converted to a QF-106 drone for weapons tests. Many of these aircraft were used for years and survived many missile engagements, but 0780 was shot down by an AIM-7 Sparrow in its first unmanned mission on 9 March 1993.

DASSAULT BR1150 ATLANTIC 1

88° Gruppo Antisomergibili, 41° Stormo, Aeronautica Militare Italiana, Catania-Sigonella, Italy, late 1980s

DASSAULT BR1150 ATLANTIC 1

Specification

- **Type** maritime patrol aircraft
- **Crew** 12
- **Powerplant** two 4549kW (6100hp) Rolls-Royce Tyne Type RTy 20 Mk 21 turboprop engines
- **Performance** max speed 658km/h (409mph); service ceiling 10000m (32,810ft); range 9000km (5592 miles)
- **Dimensions** wing span 36.30m (119ft 1in); length 31.75m (104ft 2in); height 11.33m (37ft 2in)
- **Weight** 44,500kg (98,104lb) loaded
- **Armament** up to eight bombs, depth charges or torpedoes in bomb bay; Exocet or Martel ASMs on wing pylons

The Atlantic is the only maritime patrol aircraft in service designed for the role from the outset, rather than being adapted from a commercial airliner. Its genesis was a 1957 Nato requirement for a common long-range maritime surveillance aircraft. Breguet of France (later part of Dassault) was the winning bidder with its twin-engined design with a 'double bubble' fuselage, having a pressurized main cabin and a large bomb bay underneath.

The first Breguet 1150 prototype flew in October 1961. Development and production lasted 12 years with a total of 91 built, of which 40 were for France, 20 for Germany, 18 for Italy and nine for the Netherlands. Three French and one Dutch aircraft were later transferred to Pakistan.

The Atlantic has been succeeded in French service by the Atlantique 2 (ATL 2), a new-build version with an all-new Iguane (iguana) radar and a Thomson-CSF MAD (magnetic anomaly detector). The ATL 2 is significantly more capable than its predecessor, and the first of 40 production aircraft was delivered in 1989. Italy chose to upgrade its Atlantics with many of the features of the ATL 2 from 1985–88.

The aircraft depicted was the first example delivered to the *Aeronautica Militare Italiana* (Italian Air Force) in June 1972. Since then it has served with the 88° *Gruppo Antisomergibili* (88th Anti-Submarine Squadron) at Catania, Sicily. A sister unit was based at Cagliari, Sardinia, but all Atlantics are now concentrated at Catania. Italy's Atlantics have long patrolled the Mediterranean and have kept a particular watch on movements in the Adriatic Sea during the Balkan conflicts of the 1990s. This Atlantic 1 was upgraded to near ATL 2 standard as shown by the radar 'dustbin' radome under the forward fuselage and the ESM antenna on the tip of the vertical tail.

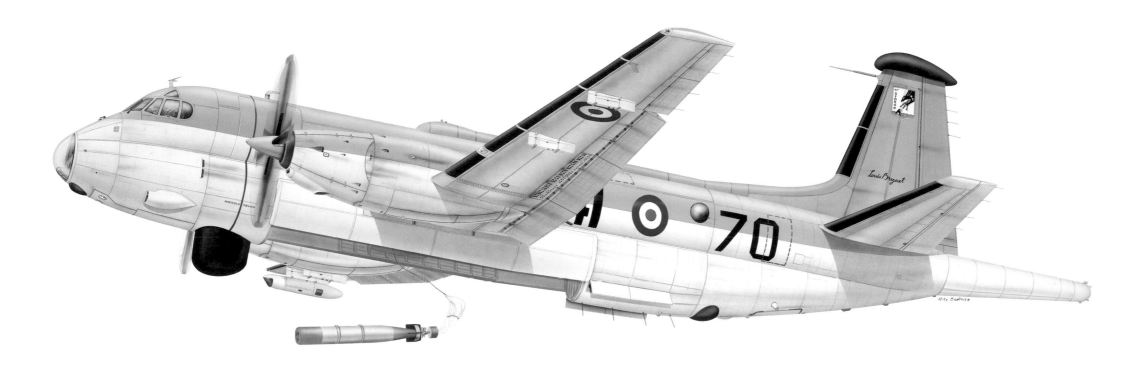

DASSAULT MIRAGE IIICZ

No. 2 Squadron, South African Air Force, AFB Hoedspruit, Republic of South Africa late 1980s

DASSAULT MIRAGE IIICZ

Specification
- **Type** supersonic fighter
- **Crew** 1
- **Powerplant** one 58.84kN (13,228lb thrust) SNECMA Atar 9C turbojet
- **Performance** max speed 2112km/h (1320mph); combat radius 290km (180 miles); service ceiling 20,000m (65,615ft)
- **Dimensions** span 8.22m (27ft); length 14.75m (48ft 5in); height 4.5m (14ft 9in)
- **Weight** loaded 12,700kg (27,998lb)
- **Armament** two 30mm (1.18in) DEFA cannon; up to 4000kg (8818lb) weapons load including Matra Magic or Atlas Kukri and Darter air-to-air missiles

The classic Mirage series of fighters began with the MD550 Mystère Delta, a sub-scale delta-winged testbed flown in 1955 and later named Mirage I. This was followed on 18 November 1956 by the slightly larger Mirage III. The pre-production Mirage IIIA was the first 'full-sized' version and led to the IIIC interceptor for the French Air Force in 1961. The multi-role Mirage IIIE fighter (and equivalent Mirage IIID trainer) was flown in 1961 and introduced provision for an AN52 nuclear bomb. The Mirage III was very successful on the export market, selling to Abu Dhabi, Argentina, Australia, Brazil, Egypt, Israel, Lebanon, Pakistan, South Africa, Spain, Venezuela and Zaire. A ground-attack version dubbed the Mirage 5 was equally successful and also saw combat action with many of its users.

The No. 2 Squadron of the South African Air Force (SAAF), known as the 'Flying Cheetahs', was active in the North African and Italian campaigns during World War II, flying mainly P-40s and Spitfires. In Korea, it used F-51D Mustangs and later F-86F Sabres in the ground-attack role, flying Vampires and Sabres on return to South Africa. In 1963, the first of many Mirages for the SAAF entered service when No. 2 Squadron received 16 Mirage IIICZ interceptors and three IIIBZ trainers. A further 39 aircraft, including IIIDs, IIIEs and IIIRs, followed.

The early 1990s saw a major drawdown in the SAAF, and most of the Mirages were retired in 1992. Many Mirage IIIDs had been converted with Israeli help to the much more capable Atlas Cheetah configuration. In October 1990, No. 2 retired its Mirages, exchanging them for Cheetahs. Moving to Louis Trichardt Air Force Base in January 1993, No. 2 Squadron is now the SAAF's sole frontline combat jet squadron and is destined to receive the Saab Gripen in the coming decade.

DASSAULT MIRAGE IVP

91e Escadre de Bombardment,
Commandement des Forces Aériennes
Stratégiques, Armée de l' Air,
Mont de Marsan, France, 1980s

DASSAULT MIRAGE IVP

Specification
- **Type** supersonic strategic bomber
- **Crew** 2
- **Powerplant** two 71.6kN (15,432lb thrust) SNECMA Atar 9K afterburning turbojets
- **Performance** max speed 2340 km/h (1454 mph); service ceiling 20,000m (65,615ft); range 2480 km (1550 miles)
- **Dimensions** wing span 11.85m (38ft 10in); length 23.50m (77ft 2in); height 5.65m (18ft 6in)
- **Weight** 31,600kg (69,666lb) max take-off
- **Armament** one ASMP nuclear cruise missile

First flown in June 1959, the Mirage IV is still in *Armée de l' Air* (French Air Force) service, albeit as a reconnaissance platform, rather than in its original role as a strategic bomber. Based on a scaling up of the Mirage III fighter, but fitted with two seats and four-wheel main undercarriage units, the Mirage IVA was intended to carry a single AN22 free-fall nuclear bomb as part of France's independent nuclear deterrent. This was regarded as a 'pre-strategic' deterrent, being unable to reach the Soviet Union itself.

Sixty-two examples were built, the first entering service in 1964. Nineteen Mirage IVs were updated to Mirage IVP (penetration) standard and equipped to carry the Air-Sol Moyenne Portée (ASMP) ramjet cruise missile. The last armed 'M4s' were retired in 1996, and the ASMP role was passed to the Mirage 2000N.

Twelve Mirage IVAs were converted in the 1970s to Mirage IVR high-altitude reconnaissance platforms, and it is the last of these that remain in service, having been used operationally over Bosnia and Afghanistan in recent years. To fulfil the reconnaissance mission, the CT-52 sensor pod under the fuselage could be configured in several ways, but typically with three low-altitude OMERA 35 film cameras, three high-altitude OMERA 36 film cameras, and a Wildt mapping film camera.

The aircraft pictured here, the seventh production Mirage IVA and one of those converted to IVP configuration in the 1980s, served with the 91st *Escadre de Bombardment*, which was comprised of two squadrons, 1/91 'Gascogne' at Mont-de-Marsan and 2/91 'Bretagne' at Cazaux. The former unit remains active with the eight or so reconnaissance Mirages. The aircraft is not currently in service, being in storage at the Chateaudun airfield.

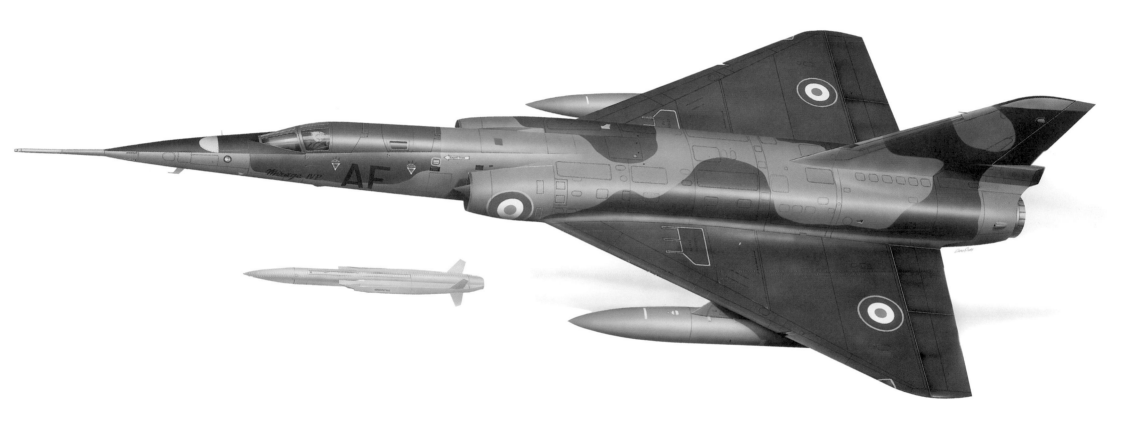

DASSAULT MIRAGE F1AZ

No. 1 Squadron, Air Defence Command, South African Air Force, AFB Hoedspruit, Republic of South Africa, 1980s

DASSAULT MIRAGE F1AZ

Specification
- **Type** single-seat fighter
- **Crew** 1
- **Powerplant** one 49.03kN (11,023lb thrust) SNECMA Atar 9K-50 turbojet engine
- **Performance** max speed 2125km/h (1320mph); service ceiling 20,000m (65,615ft)
- **Dimensions** wing span 8.4m (27ft 6.75in); length 15.3m (50ft 2.5in); height 4.5m (15ft 9in)
- **Weight** 16200kg (35,715lb) loaded
- **Armament** two internal DEFA 553 30mm (1.18in) cannon; max ordnance load of 13,889 lb (6300kg), including Matra Magic or Atlas Kukri and Darter air-to-air missiles

The Mirage F1 was Dassault's successor to its highly successful Mirage III/5 delta series and was developed to meet an *Armée de l'Air* requirement for an all-weather interceptor. Although powered by a version of the SNECMA Atar 9 engine as used on the Mirage III, the F1 forsook that aircraft's delta configuration for a high-mounted wing and conventional tail surfaces. The prototype first flew in December 1966, and the Mirage F1C fighter entered French service in May 1973, along with the F1B two-seater.

The Mirage F1 has been widely exported, and has seen action with a number of its users, notably Iraq. Only South Africa and Libya bought the F1A version, which was without radar, although it had a laser rangefinder.

The No. 1 Squadron of the South African Air Force (SAAF) received 32 F1AZ models beginning in 1975, although they were not publicly acknowledged for several years. These were followed later by 16 F1CZs for No. 3 Squadron. From the late 1970s to the late 1980s, the SAAF Mirages were used for ground-attack missions over Angola and South West Africa (Namibia).

One F1CZ pilot destroyed two Angolan MiG-21s in separate combats in 1981 and 1982, one with cannon and the other with a Matra Magic missile. Other air-to-air weapons included the similar V3 Kukri and V3C Darter, and attack weapons were Matra rocket pods and bombs.

Although one or two F1CZs were tested with the Klimov RD-33 engine as used in the MiG-29, a programme to re-engine the entire fleet was not implemented, and the F1s were retired at the end of 1997. F1AZ number 231 was one of 22 F1AZs put up for sale alongside 11 of the F1CZs.

DASSAULT MIRAGE 2000B

Escadrille 3/2 'Alsace', Commandement de la Force Aérienne de Combat, Armée de l'Air, Dijon-Longvic, France, 1985

The Dassault Mirage 2000 was chosen in December 1975 to be the next-generation fighter for the *Armée de l'Air*, and the first of five prototypes took to the air in March 1978. With the Mirage 2000, Dassault returned to the delta configuration of the Mirage III, using negative longitudinal stability and a fly-by-wire flight control system to eliminate many of the shortcomings of a conventional delta. As such, the Mirage 2000 has the Mirage III/5 series' large internal volume and low drag, but has improved agility, slow-speed handling and lower landing speed.

The first of 30 production Mirage 2000Cs made its maiden flight in November 1982, and deliveries began in April 1983. The Mirage 2000B tandem two-seat trainer first flew in August 1983. It loses some internal fuel and both cannon in order to accommodate the second cockpit, although it is only 19cm (7.5in) longer than the 2000C. Full weapons capability is retained.

The Mirage 2000 has had considerable export success, with each customer having its own two-seat version. Abu Dhabi's two-seat trainers are known as Mirage 2000DADs, India's are Mirage 2000THs and Peru's are Mirage 2000DPs. The two-seat trainer formed the basis of the *Armée de l'Air*'s Mirage 2000N nuclear-strike variant.

This aircraft was the thirty-first two-seater to be built and was delivered to *Escadrille* 2/3 'Champagne' in March 1985. It was one of four two-seaters in this unit, which phased out the Mirage IIIE in July that year. When *Escadrille* 3/2 'Alsace' (EC.2 – redesignated EC 01.030 in the mid-1990s) was declared fully operational, the two-seaters were passed on. In 2003, it was in service at Orange with EC02.005 'Ile de France', coded 5-OX.

DASSAULT MIRAGE 2000B

Specification
- **Type** two-seat interceptor fighter
- **Crew** 2
- **Powerplant** one 64.3kN (14,462lb thrust) SNECMA M53-P2 turbofan engine
- **Performance** max speed 2338km/h (1453mph); service ceiling 18,000m (59,055ft); 1850km (1150 miles)
- **Dimensions** wing span 9.13m (28ft 11.5in); length 14.36m (47ft 8.75in); height 5.20m (17ft 0.75in)
- **Weight** 17,000kg (37,478lb) loaded
- **Armament** two DEFA 534 30mm (1.18in) cannon with 125 rounds each; weapons load up to 6300kg (13,890kg) including Matra Magic 2 and Super 530F air-to-air missiles, conventional or laser-guided bombs or AS30L laser-guided missiles

DASSAULT SUPER ETENDARD

14 e Flotille, Aéronavale, Landivisiau, France, late 1980s

DASSAULT SUPER ETENDARD

Specification
- **Type** carrier-based attack aircraft
- **Crew** 1
- **Powerplant** one 49.05kN (11,023lb thrust) SNECMA Atar 8K50
- **Performance** max speed 1380 km/h (857mph); service ceiling 13,700m (44,950ft); range 1700 km (1056 miles)
- **Dimensions** wing span 9.60m (31ft 6in); length 14.31m (46ft 11.5in); height 3.86m (12ft 8in)
- **Weight** 12,000kg (26,455lb) max take-off
- **Armament** two 30mm (1.18in) DEFA 552A cannon with 125 rounds each; weapons include bombs and rockets, AS30L laser-guided missiles, one AM39 Exocet, one ASMP nuclear missile, Magic 2 air-to-air missiles

Originally designed for a Nato requirement for a lightweight tactical assault fighter, the Dassault Etendard first flew in July 1956. Although it lost out to the Fiat G.91, the Etendard was developed to provide a missile-armed strike aircraft for the French Navy, or *Aéronavale*.

The initial production Etendard IVM served from the carriers *Clemenceau* and *Foch* from 1961–80. Some were upgraded to IVP tanker/reconnaissance standard, but the attack role was taken over by the much improved Super Etendard, which first flew in 1978 and added Agave radar in the nose and Exocet anti-ship missile (ASM) capability.

In the 1980s, five were leased to Iraq, which used them to attack Iranian civil and military shipping. Argentina's Navy had five Super Etendards and five Exocets in 1982, and sank HMS *Sheffield* and the freighter *Atlantic Conveyor* during the Falklands conflict. French 'Sue's were used on bombing missions over Lebanon in the 1980s and Bosnia in the 1990s. Although the Rafale is slated to replace the Super Etendard in *Aéronavale* service, the remaining unit is expected to serve for some years to come.

The unit of the aircraft depicted here, 14F, was disbanded in July 1991, leaving 11F and 17F as the remaining Super Etendard units.

DASSAULT/DORNIER ALPHA JET A

Jagdbombergeschwader 41, Taktische Division, Luftflotten Kommando, Luftwaffe, Husum, Federal Republic of Germany late 1980s

DASSAULT/DORNIER ALPHA JET A

Specification
- **Type** two-seat jet trainer/light attack aircraft
- **Crew** 2
- **Powerplant** two 13.24kN (2976lb thrust) SNECMA/Turboméca Larzac 04-C6 turbofan engines
- **Performance** max speed 1000km/h (621mph); service ceiling 14630m (48,000ft); range 2460km (1780 miles)
- **Dimensions** wing span 9.11m (29ft 10.75in); length 11.75m (38ft 6.5in); height 4.19m (31ft 9in)
- **Weight** 8000kg (17,637lb) loaded
- **Armament** one 27mm (1.06in) IWKA-Mauser cannon in removable pod; up to 2500kg (5511lb) of bombs and rockets

The Alpha Jet was a collaborative project between Dassault of France and Dornier of Germany to produce a new advanced trainer. During development, which began in 1969, the German requirement diverged so that its aircraft were specified as light attack aircraft to replace the Fiat G-91. The French prototype of the Alpha Jet flew in 1973, with another flying in Germany a year later.

France ordered 175 of the Alpha Jet E (Ecole), while West Germany took the same number of the Alpha Jet A (Appui Tactique). Both aircraft were weapons capable, but the German aircraft had a head up display (HUD) and a navigation/attack system. The French aircraft had a more rounded nose, which gave better spinning characteristics, and Martin-Baker Mk 4 ejection seats rather than the American Stencel S-111 model.

The Alpha Jet has been nearly as successful as the BAe Hawk in the export market, new examples being sold to Qatar, Ivory Coast, Belgium, Morocco, Togo, Cameroon, Nigeria and Egypt. German service began in 1979, and the last aircraft was delivered in 1985. They were used as light attackers, forward air control trainers, conversion trainers and to give fast jet experience to prospective Tornado navigators. Some crews were trained to destroy enemy helicopters. During the 1991 Gulf War, some *Luftwaffe* Alpha Jets were despatched to Erhac, Turkey, to maintain Nato's commitment to defend that country. Alpha Jet A 40+15 was assigned to *Jagdbombergeschwader* (JBG) 41, one of three fighter-bomber wings to operate the type. The *Luftwaffe* withdrew the Alpha Jet from the combat role in 1993 and 50 were given to Portugal, including 40+15, which was issued to one of two squadrons of *Grupo Operativo* 111 at Beja. A few *Luftwaffe* aircraft remained in use as trainers until 1997. The remaining surplus *Luftwaffe* aircraft are likely to find new customers.

DOUGLAS A1-H SKYRAIDER

1st Special Operations Squadron,
556th Special Operations Wing,
United States Air Force, Nahkon Phanom
Royal Thai Air Force Base, Thailand, 1972

DOUGLAS A1-H SKYRAIDER

Specification
- **Type** close air support aircraft
- **Crew** 1
- **Powerplant** one 2014kW (2700hp) Wright R-3350-26WA Duplex Cyclone 18-cylinder air-cooled radial engine
- **Performance** max speed 564km/h (350mph); service ceiling 7925m (26,000ft); range 2215km (1316 miles)
- **Dimensions** wing span 15.24m (50ft); length 11.84m (38ft 10in); height 3.66m (12ft)
- **Weight** 11,340kg (20,000lb) max take-off
- **Armament** two 20mm (0.79in) cannon in the wing

The capable and durable Skyraider served throughout the Vietnam War, beginning with deliveries to the South Vietnamese Air Force (VNAF) in 1961 and ending with the same air arm with the fall of Saigon in 1975. Many of the Skyraiders serving at the end of the conflict had seen hard action with the US Navy, US Air Force (USAF) and VNAF before eventual capture by the North Vietnamese.

In its initial attack form, the 'Able Dog' had a nuclear role, but the type was made famous as a close air support aircraft in both the Korean and Vietnam wars. Its long endurance and ability to carry a wide range of ordnance on its 15 wing pylons made it ideal for orbiting the battlefield and striking when called upon.

Built as an AD-6 (Bureau Number 135257) for the US Navy, this aircraft was transferred to the US Air Force (USAF) when the Navy retired the single-seat Skyraider from carrier operations in 1968. After refurbishment in the United States and installation of USAF equipment and a seat extractor system, it was assigned to the 1st Special Operations Squadron (SOS) of the 556th Special Operations Wing (SOW) at Nahkon Phanom Royal Thai Air Force Base.

In October 1971, the 1st SOS had 28 Skyraiders of four different models (A-1E, G, H and J). This unit was particularly active in the 'Sandy' role, providing close air support and helicopter escort for search-and-rescue missions for pilots downed over South Vietnam, Cambodia and Laos. In order to suppress enemy attempts to capture aviators on the ground, the 'Spad' could carry a variety of rockets, including three-round 'bazooka' tubes, seven- and 19-shot 70mm (2.75in) folding-fin rocket launchers and four-shot 127mm (5in) Zuni rocket pods. 'Midnight Cowboy' was usually flown by Rick Drury, author of *My Secret War*. This Skyraider was eventually transferred to the VNAF as US forces withdrew from Vietnam.

DOUGLAS A-4S SKYHAWK

No. 143 'Phoenix' Squadron,
Republic of Singapore Air Force,
Changi Air Base, Singapore
late 1980s

DOUGLAS A-4S SKYHAWK

Specification
- **Type** jet fighter-bomber
- **Crew** 1
- **Powerplant** one 37.37kN (8400lb thrust) Curtiss-Wright J65-W-20 turbojet engine
- **Performance** max speed 1064km/h (661mph); service ceiling 13,716m (45,000ft); range 2680km (1665 miles)
- **Dimensions** wing span 8.38m (27ft 6in); length without probe 11.70m (38ft 5in); height 4.27m (14ft 1in)
- **Weight** 10,206kg (22,500lb) loaded
- **Armament** two 30mm (1.18in) ADEN cannon; ordnance of up to 2268kg (5000lb) including conventional bombs and rockets and AIM-9P Sidewinder missiles

The A-4 Skyhawk is one of the classic designs of post-war military aviation, being both lighter and stronger than the US Navy thought possible when it asked Ed Heinemann for proposals for a new carrier-based attack aircraft in 1952. The X44D-1 Skyhawk prototype was flown in June 1954, and production models entered service in 1956.

The A-4B was the first fully operational model, fitted with an inflight-refueling probe and able to carry a wide range of conventional or nuclear weapons. In all, 2960 Skyhawks were built, 542 of them A-4Bs, but production of new models continued until 1979. Four nations ordered new A-4s from Douglas, but a further five took surplus US Navy and US Marine Corps models. Both Argentina and Singapore bought large numbers of refurbished A-4Bs for their air arms.

A-4S number 681 was built for the US Navy as A-4B Bureau Number 145046 and is known to have flown with Reserve squadron VA-209 'Air Barons' before delivery to Singapore in 1972. Although later deliveries of A-4s were converted to 'Super Skyhawk' configuration with F404 turbofans and modern avionics, this was not one of them, being sold to Celtrad Metal Industries for scrap.

In Singapore service, the A-4 has been used in both the fighter and bomber roles and still serves with three squadrons. Until the Royal Singapore Air Force (RSAF) acquired tanker aircraft, it was not uncommon to see some of its A-4Bs without refuelling probes as a weight- and drag-saving measure.

No. 143 Squadron moved from Changi to Tengah when the former airfield was rebuilt as the country's international airport. In 1997, it became the first RSAF squadron to make the transition to the F-16C/D Falcon.

DOUGLAS EA-3B SKYWARRIOR

VQ-2, Detachment C,
'World Watchers', CVW-15,
US Navy, USS Carl Vinson, 1983

DOUGLAS EA-3B SKYWARRIOR

Specification
- **Type** carrier-based electronic intelligence gathering aircraft
- **Crew** 7
- **Powerplant** two 57.5kN (12,400lb thrust) Pratt & Whitney J57-10 turbojet engines
- **Performance** max speed 995km/h (618mph); service ceiling 12,495m (41,000ft); range 4667km (2900 miles)
- **Dimensions** wing span 22.1m (72ft 6in); length 23.27m (76ft 4in); height 6.95m (22ft 10in)
- **Weight** 38,102kg (84,000lb) max take-off
- **Armament** none

The Douglas Skywarrior was the first all-jet bomber designed for aircraft-carrier use and was conceived in a 1947 US Navy specification for an aircraft able to carry a 10,000 lb (4536kg) payload over 2000 nautical miles (3700 km) and return safely to its carrier. Douglas produced the XA3D-1 Skywarrior prototype which flew in October 1952. The original Westinghouse J40 engines proved inadequate to meet the required performance, but the podded design enabled a change to the much better Pratt & Whitney J57 for the A3D-1, which entered service in 1956.

As a bomber, the Skywarrior, usually known as the 'Whale', saw some action in Vietnam, but was mainly used as a tanker and/or an electronic warfare platform. Other variants served as transports or photographic reconnaissance aircraft. The A3D-2Q, later designated EA-3B, was designed for electronic reconnaissance or 'ferreting' of enemy radar emissions. Twenty-six of the 283 Skywarriors were built as A3D-2Qs (later EA-3Bs) and served with the US Navy's electronic intelligence or VQ squadrons.

This 'Queer Whale', Bureau No. 144849, is illustrated in the markings of VQ-1 'World Watchers' when on a detachment to the USS *Carl Vinson* for a world-circling cruise in 1983. The EA-3Bs were the last Skywarriors in regular service, seeing use in Operation Desert Storm. The last active aircraft were retired at Rota, Spain, in October 1991. Their role was replaced by the ES-3A Shadow aboard carriers and EP-3 Orions from land bases. Bureau No. 144849 is known to have also served with electronic aggressor VAQ-34. It was delivered to storage at Davis-Monthan Air Force Base, Arizona. in July 1990, where it remains.

EMBRAER EMB111A (P-95A) BANDEIRULHA

*1°/7° Grupo de Aviaçio 'Orungan',
IIa Força Aérea, Comando Aérotactico,
Força Aérea Brasileira, Base Aérea
de Salvador, Salvador, Brazil, late 1980s*

EMBRAER EMB111A (P-95A) BANDEIRULHA

Specification

- **Type** maritime surveillance and patrol aircraft
- **Crew** 7
- **Powerplant** two 559kW (750hp) Pratt & Whitney Canada PT6A-34 turboprop engines
- **Performance** max speed 360km/h (223mph); service ceiling 7770m (25,492ft); range 2945km (1830 miles)
- **Dimensions** wing span 15.95m (52ft 4in); length 14.91m (48ft 11in); height 4.91m (16ft 2in)
- **Weight** 7000kg (15,432lb) loaded
- **Armament** up to 608kg (1340lb) of ordnance, including 70mm (2.75in) FFAR or 5in (127mm) HVAR rockets, smoke floats, flares or chaff

---

Built to a *Força Aérea Brasileira* (FAB – Brazilian Air Force) requirement for a light transport, the Embraer EMB-110 Bandeirante (pioneer) entered FAB service in 1973 as the C-95. Various specialized versions have been acquired among the 80 or so that have entered FAB service. The EC-95 or EMB-110A/P1 was the first, and is used to calibrate airport landing aids. The photographic reconnaissance model is the R-95 or EMB-110B, and the specialsized search-and-rescue version is the SC-95 or EMB-110P1K Bandeirusca. Known officially as the Bandeirante Patrulha (patroller), the P-95 or EMB.111 is also called the Bandeirulha. The Bandeirante formed the basis of a successful civilian commuter airliner and established Embraer in the commercial market, leading to today's range of turboprop and jet airliners.

The 1°/7° *Grupo de Aviaçio* (GAV) has been based at Salvador in the state of Bahia since 1947, with the mission of patrolling and protecting that stretch of Brazil's enormous coastline. The unit badge depicts an Oraungang, a mythical four-armed winged African deity that symbolizes the sky in struggle with the sea. The group operated the B-25 Mitchell, Lockheed PV-1 Ventura, PV-2 Harpoon and P-2 Neptune before it received the P-95.

The original P-95, of which 21 were procured, was followed by 10 P-95Bs with improved avionics and a strengthened airframe. The Bandeirulha is equipped with a Supersearcher radar and can carry a variety of types of rocket under its wings for use against surface vessels and can also drop flares and smoke floats to mark subsurface targets. Wingtip fuel tanks allow missions of up to nine hours' duration and a powerful searchlight permits searching at night.

ENGLISH ELECTRIC (BAC) CANBERRA PR.9

No. 39 Squadron (1 PRU)
Royal Air Force,
Wyton, Cambridgeshire, 1980s

ENGLISH ELECTRIC (BAC) CANBERRA PR.9

Specification
- **Type** jet reconnaissance aircraft
- **Crew** 2
- **Powerplant** two 50kN (11,250lb thrust) Rolls-Royce RA24 Avon Mk 26 turbojets
- **Performance** max speed 901km/h (560mph); service ceiling over 18,288m (60,000ft); range 8159km (5,070 miles)
- **Dimensions** wing span 22.30m (69ft 5in); length 20.31m (66ft 8in); height 4.77m (15ft 8in)
- **Weight** 26,082kg (57,500lb) loaded
- **Armament** none

The first photoreconnaissance (PR) Canberras were the PR.3 and PR.7, the latter having extra wing fuel and more powerful engines. The PR.57 was an export version of the Mk 7 for India of which a dozen were supplied. The PR.9 introduced a revised wing with a broader-chord inner wing and extended outer wings. A new nose section was fitted, which hinged to the right to allow entry by the navigator. The pilot's canopy opened unlike that on the B(I)8. The new nose housed an F95 forward-facing camera at the tip and another oblique F95 at the rear of the compartment. Two F96 cameras with lenses up to 1220mm (48in) focal length were mounted in front of the wing roots. Up to three more F96s could be carried in the rear fuselage. An infrared linescan system allowed the terrain under the flight path to be mapped by day or night. An optional Electro-Optical Long-Range Oblique Photographic sensor (EO-LOROP) records imagery in digital format on magnetic tape.

Twenty-three production PR.9s were built under licence by Shorts in Belfast between 1958 and 1962. No. 39 Squadron (also known as 1 Photo Reconnaissance Unit) has operated this version since 1962 and have taken part in many operations, from monitoring Soviet ports during the Cuban Missile Crisis in 1962 to tracking refugee movements in the Congo in the late 1990s. Chile received two ex-RAF PR. 9s after the Falklands War, but it seems likely that RAF aircraft were also operated in Chilean markings during the conflict to keep an eye on bases in neighbouring Argentina. During the 1980s the RAF reduced its Canberra force greatly and XH174 was one of many aircraft scrapped – a move that was later regretted when the PR.9 continued in service later than expected. Its nose section is preserved at RAF Shawbury.

FAIRCHILD A-10A THUNDERBOLT II

81st Fighter Squadron, 52nd Fighter Wing, USAFE, Spangdahlem, Germany, late 1980s

FAIRCHILD A-10A THUNDERBOLT II

Specification
- **Type** close support aircraft
- **Crew** 1
- **Powerplant** two 40.32kN (9065lb thrust) General Electric TF34-GE-100 turbofans
- **Performance** max speed 706km/h (439mph); service ceiling 13,636m (45,000ft); range 3947km (2454 miles) ferry range with two drop tanks
- **Dimensions** wing span 17.53m (57ft 6in); length 16.26m (53ft 6in); height 4.47m (14ft 8in)
- **Weight** 22,680kg (50,000lb) max take-off
- **Armament** one GAU-8 Avenger 30mm (1.18in) cannon with 1350 rounds; max ordnance load of 7758kg (16,000lb) including bombs, rockets and AGM-65 Maverick missiles

The Fairchild A-10A is one of the most specialized modern combat aircraft to enter service, having been designed to destroy Soviet armour on the European central front using its massive 30mm (1.18in) cannon as its primary weapon. The first A-10 flew in May 1972 and beat the Northrop A-9 to win a US Air Force (USAF) competition in early 1973.

The A-10's unusual appearance, which resulted in the nickname 'Warthog', resulted largely from the need to duplicate and separate critical systems such as engines and control surfaces. The pilot is protected by a 'bathtub' of titanium armour to protect against ground fire, and the wing and fuselage have 11 weapons pylons that can carry a combination of bombs, rockets and missiles. The A-10 saw a great deal of action in both US–Iraq wars and proved its ability to absorb large amounts of battle damage and keep flying. One was credited with an air-to-air kill in 1991, when it destroyed an Iraqi Mi-8 helicopter with its cannon.

This late-production Fairchild A-10A is in the colours of the 81st Fighter Squadron 'Black Panthers' of the 52nd Fighter Wing. The 81st flew the original Republic P-47 Thunderbolt from English bases during World War II and received the A-10 Thunderbolt II in 1993. The 81st's two sister squadrons fly the F-16C in the defence suppression role. The 81st flew many missions over the former Yugoslavia during Operation Allied Force in 1999. One notable mission was in supporting the rescue of an F-117 pilot downed over Serbia, for which the A-10 pilot received the Silver Star.

By July 1994, A-10 82-0646 had joined the 118th Fighter Squadron 'Flying Yankees' of the Connecticut Air National Guard, with which it still serves. The 81st continues to fly the A-10 at Spangdahlem.

Keith Fretwell

GENERAL DYNAMICS F-16B FIGHTING FALCON

253 Tayeset, Tsvah Haganah Le Israeli – Hey' l Ha' avir, Ramon, Israel, 1981

GENERAL DYNAMICS F-16B FIGHTING FALCON

Specification
- **Type** two-seat fighter-attack aircraft
- **Crew** 2
- **Powerplant** one 65.26-kN (14,670-lb) thrust Pratt & Whitney F100-P-100 turbofan
- **Performance** max speed more than 2124km/h (1320mph); service ceiling over 15,240m (50,000ft); range (ferry) 3891km (2418 miles)
- **Dimensions** wing span 9.45m (31ft 0in); length 14.53m (47ft 8in); height 5.01m (16ft 5in)
- **Weight** 14,968kg (33,000lb) loaded
- **Armament** one 20mm (0.79in) M61A1 cannon; max ordnance up to 6894kg (15,200lb)

The *Tsvah Haganah Le Israeli – Hey' l Ha' avir* (Israeli Defence Force/Air Force) is the biggest user of the General Dynamics (now Lockheed Martin) F-16, operating more than 230 Fighting Falcons since the early 1980s, with new versions continuing to enter service. Initial deliveries to Israel in 1980 consisted of 67 F-16As and eight F-16Bs. All the F-16Bs and 18 of the F-16As were originally destined for Iran, but were not delivered due to the Islamic revolution of 1979. These deliveries were followed by 81 F-16Cs and 54 F-16Ds, plus 35 surplus F-16As and 15 more F-16Bs.

The F-16B is mainly used as a conversion trainer, unlike the later F-16D two-seaters which have extensive modifications for the 'Wild Weasel' defence suppression role. In Israeli service, the F-16A and B are known as the Netz (Hawk), the F-16Cs as the Barak (Lightning) and the F-16Ds as the Brakeet (Thunderbolt).

Israel's F-16s were soon in action. Eight F-16As were used on the raid on Iraq's Osirak nuclear reactor in June 1981 and they hit the target with 16 908kg (2000lb) 'dumb' bombs. Twenty air-to-air kills have been claimed by Israeli F-16 pilots. Among the first were two against Syrian Mi-8 helicopters in April 1981, one destroyed with cannon and another with a Maverick air-to-ground missile.

The first scored using the Python 3 air-to-air missile depicted here was against Syrian MiG-23s in June 1982, during the invasion of Lebanon. No kills have been attributed since that conflict, although the F-16s have performed a number of strike missions in Lebanon and Syria. F-16 B '004' was one of the first aircraft delivered from Fort Worth in July 1980 and is believed to serve with 253 *Tayeset* (squadron). This is the first squadron to make the transition to the F-16I Sufa (Storm), a very advanced two-seat variant for long-range strike.

GRUMMAN A-6E INTRUDER

Marine Attack Squadron (All Weather) 121, 'Green Knights', United States Marine Corps, Marine Corps Air Station Cherry Point, South Carolina, late 1980s

GRUMMAN A-6E INTRUDER

Specification
- **Type** all-weather carrier-based attack bomber
- **Crew** 2
- **Powerplant** two Pratt & Whitney J52-P-8B turbojets rated at 41.4kN (9300lb thrust)
- **Performance** max speed 1297km/h (806mph); service ceiling 12,925m (42,200ft); range (fully loaded) 1627km (1011 miles)
- **Dimensions** wing span 16.15m (53ft); length 16.69m (54ft 9in); height 4.93m (16ft 2in)
- **Weight** 27,397kg (60,400lb) loaded
- **Armament** up to 8165kg (18,000lb) of conventional or precision bombs, guided missiles including AGM-62 Walleye, AGM-84 Harpoon, AGM-88 HARM and AGM-123 Skipper

The Grumann A-6 Intruder was originally flown as the YA2F-1 in April 1960, having been selected for the US Navy's all-weather attack aircraft requirement in 1957. Unlike previous navy jet bombers, it was relatively small, with only a two-man crew, seated side by side. All weapons were carried externally on wing and fuselage pylons, rather than in an internal bomb bay. The bulbous nose contained a powerful Norden multi-mode radar with terrain-following capability. As part of a sophisticated navigation and attack package, this allowed the Intruder to strike targets at night and in bad weather, following a long run at low level to avoid radar detection.

Despite some initial problems, and a high initial loss rate, the A-6 went on to be the most effective night-attack platform in Vietnam. In all, 69 US Navy and 25 US Marine Corps (USMC) Intruders were lost on combat missions, a low figure in relation to their total numbers.

In 1969, USMC Skyhawk squadron VMA-121 made the transition to the A-6A, and it was reconstituted as Marine Attack Squadron (All Weather) 121, or VMA(AW)-121, the additional letters signifying its new all-weather role. For the next 20 years, the 'Green Knights' it the A-6 until they became the first USMC squadron to fly the two-seat night-attack version of the F/A-18 Hornet in 1993.

Built as an A-6A, this particular aircraft was one of those upgraded to A-6E configuration and later given the Target Recognition Attack Multi-Sensor (TRAM) turret under the nose, which integrated the Forward Looking Infrared (FLIR) and laser sensors used for target identification and self-contained laser guided bomb delivery. VMA(AW)-121 was the first Intruder squadron to receive the TRAM system.

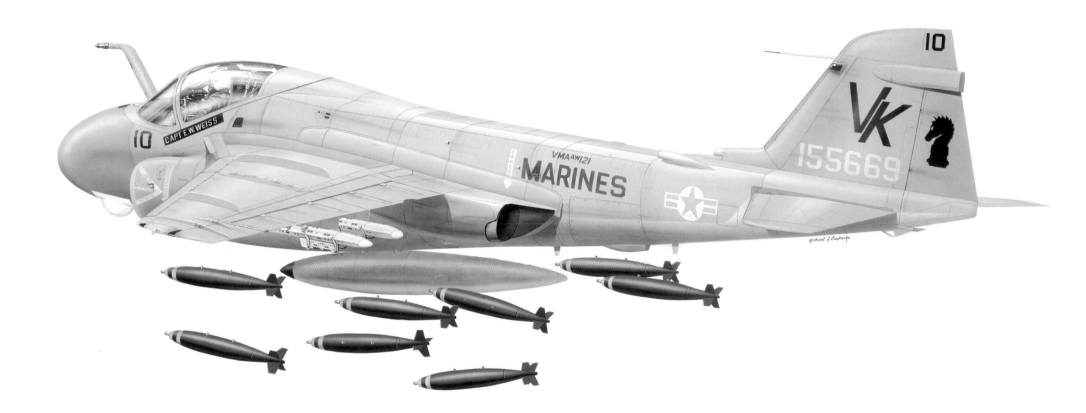

GRUMMAN E-2C HAWKEYE

Carrier Airborne Early Warning Squadron VAW-123 'Screwtops', Air Wing 1 United States Navy, USS America 1986

GRUMMAN E-2C HAWKEYE

Specification
- **Type** carrier-based early warning aircraft
- **Crew** 5
- **Powerplant** two 3661kW (4910hp) Allison T56-A425 turboprop engines
- **Performance** max speed 598km/h (358mph); service ceiling 9100m (30,000ft); range 2583km (1754 miles)
- **Dimensions** wing span 24.56m (80ft 7in); length 17.54m (57ft 7in); height 5.58m (18ft 4in)
- **Weight** 23,850kg (53,000lb)
- **Armament** none

Since 1964 the E-2 Hawkeye has been the US Navy's carrier-borne early warning platform, replacing the E-1 Tracer, which was based on the same airframe as the S-2 Tracker. Unlike the Tracer, with its fixed teardrop radar housing, the Hawkeye has a rotating radar dome or radome. The current generation is the E-2C, which first flew in January 1971 and had been upgraded in stages with different radars. The most recent E-2C Group III has the APS-145 with high resistance to jamming and an overland surveillance capability. E-2s have been sold to Taiwan, France, Japan, Egypt, Singapore, Israel and Mexico.

VA-123 'Screwtops' received the E-2C in 1972 and was a part of Air Wing 3 (CVW-3) aboard USS Saratoga through the 1970s. In October 1980, the squadron transferred to CVW-11 aboard the USS America (CV-66) and in 1981 joined CVW-1. It made several deployments on America until 1997 when the ship was decommissioned.

The squadron was involved in 1986 Gulf of Sidra operations off the coast of Libya, and were directly involved in the first combat use of the HARM (High speed Anti-Radiation Missile) and Harpoon weapon systems. During the 1991 Gulf War they were the only E-2 squadron to operate in both the Red Sea and Arabian Gulf. The Screwtops also flew in support of Operations Deny Flight and Deliberate Force over Bosnia-Herzegovina and Operation Southern Watch over Iraq. Before the rotodome-equipped EC-130V Hercules became available, the US Coast Guard leased nine Hawkeyes from the Navy, including 158641, the fourth production E-2C, which was reserialed 3507. They were based at St. Augustine, Florida and were later all returned to the Navy except for one lost in an accident in 1990.

Michael A. Badrocke

GRUMMAN EA-6B PROWLER

Detachment Yankee, Marine Tactical Electronic Warfare Squadron 2 'Playboys', US Marine Corps, Carrier Air Wing 1, USS America, 1986

The EA-6A was a version of the two-seat A-6 Intruder for the US Marine Corps (USMC), designed to replace the elderly EF-10 Skyknight in the role of jamming North Vietnamese radars. The task of detecting, interpreting and suppressing enemy emitters put a heavy workload on the single crewman; in 1971, the first four-seat EA-6B entered service. The first prototype had flown in May 1968 and was structurally similar to the A-6, but with a new forward fuselage and the more powerful -P408 version of the J52 engine.

Like the EA-6A, the Prowler had a large fairing on the top of the fin containing receivers for the ALQ-99 electronic warfare system and usually carried four ALQ-99 jamming pods. US Navy Electronic Attack Squadron 132 (VAQ-132) 'Scorpions' introduced the Prowler to combat in Vietnam in 1972. The Prowlers in service today have gone through many capability upgrade programmes to meet new threats.

In 1986, Detachment Yankee (Det. Y) of Marine Tactical Electronic Warfare Squadron 2 (VMAQ-2) 'Playboys' made a cruise with Carrier Air Wing 1 (CVW-1), participating in the strikes against Libya in April 1986, supplying jamming for the carrier-based Intruders and other strike aircraft. The squadron flew from Bahrain in Desert Storm, and also many missions over Bosnia and Kosovo from bases in Italy.

The Prowler was only cleared to carry offensive weapons in the form of the AGM-88 HARM missile shortly before it used them in combat for the first time in 1991 over Iraq and Kuwait. More active suppression of enemy air defences missions were flown over the former Yugoslavia in the 1990s and in Iraq in 2003. In 1998, the Prowler became a joint force asset, with US Air Force (USAF) crew in each aircraft and whole units dedicated to supporting USAF missions when required.

GRUMMAN EA-6B PROWLER

Specification
- **Type** carrier-based electronic warfare platform
- **Crew** 4
- **Powerplant** two 49.8kN (11,200lb thrust) Pratt & Whitney J52-P408 turbojets
- **Performance** Max speed 774km/h (481 mph); service ceiling 12,186m (40,000ft); range 1574km (978 miles)
- **Dimensions** wing span 16.15m (53ft); length 17.98m (59ft); height 4.57m (15ft)
- **Weight** 27,921kg (61,500lb) max take-off
- **Armament** up to four AGM-88 HARM high-speed anti-radiation missiles

GRUMMAN OV-1D MOHAWK

*73rd Combat Intelligence Company,
2nd Military Intelligence Battalion,
US Army, Europe, late 1980s*

GRUMMAN OV-1D MOHAWK

Specification
- **Type** battlefield reconnaissance aircraft
- **Crew** 2
- **Powerplant** two 1044kW (1400hp) Lycoming T53-L-701 turboprop engines
- **Performance** max speed 491km/h (305mph); service ceiling 7620m (25,000ft); range 1625km (1010 miles)
- **Dimensions** wing span 14.63m (48ft); length 13.69m (44ft 11in); height 3.96m (13ft)
- **Weight** 8215kg (18,110lb) loaded
- **Armament** none

In early 1956, Grumman was one of six companies to offer an aircraft to meet a US Army battlefield surveillance platform, and in 1957 it was awarded a contract to develop its G-134 design, which met the criteria of having a two-man crew, turboprop engines, bad-weather flying capability and good short-field performance. The prototype flew in April 1959 and was designated the YAO-1AF Mohawk in line with the Army tradition of using the names of Native American tribes for aircraft.

The Mohawk entered service in 1961, and in Vietnam in September 1962, just in time to become the OV-1A under the new designation system. Later OV-1As had up to six weapons pylons and could carry smoke rockets, fuel tanks or occasionally offensive weapons. The Mohawk was often at the centre of controversy over whether the US Army should operate fixed-wing combat aircraft.

The OV-1D was able to take either the SLAR or the infrared system, which could be changed in about one hour. There were 37 new-build OV-1Ds, and 108 of the earlier models were rebuilt to this standard. In total, 380 Mohawks were built. The example illustrated was one of those converted from an OV-1C. A number were configured as electronic intelligence (Elint) gathering platforms as the RV-1C and RV-1D, under the 'Quick Look' programme.

This aircraft was delivered in March 1968 and served with the 1st and 2nd Military Intelligence Battalions of the US Army in Germany. It was struck off the inventory at Wiesbaden in August 1993 and scrapped in October. The Mohawk itself was withdrawn from the inventory in 1996, but 23 were supplied to Argentina, where they still serve.

GRUMMAN S-2E TRACKER

Aviación de la Marina Venezolana,
Puerto Cabello, Venezuela, late 1980s

GRUMMAN S-2E TRACKER

Specification
- **Type** carrier/land-based anti-submarine aircraft
- **Crew** 4
- **Powerplant** two 1137kW (1525hp) Wright R-1820-82-WA Cyclone radial piston engines
- **Performance** max speed 384km/h (242mph); service ceiling 5486m (18,000ft); range 1609km (1000 miles)
- **Dimensions** wing span 22.13m (72ft 7in); length 13.26m (43ft 6in); height 5.06m (16ft 7in)
- **Weight** 13,234kg (29,150lb) loaded
- **Armament** two torpedoes, two depth bombs or four depth charges in weapons bay; six underwing racks for 113kg (250lb) bombs or 127mm (5in) rockets

The Grumman Tracker was the US Navy's first carrier-based aircraft combining the roles of anti-submarine hunter and killer in one airframe. Originally designated the S2F-1, which led to the nickname 'Stoof', the first example was flown in December 1952 and the initial model entered service in February 1954. Various improved models followed and from late 1962 the series was redesignated S-2. The last new-built version (all later models being rebuilds) was the S-2E, which differed from its predecessors by having an additional small radome behind the belly search radar and many internal equipment changes. A new computerized system greatly improved the range of the magnetic anomaly detection (MAD) equipment in finding submerged submarines.

A total of 252 S-2Es was built, some for export. The Tracker was widely used by foreign operators, including Argentina, Australia, Brazil, Canada, Italy, Japan, the Netherlands, South Korea, Peru, Taiwan, Turkey, Uruguay and Venezuela. Several of these countries operated Trackers from their small aircraft-carriers. Taiwan and Argentina still use the type in S-2T Turbo Tracker form with modern turboprop engines. The Tracker has also proved popular as a fire-bomber in the United States and France.

The *Marina Venezolana* (Venezuelan Navy) received six former US Navy S-2Es in 1974–75 and two more in 1982 for land-based anti-submarine warfare and coastal patrol. AS-0103 was delivered in 1974 and spent some time in Florida for crew training before delivery to Venezuela. After many years of service, it was withdrawn from use in 1987 and was last noted in 1998, stored at its former base of Puerto Cabello. The *Marina Venezolana* would like to buy secondhand P-3 Orions if funding were available.

HAWKER HUNTER F.MK 56

No. 122 Squadron,
Indian Air Force
Jaisalmer, 1971

HAWKER HUNTER F.MK 56

Specification
- **Type** single-seat day fighter
- **Crew** 1
- **Powerplant** one 44.48kN (10,000lb thrust) Rolls Royce Avon 203 turbojet engine
- **Performance** max speed 1150km/h (715mph); service ceiling 15,707m (51,000ft); combat radius 713km (443 miles)
- **Dimensions** wing span 10.2m (33ft 8in); length 14m (45ft 11in); height 4.01m (13ft 2in)
- **Weight** 5795kg (12,760lb) loaded
- **Armament** four 30mm (1.18in) Aden cannon

Hawker's classic Hunter first flew in July 1951, sharing a common ancestor with the Sea Hawk naval fighter in the P.1040 prototype of 1947. At this time, the British aviation industry led the world in jet engines, but came to swept wings later than the United States and Soviet. The Hunter became the first British-built swept-wing fighter and was the backbone of Royal Air Force (RAF) day-fighter squadrons from 1954.

The definitive RAF Hunter was the F.Mk 6, powered by the Avon 203 engine rated at 44.48kN (10,000lb thrust). The so-called 'big-bore' Hunter equipped eighteen RAF squadrons and was the only pure fighter version in British use after 1963. Derivatives of the F.6 were exported to a number of countries, including Belgium, Denmark, India, Oman, Peru, Saudi Arabia, Sweden and Switzerland.

India took more than 200 Hunters, which equipped seven squadrons and saw considerable action in the 1965 and 1971 wars with Pakistan. The bulk of India's Hunters were F.6s delivered as the F.Mk 56. Deliveries after the 1965 war were mostly the F.Mk 56A, which was equivalent to the FGA.9, optimized for ground attack and operations in 'hot and high' conditions. In air combat, the Hunter came off second-best to the F-86F Sabre, but was extremely effective at destroying armoured vehicles and was in fact instrumental on one occasion in preventing the capture of an important fort by driving off the attacking forces.

The Indian Hunters had an especially long career and were almost certainly the last of their type in military service, used as conversion trainers for the Indian Air Force's Western aircraft types and for target towing and general duties at least until 1999.

HAWKER HUNTER FGA.MK 73A

No. 6 Squadron,
Sultan of Oman's Air Force,
Thumrait Air Base, Oman, 1977

HAWKER HUNTER FGA.MK 73A

Specification
- **Type** single-seat ground attack fighter
- **Crew** 1
- **Powerplant** one 44.7kN (10,050lb thrust) Rolls-Royce RA.28 Avon 207 turbojet engine
- **Performance** max speed 1150km/h (715mph); service ceiling 15,707m (51,000ft); combat radius 713km (443 miles)
- **Dimensions** wing span 10.2m (33ft 8in); length 14m (45ft 11in); height 4.01m (13ft 2in)
- **Weight** loaded 5795kg (12,760lb)
- **Armament** four 30mm (1.18in) cannon; up to 908kg (2000lb) of bombs or 12 76.2mm (3in) rockets or two rocket pods

The FGA.9 (Fighter Ground Attack) version of the Hunter was built mainly for Far East use, with better air conditioning and other 'tropical' features. This version could carry larger fuel tanks and bombs or rockets, and saw action with the Royal Air Force (RAF) in Borneo, Malaya and Aden. The FGA.9 was sold under various designations to Abu Dhabi, Chile, Iraq, Jordan, Kenya, Kuwait, Lebanon, Oman, Qatar, Rhodesia and Somalia. Oman's aircraft were designated the FGA.Mk 73A, although a variety of different models were used over the years, based at Thumrait, in the south of the Gulf state.

The first Hunters in Oman were RAF aircraft, F.Mk 6s of Nos 8 and 208 Squadrons that were donated to the Sultan of Oman's Air Force (SOAF) when Britain withdrew from 'East of Suez'. Oman received its own refurbished Hunters in August 1975, and they were soon used in action against Yemeni-backed rebels trying to win independence for the province of Dhofar; they were flown mainly by RAF pilots on temporary attachment and ex-RAF pilots on contract to the Sultan.

On numerous occasions, the Hunters and Strikemasters of the SOAF prevented isolated outposts from being overrun by rebel tribesmen by strafing and rocketing advancing forces. The major combat was over in 1976, but sporadic missions were flown for a number of years during which a number of Hunters were lost to ground fire. These were replaced by surplus aircraft from Jordan and Kuwait, giving the SOAF a mixture of diverse although basically similar aircraft.

The last of Oman's Hunters was retired in November 1993. This aircraft, No. 825, was one of those supplied by Jordan, and was last reported preserved at the gate of Gallah Air Base, Muscat.

HAWKER SIDDELEY HARRIER GR.MK.3

No. 1 Squadron, Royal Air Force,
RAF Wittering, Northamptonshire, 1982

HAWKER SIDDELEY HARRIER GR.MK.3

Specification
- **Type** V/STOL strike aircraft
- **Crew** 1
- **Powerplant** one 9739kg (21,500lb thrust) Rolls-Royce Pegasus Mk 103 turbojet
- **Performance** max speed 1176km/h (730mph); service ceiling 15,605m (51,200ft); range 5560km (3455 miles) with one inflight refuelling
- **Dimensions** wing span 7.7m (25ft 3in); length 13.87m (45ft 6in); height 3.45m (11ft 4in)
- **Weight** 11,340kg (25,000lb) loaded
- **Armament** one 30mm (1.18in) Aden gun; up to 2268kg (5000lb) of stores on underwing and underfuselage points

One of the most important and certainly the most revolutionary combat aircraft to emerge during the post-war years, the Hawker Siddeley Harrier VSTOL tactical fighter-bomber began as a private venture in 1957, two prototypes and four development aircraft being ordered under the designation P.1127. The initial prototype made its first tethered hovering flight on 21 October 1960 and began conventional flight trials on 13 March 1961.

In 1962, Britain, the United States and West Germany announced a joint order for nine Kestrels, as the aircraft was now known, for evaluation by a tripartite handling squadron at RAF West Raynham in 1965. In its single-seat close support and tactical reconnaissance version, the aircraft was ordered into production for the Royal Air Force (RAF) as the Harrier GR.Mk.1, the first of an initial order of 77 machines flying on 28 December 1967. The Harrier GR.3, which saw combat in the Falklands War of 1982, was a development of the Harrier GR.1, being fitted with improved attack sensors, electronic countermeasures and a more powerful engine.

The simplicity and flexibility inherent in the Harrier design proved their worth in service in Germany. In time of war, the Harrier was to be deployed away from established airfields, which were vulnerable to attack. Instead it was to be operated from short, rough strips of ground and hidden in camouflaged 'hides', from which it would attack the enemy's approaching armoured formations.

Originally a Harrier Mk 1, XV740 first flew on 3 July 1968 and carried out trials at Boscombe Down before being delivered to No 4 Squadron at Wildenrath, Germany, in 1975. It was later allocated to No 1 Squadron at Wittering.

HAWKER SIDDELEY (BAE) NIMROD MR MK.2P

Kinloss Maritime Wing,
Royal Air Force Strike Command,
Royal Air Force, RAF Kinloss, Scotland
late 1980s

HAWKER SIDDELEY (BAE) NIMROD MR MK.2P

Specification

- **Type** long-range maritime patrol aircraft
- **Crew** 12
- **Powerplant** four 54kN (12,140lb thrust) Rolls-Royce RB168-20 Spey 250 turbofan engines
- **Performance** max speed 926km/h (575mph); service ceiling 12,800m (42,000ft); range 9266km (5758 miles)
- **Dimensions** wing span 35.0m (114ft 10in); length 38.63m (126ft 9in); height 8.60m (29ft 8.5in)
- **Weight** 80,514kg (177,500lb) loaded
- **Armament** internal bay for up to nine torpedoes, bombs and depth charges; Sidewinder air-to-air missiles can be carried on underwing pylons for self-defence

Development of the Nimrod began in 1964 to create a replacement for the Avro Shackleton in the maritime patrol role. The airframe was based on that of the de Havilland Comet, the first jet airliner in commercial service. The fuselage was modified to have a large internal weapons bay, a radar nose was fitted and the turbojet engines were replaced by Spey turbofans. The new tail had a large ESM fairing on the tip and a magnetic anomaly detector (MAD) boom behind.

The first of 46 Nimrod MR.1s entered Royal Air Force (RAF) service in October 1969. In 1975, 32 were upgraded to MR.2 standard with modernized electronics. A later upgrade saw an inflight refuelling probe added and additional ESM pods fitted on the wingtips. As such the designation changed to MR.2P, although the 'P' was dropped in the mid-1990s. Three Nimrods were completed as the R.1 electronic intelligence aircraft for No. 51 Squadron and have been involved on the periphery of numerous conflicts and periods of tension.

The MR.2s are pooled between the squadrons of the Kinloss Maritime Wing, which consists of No. 42(R), 120, 201 and 206 Squadrons. As such they do not wear individual unit markings except for special airshow colour schemes. During the 1991 Gulf War, four Nimrod MR.2s were detached to Seeb, Oman, to support coalition naval operations in the Persian Gulf and Gulf of Oman. Six Nimrods were deployed in support of Operation Telic, the British contribution to the 2003 Iraq war. The 2002 Fincastle Trophy for Commonwealth anti-submarine crews was won by a crew of No. 201 Squadron flying Nimrod XV248 out of Kinloss.

Eighteen of the Mk.2 Nimrods are to be converted to MR.4 standard with new radar and electronics, and greatly enhanced weapons capabilities. The rebuilt aircraft will get new serial numbers in the ZJ500 series.

ISRAELI AIRCRAFT INDUSTRIES KFIR C.2

Israeli Air Force, mid-1980s

IAI KFIR C2

Specification
- **Type** fighter-bomber
- **Crew** 1
- **Powerplant** one 8119kg (17,900lb thrust) General Electric J79-J1E turbojet
- **Performance** max speed 2445mph (1520mph); service ceiling 17,680m (58,000ft); combat radius 346km (215 miles)
- **Dimensions** wing span 8.22m (26ft 11in); length 15.65m (51ft 4in); height 4.55m (14ft 11in)
- **Weight** 16,200kg (35,715lb) loaded
- **Armament** one 30mm (1.18in) cannon; up to 5775kg (12,732lb) of external ordnance

The Israeli Aircraft Industries (IAI) Kfir (Lion Cub) was developed as an expedient after France imposed an embargo on the sale of combat aircraft to Israel. It was basically a Dassault Mirage III airframe married with a General Electric J79 turbojet. IAI produced 27 Kfir C.1s, which equipped two squadrons of the Israeli Air Force; after replacement by the improved C.2, all but two were leased to the US Navy for aggressor training, bearing the designation F-21A. The Kfir C.2, which appeared in 1976, was the major production version, with 185 examples being delivered. Most C.2s were upgraded to C.7 standard between 1983 and 1985.

The Kfir saw a great deal of action in Lebanon's Bekaa Valley in the 1980s. The type was exported to Colombia, Ecuador and Sri Lanka. By the end of the twentieth century, the Israeli Air Force's surviving Kfirs were serving with reserve units only, these being No. 149 Squadron at Hatzor and Nos 132, 141 and 251 Squadrons at Nevatim.

The aircraft illustrated here is shown as it would have appeared in the mid-1980s, with two-tone brown and green over light grey camouflage and a typical lack of squadron markings. It is carrying two Shafrir 2 air-to-air missiles, developed from the US AIM-9B Sidewinder, underwing fuel tanks and 227kg (500lb) Mk 82 bombs. The Kfir C.7 introduced an additional pair of weapons pylons, one under each engine intake, with a corresponding increase in weapons load. The Kfir C.7 was also equipped to deliver laser-guided bombs.

KAWASAKI (LOCKHEED) P-2J NEPTUNE

*Dai-4 Kokutai (Squadron VP-4),
2 Kokugun (Air Wing), 1 Japanese
Maritime Self-Defence Force, Hachinoe,
Japan, 1970*

KAWASAKI (LOCKHEED) P-2J NEPTUNE

Specification

- **Type** maritime patrol aircraft
- **Crew** 12
- **Powerplant** two 2125kW (2850hp) General Electric T64-IHI-10 turboprop engines and two 1397kg (3085lb) thrust J3-IHI-7C auxiliary turbojets
- **Performance** max speed 648km/h (403mph); service ceiling 9150m (30,000ft); range 4450km (2764 miles)
- **Dimensions** wing span 29.78m (97ft 8.5in); length 29.23m (95ft 10.75); height 8.94m (29ft 4in)
- **Weight** 34,019kg (75,000lb) loaded
- **Armament** full range of maritime offensive stores internally; provision for air-to-surface missiles on underwing racks

The first land-based aircraft designed specifically for the long-range maritime reconnaissance role, the Lockheed Neptune was destined to be one of the longest-serving military aircraft ever built. The first of two XP2V-1 prototypes flew on 17 May 1945, orders already having been placed for 15 pre-production and 151 production P2V-1s. Deliveries to the US Navy began in March 1947, by which time another variant, the P2V-2, had also flown.

The next variant was the P2V-3, and another engine change produced the P2V-4, which carried underwing fuel tanks. The P2V-5 Neptune was the first variant to be supplied to foreign air arms, 36 P2V-5Fs being supplied to the Royal Air Force (RAF) as Neptune MR.1s. The P2V-5F was fitted with two Westinghouse J34-WE-36 turbojets in underwing pods outboard of the main engine nacelles. The P2V-6 (P2F) Neptune had a minelaying capability in addition to its ASW role; 83 were delivered to the US Navy and 12 to France's *Aéronavale*. The last production version was the P2V-7.

The Kawasaki-built P-2J, seen here, was originally known as the P2V-7kai (for *kaizo*, meaning 'modified'). It was a radical redesign of the P2V-7, incorporating turboprop powerplants and other changes.

The turbine-powered P-2J, 83 of which were built by Kawasaki, was the last operational Neptune in the world. It was replaced in Japanese Maritime Self-Defence Force (JMSDF) service by the P-3C Orion. Three aircraft were converted to the target tug role as UP-2Js.

LOCKHEED C-141B STARLIFTER

*437th Military Airlift Wing,
United States Air Force, Charleston Air
Force Base, South Carolina, 1977*

LOCKHEED C-141B STARLIFTER

Specification
- **Type** strategic heavy lift transport
- **Crew** 4
- **Powerplant** four 9526kg (21,000lb thrust) Pratt & Whitney TF33-7 turbofan engines
- **Performance** max speed 912km/h (567mph); service ceiling 12,800m (42,000ft); range 10,370km (6445 miles)
- **Dimensions** wing span 48.74m (159ft 11in); length 51.29m (168ft 3in); height 11.96m (39ft 3in)
- **Weight** 155,582kg (343,000lb)
- **Payload** 32,161kg (70,848lb)

First flown on 17 December 1963, the C-141A StarLifter heavy-lift strategic transport was designed to provide the US Air Force (USAF) Military Air Transport Service with a high-speed global airlift and strategic deployment capability. Deliveries to the USAF began in April 1965, and the aircraft ultimately equipped 13 squadrons of Military Airlift Command, with 277 examples being built in total.

Starting in 1976, all surviving C-141A aircraft were upgraded to C-141B standard, the fuselage being stretched by 7.11m (23ft 4in). In Operation Desert Shield in 1990, during the build-up to the Gulf War, a C-141B from the 437th Military Airlift Wing (MAW) at Charleston Air Force Base, South Carolina, was the first American aircraft into Saudi Arabia, transporting an Airlift Control Element (ALCE) from the 438th MAW at McGuire Air Force Base, New Jersey. In the following year, Starlifters completed the most airlift missions (7,047 out of 15,800) in support of the Gulf War. They also carried more than 41,400 passengers and 139,600 tons of cargo. Eighty percent of Air Force C-141Bs were used in Operations Desert Shield and Desert Storm, while the rest were flying high-priority missions elsewhere around the world.

Thirteen C-141Bs of the 437th Airlift Wing (AW) were equipped for the Special Operations Low Level (SOLL) role with increased survivability measures, the most obvious being the addition of a FLIR turret beneath the nose.

Still based at Charleston Air Force Base, the 437th Airlift Wing now operates the C-17 Globemaster III transport, which is about the same size as the C-141, able to carry twice the payload.

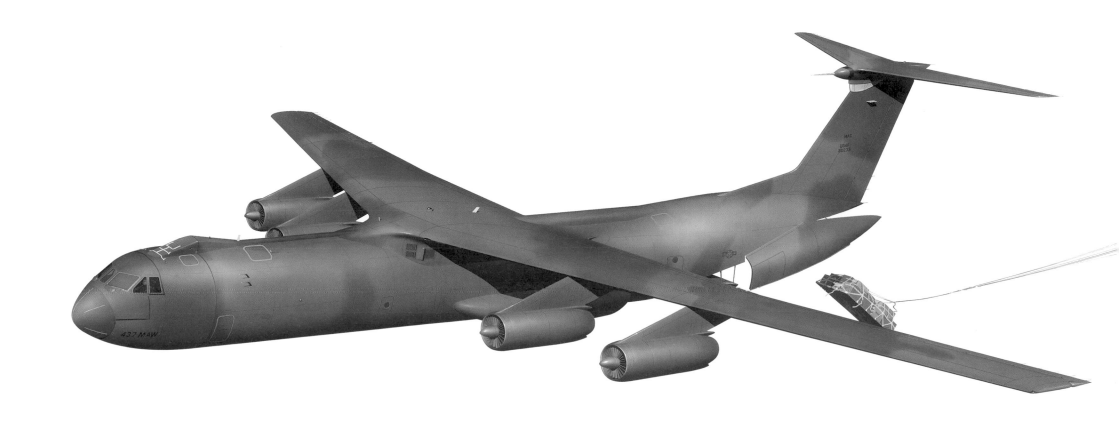

LOCKHEED S-3A VIKING

Sea Control Squadron 32 'Norsemen',
United States Navy, USS America,
Atlantic Fleet, 1985

LOCKHEED S-3A VIKING

Specification
- **Type** anti-submarine warfare aircraft (S-3A/B)
- **Crew** 4
- **Powerplant** two 4207kg (9275lb) General Electric TF34-GE-2 turbofans
- **Performance** max speed 814km/h (506mph); service ceiling 10,670m (35,000ft); range 3705km (2302 miles)
- **Dimensions** wing span 20.93m (68ft 8in); length 16.26m (53ft 4in); height 6.93m (22ft 9in
- **Weight** 19,278kg (42,500lb) loaded
- **Armament** up to 907kg (2000lb) of ASW stores; two underwing pylons for bombs, rockets, missiles etc

The Lockheed S-3A Viking was designed in response to a 1969 US Navy requirement for a carrier-borne ASW system built around a Univac digital computer. The prototype flew for the first time on 21 January 1972, and 93 production SA-3As had been ordered by the end of 1973, deliveries beginning to Sea Control Squadron 41 (VS-41), an operational training unit, in March 1974. The last of 187 Vikings was delivered to the US Navy in 1978.

The Viking fleet was substantially updated to S-3B standard in the early 1990s, some aircraft being converted to the electronic warfare role as ES-3As. The ES-3A Shadow provided indications and warnings for the battle group commander, and was normally assigned to the command and control warfare commander, for tasking and mission assignment.

The heart of the Shadow was an avionics suite based on the Aries II system of the land-based EP-3E Orion. The Shadow's fuselage was packed with sensor stations and processing equipment, and the exterior sports over 60 antennae. The ES-3A Shadow crew comprised a pilot, an NFO and two systems operators. Advanced sensor, navigation and communications systems allowed the Shadow's four-person crew to collect extensive data and distribute high-quality information through a variety of channels to the carrier battle group. This gave the battle group commander a clear picture of potential airborne, surface and subsurface threats. Missions flown by the detachment included over-the-horizon targeting, strike support, war at sea and reconnaissance. The Shadow's career was short-lived, the US Navy deciding to terminate the ES-3A programme in 1999.

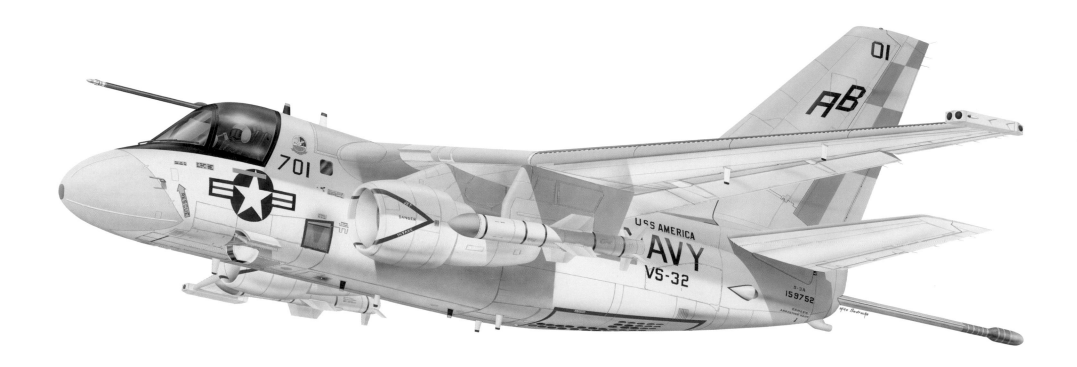

LOCKHEED SR-71 BLACKBIRD

9th Strategic Reconnaissance Wing,
United States Air Force,
Beale Air Force Base, California, 1980s

LOCKHEED SR-71 BLACKBIRD

Specification
- **Type** reconnaissance aircraft
- **Crew** 2
- **Powerplant** two 14,742kg (32,500lb) thrust Pratt & Whitney JT11D-20B turbojets
- **Performance** max speed 3220km/h (2000mph) at 24,385m (80,000ft); service ceiling 24,385m (80,000ft); range 4800km (2983 miles)
- **Dimensions** wing span 16.94m (55ft 7in); length 32.74m (107ft 5in); height 5.64m (18ft 6in); wing area 149.10m² (1605sq ft)
- **Weight** 78,017kg (172,000lb) loaded
- **Armament** none

Work on the SR-71 system began in 1959, when a team led by Clarence L. Johnson, Lockheed's Vice President for Advanced Development Projects, embarked on the design of a radical new aircraft to supersede the Lockheed U-2 in the strategic reconnaissance role. The prototype SR-71A flew for the first time on 22 December 1964.

The first aircraft to be assigned to Strategic Air Command, an SR-71B two-seat trainer (61-7957), was delivered to the 4200th Strategic Reconnaissance Wing (SRW) at Beale Air Force Base, California, on 7 January 1966. On 25 June 1966, with SR-71 deliveries continuing, the 4200th SRW was redesignated the 9th SRW. Then, in the spring of 1968, it was decided to deploy four SR-71s to Kadena Air Base, Okinawa, for operations over Southeast Asia. The first SR-71 mission over Vietnam was flown in April 1968, with up to three missions per week being flown thereafter.

SR-71 operations from the United Kingdom began on 20 April 1976. Two SR-71s were stationed in the United Kingdom at any one time, the aircraft flying stand-off surveillance missions over the Soviet Arctic, the Baltic and the Mediterranean. On 15 and 16 April 1986, two UK-based SR-71s carried out post-strike reconnaissance following the attacks on Libya (Operation Eldorado Canyon) by F-111s and US Navy aircraft. The SR-71A was officially retired in 1990, but two aircraft were subsequently reactivated in 1995 for further operations.

The Lockheed SR-71A pictured here (64-17964) flew for the last time on 20 March 1990 and is currently on display at Offutt Air Force Base, Nebraska.

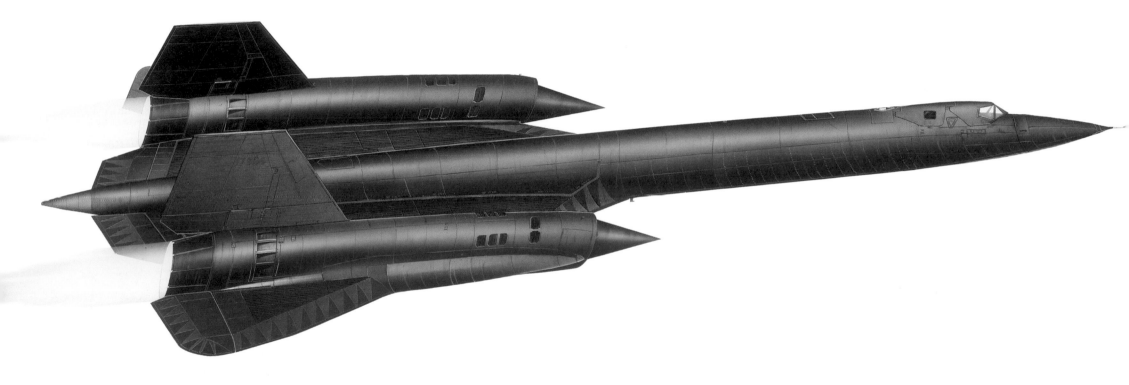

MARTIN B-57G CANBERRA

13th Tactical Bombing Squadron,
8th Tactical Fighter Wing, United States
Air Force, Ubon Air Base, Thailand, 1972

MARTIN B-57G CANBERRA

Specification
- **Type** : night interdictor
- **Crew** 2
- **Powerplant** two 3226kg (7200lb) thrust Wright J65-W5 turbojets
- **Performance** max speed 937km/h (582mph); service ceiling 14,630m (48,000ft); range 3710km (2300 miles)
- **Dimensions** wing span 19.51m (64ft); length 19.96m (66ft 6in); height 4.75m (15ft 7in)
- **Weight** 24,950kg (55,000lb) loaded
- **Armament** four 227kg (500lb) Paveway laser-guided bombs on underwing racks

Late in 1967, three Martin B-57B Canberras were experimentally fitted with a Low Light Level TV (LLLTV) system in a pod under the port wing, and operational trials with this equipment took place from December 1967 to August 1968, mostly over the Ho Chi Minh Trail on the Vietnam–Cambodia border. Results were sufficiently encouraging for the US Air Force (USAF) to award contracts to Martin and Westinghouse, which supplied the equipment, for the modification of 16 B-57s as night interdictors under a programme called Tropic Moon.

As well as being fitted with the LLLTV, a redesigned nose section containing forward-looking infrared equipment and a laser guidance system were added. The modified aircraft, designated B-57G, could carry the same ordnance as the B-57B, except that the laser guidance system now made it possible to fit four 227kg (500lb) 'smart' bombs on underwing pylons.

The first B-57G was delivered to the 13th Tactical Bombing Squadron (TBS) in July 1969, this unit deloying to Ubon in Thailand in September 1970 as part of the 8th Tactical Fighter Wing, USAF. The Tropic Moon B-57Gs went into action over the Ho Chi Minh Trail almost immediately and continued operations until April 1972, when the 13th TBS was withdrawn from Vietnam and deactivated. During operations in Vietnam, only one B-57G was lost, as the result of a collision – its crew was rescued.

After their withdrawal from Vietnam, the B-57Gs of the 13th TBS were assigned to the 190th Bombardment Group (Tactical) of the Kansas Air National Guard where they served until 1974, before being placed in storage at Davis-Monthan Air Force Base, Arizona.

MCDONNELL DOUGLAS
A-4M SKYHAWK II

VMA-223 'Bulldogs', US Marine Corps, Marine Corps Air Station, Iwakuni, Japan 1983

The United States Marine Corps (USMC) operated the McDonnell Douglas A-4 Skyhawk from 1957 and had, by 1969, received all the US versions from the A-4A through to the TA-4F. In that year, it decided against purchase of the A-7 Corsair II in favour of a new version known as the A-4M Skyhawk II. This had the most powerful version of the J52 engine, the P408, as well as self-starting capability and a raised cockpit and enlarged canopy for better visibility. A much improved navigation and attack system and a head-up display (HUD) made the 'Mike' a much more effective attack platform. Later model Ms had an ALR-45 radar warning system in a fairing atop the tail fin.

The 'Bulldogs' of VMA-223 were formed in Hawaii in 1942 and went on to have a distinguished career during World War II flying the F4F Wildcat and F4U Corsair at Guadalcanal, in the Philippines and at Okinawa. Receiving F9F Panther jets in 1950, the squadron flew the FJ-4B Fury from 1957 to 1961, when it received the A-4B Skyhawk. From 1965 to 1970, the squadron was based in the Far East, mainly at Chu Lai in South Vietnam, where it flew many thousands of close-support missions in support of Marines on the ground and other friendly forces.

In 1975, the 'Bulldogs' received the first of its A-4Ms, which it flew from Cherry Point, South Carolina, with two six-month deployments to Iwakuni, Japan in 1981 and 1983. In September 1987 the squadron transitioned to the AV-8B Harrier II, which it still flies today. After service with VMA-223, the A-4M illustrated was issued to training squadron VMAT-102. On 12 June 1985, while flying a simulated air combat mission, it flew into the ground near Yuma, Arizona, and was destroyed – the pilot managed to eject to safety.

MCDONNELL DOUGLAS A-4M SKYHAWK II

Specification
- **Type** light attack bomber
- **Crew** 1
- **Powerplant** one 49.82kN (11,200lb thrust) Pratt & Whitney J52-P408 turbojet engine
- **Performance** max speed 1083km/h (673mph); service ceiling 13,500m (44,300ft); range km (miles)
- **Dimensions** wing span 8.38m (27ft 6in); length 12.27m (40ft 3in); height 4.65m (15ft 3in)
- **Weight** 11,113kg (24,500lb) loaded
- **Armament** two 20mm (0.79in) Colt Mk 12 cannon with 100 rounds each; up to 4153kg (9155lb) of ordnance, including conventional, laser-guided or nuclear bombs, rockets and gun pods

MCDONNELL DOUGLAS F-4B PHANTOM II

Fighter Squadron 111 'Sundowners', United States Navy, USS Coral Sea, Vietnamese waters, 1972

One of the most potent and versatile combat aircraft ever built, the McDonnell (later McDonnell Douglas) F-4 Phantom II stemmed from a 1954 project for an advanced naval fighter. The XF4H-1 prototype flew for the first time on 27 May 1958. Twenty-three development aircraft were procured, followed by 45 production machines for the US Navy. These were originally designated F4H-1F, but this was later changed to F-4A. The F-4B was a slightly improved version with J79-GE-8 engines, and between them the F-4A and F-4B captured many world records over a four-year period.

Carrier trials were carried out in 1960, and in December that year the first examples of the Phantom were delivered to training squadron VF-121. The first fully operational Phantom squadron, VF-114, was commissioned with F-4Bs in October 1961, and in June 1962 the first US Marine Corps (USMC) deliveries were made to Marine Fighter Squadron (All Weather) 314, or VMF(AW)-314. Total F-4B production was 649 aircraft. The successor to the F-4B in US Navy/USMC service was the F-4J, which possessed greater ground-attack capability; the first of 522 production aircraft was delivered in June 1976.

The Phantom proved itself many times over in combat with MiG-17s and MiG-21s over North Vietnam. This particular aircaft, an F-4B of US Navy Fighter Squadron 111 (VF-111) 'Sundowners', was flown by Lieutenant Garry L. Weigand (pilot) and Lieutenant (jg) William C. Freckleton (RIO) when they shot down a MiG-17 on 6 March 1972. Note the kill marking on the intake splitter plate.

MCDONNELL DOUGLAS F-4B PHANTOM II

Specification

- **Type** carrier-based fighter-bomber
- **Crew** 2
- **Powerplant** two 8119kg (17,900lb) thrust General Electric J79-GE-8 turbojets
- **Performance** Max speed 2390km/h (1485mph); service ceiling 26,308km/h (58,000lb); range 2817km (1750 miles)
- **Dimensions** Wing span 11.70m (38ft 5in); length 17.76m (58ft 3in); height 4.96m (16ft 3in)
- **Weight** 26,308kg (58,000lb) loaded
- **Armament** one 20mm M61A1 Vulcan cannon and four AIM-7 Sparrow AAMs recessed under fuselage; up to 5888kg (12,980lb) of ordnance and stores on underwing pylons

MCDONNELL DOUGLAS F-4J PHANTOM II

No. 74 (Tiger) Squadron, Royal Air Force,
RAF Wattisham, Suffolk, 1984

MCDONNELL DOUGLAS F-4J PHANTOM II

Specification
- **Type** interceptor
- **Crew** 2
- **Powerplant** two 8119kg (17,900lb) thrust General Electric J79-GE-17 turbojets
- **Performance** max speed 2390km/h (1485mph); service ceiling 26,308km/h (58,000lb); range 2817km (1750 miles)
- **Dimensions** wing span 11.70m (38ft 5in); length 17.76m (58ft 3in); height 4.96m (16ft 3in)
- **Weight** 26,308kg (58,000lb) loaded
- **Armament** one 20mm (0.79in) M61A1 Vulcan cannon and four AIM-7 Sparrow air-to-air missiles recessed under fuselage; up to 5888kg (12,980lb) of ordnance and stores on underwing pylons

In the early 1980s, the primary air defence interceptor of the Royal Air Force (RAF) was the McDonnell Douglas F-4K Phantom FGR.2. At this time, for various reasons, the UK Ministry of Defence was concerned that the air defence commitment could not be adequately met because of a shortage of these aircraft, so it was decided to purchase 15 refurbished F-4J Phantoms from the US Navy. These were to be operated by No. 74 Squadron, which had flown Lightnings in the air defence role at Tengah, Singapore, until 1971, when it disbanded.

On 19 October 1984, No. 74 Squadron re-formed at RAF Wattisham, Suffolk, where it received its F-4Js, which were known as the Phantom F.Mk.3 in RAF service. The aircraft initially wore their US Navy overall light blue-grey finish, before being repainted in RAF grey. No. 74 Squadron shared the air defence task at Wattisham with the Phantom FGR.2s of No. 56 Squadron, gradually replacing its F-4Js with FGR.2s relinquished by other squadrons. The Phantom remained in service in the air defence role – which in the 1980s it had shared with the two surviving Lightning squadrons (Nos 5 and 11) – until the early 1990s, when the task was taken over by the Tornado F.3.

The Phantom pictured here bears the distinctive 'Tiger' badge of No. 74 Squadron, which was first formed in July 1917, during World War I. It disbanded in October 1992, but re-formed as No. 74 (Reserve) Squadron, flying Hawk jet trainers with No. 4 Flying Training School at RAF Valley, Anglesey.

MCDONNELL DOUGLAS F/A-18A HORNET

Marine Fighter Attack Squadron 314 'Black Knights', Carrier Air Wing 13, USS Coral Sea, Mediterranean, 1986

MCDONNELL DOUGLAS F/A-18A HORNET

Specification
- **Type** tactical strike aircraft
- **Crew** 1
- **Powerplant** two 7264kg (16,000lb) thrust General Electric F404-GE-400 turbofans
- **Performance** max speed 1912km/h (1183mph); service ceiling 15,240m (50,000ft); combat radius 1065km (662 miles)
- **Dimensions** wing span 11.43m (37ft 6in); length 17.07m (56ft); height 4.66m (15ft 3´in)
- **Weight** 25,401kg (56,000lb) loaded
- **Armament** one 20mm (0.79in) M61A1 Vulcan cannon; external hardpoints with provision for up to 7711kg (17,000lb) of stores

While the F-14 replaced the Phantom in the naval air superiority role, the aircraft that replaced it in the tactical role (with both the US Navy and US Marine Corps) was the McDonnell Douglas F-18 Hornet. First flown on 18 November 1978, the prototype Hornet was followed by 11 development aircraft.

The first production versions were the fighter/attack F/A-18A and the two-seat F/A-18B operational trainer; subsequent variants are the F/A-18C and F/A-18D, which have provision for AIM-120 air-to-air missiles and Maverick infrared missiles, as well as an airborne self-protection jamming system. The aircraft also serves with the Canadian Armed Forces as the CF-188 (138 aircraft). Other customers are Australia (75), Finland (64), Kuwait (40), Spain (72) and Switzerland (34). Total US deliveries, all variants, were 1150 aircraft.

The Hornet first saw combat during the Libyan confrontation of 1986, when the type flew ship-to-shore strikes and defence suppression missions. The type featured prominently in Operation Desert Storm in 1991, where it flew the bulk of US Navy/US Marine Corps (USMC) offensive operations, and has since taken part in many Nato peacekeeping operations, notably in the Balkans.

Operating from the USS *Coral Sea*, the Hornets of Marine Fighter Attack Squadron 314 (VMFA-314) were engaged in attacks on Libyan surface-to-air missile sites during Operations El Dorado Canyon and Prairie Fire in 1986. The units usual VW tail code was replaced by AK, denoting its inclusion within Carrier Air Wing 13 (CVW-13) aboard the *Coral Sea* for this deployment.

MCDONNELL DOUGLAS/BRITISH AEROSPACE AV-8B HARRIER II

Marine Attack Squadron 542, United States Marine Corps, Marine Air Station Cherry Point, North Carolina, 1980s

MCDONNELL DOUGLAS/BRITISH AEROSPACE AV-8B HARRIER II

Specification
- **Type** short take-off, vertical landing (STOVL) strike aircraft
- **Crew** 1
- **Powerplant** one 10,796kg (23,800lb) thrust Rolls-Royce 402-RR-408 vectored thrust turbofan
- **Performance** max speed 1065km/h (661mph); service ceiling 15,240m (50,000ft); combat radius 277km (172 miles) with 2722kg (6000lb) payload
- **Dimensions** wing span 9.25m (30ft 4in); length 14.12m (46ft 4in); height 3.55m (11ft 7in)
- **Weight** 14,061kg (31,000lb) loaded
- **Armament** one 25mm (0.98in) GAU-12U cannon; six external hardpoints with provision for up to 7711kg (17,000lb) or 3175kg (7000lb) of stores (short and vertical take-off, respectively)

Although it was the British who were responsible for the early development of this remarkable aircraft, it was the US Marine Corps (USMC) which identified the need to upgrade its original version, the AV-8A.

The prototype YAV-8B Harrier II first flew in November 1978, followed by the first development aircraft in November 1981, and production deliveries to the USMC began in 1983. The first production AV-8B was handed over to Training Squadron VMAT-203 at Cherry Point, North Carolina, on 16 January 1984.

Operational Harrier pilots were assigned to Marine Air Group 32 (MAG-32), the first tactical squadron (VMA-331) reaching initial operational capability with the first batch of 12 aircraft early in 1985. The squadron's strength had risen to 15 in the autumn of 1986 and had reached the full complement of 20 by March 1987.

Delivery of the Royal Air Force (RAF) equivalent, the Harrier GR5, began in 1987; production GR5s were later converted to GR7 standard. This version, general similar to the USMC's night-attack AV-8B, has FLIR, a digital moving map display, night-vision goggles for the pilot and a modified head-up display. The Spanish and Italian navies also operated the AV-8B. Harrier IIs fitted with the latest avionics upgrades are known as the Harrier II Plus.

Known as the 'Flying Tigers', VMA-542 is based at Marine Air Station Cherry Point and is part of Marine Air Group 14 (MAG-14). The squadron's insignia includes a yellow triangular 'tiger skin' design on the rudder, and a tiger's head badge on the nose. Pictured here is a AV-8B Harrier II Plus of VMA-542.

MCDONNELL DOUGLAS KC-10A EXTENDER

9th Air Refueling Squadron, 22nd Air Refueling Wing, USAF Strategic Air Command, March AFB, California, 1980s

MCDONNELL DOUGLAS KC-10A EXTENDER

Specification
- **Type** aerial tanker and transport
- **Crew** 4
- **Powerplant** three 23,625kg (52,500lb) thrust General Electric CF6-50C2 turbofans
- **Performance** max speed 996km/h (619mph); service ceiling 12,727m (42,000ft); range 7079km (4400 miles)
- **Dimensions** wing span 50m (165ft 4.5in); length 54.4m (181ft 7in); height 17.4m (58ft 1in)
- **Weight** 265,500kg (590,000lb)
- **Payload** 76,560kg (170,000lb) maximum

The McDonnell Douglas KC-10 flight refuelling tanker was based on the DC-10 Series 30CF convertible freighter. The KC-10 first flew on 30 October 1980 and entered service as the KC-10A in 1981. The type is operated by the 305th Air Mobility Wing, McGuire Air Force Base, New Jersey, and the 60th Air Mobility Wing, Travis Air Force Base, California. Air Force Reserve Associate units are assigned to the 349th Air Mobility Wing at Travis, and the 514th Air Mobility Wing at McGuire.

During Operations Desert Shield and Desert Storm in 1991, the KC-10 fleet provided inflight refuelling to aircraft from the US armed forces, as well as those of other coalition forces. In the early stages of Operation Desert Shield, inflight refuelling was key to the rapid airlift of material and forces. In addition to refuelling airlift aircraft, the KC-10, along with the smaller KC-135, moved thousands of tons of cargo and thousands of troops in support of the massive Persian Gulf build-up.

The KC-10 fleet was prominent during Operation Allied Force, the Nato air campaign against Yugoslavia which began on 24 March 1999. The mobility portion of the operation began in February and was tanker-dependent. By early May 1999, some 150 KC-10s and KC-135s deployed to Europe where they refuelled bombers, fighters and support aircraft engaged in the conflict. The KC-10 flew 409 missions throughout the entire Allied Force campaign and continued support operations in Kosovo. More recently, KC-10s were deployed in support of operations in Afghanistan and Iraq.

A KC-10A Extender is seen here with flight refuelling boom extended.

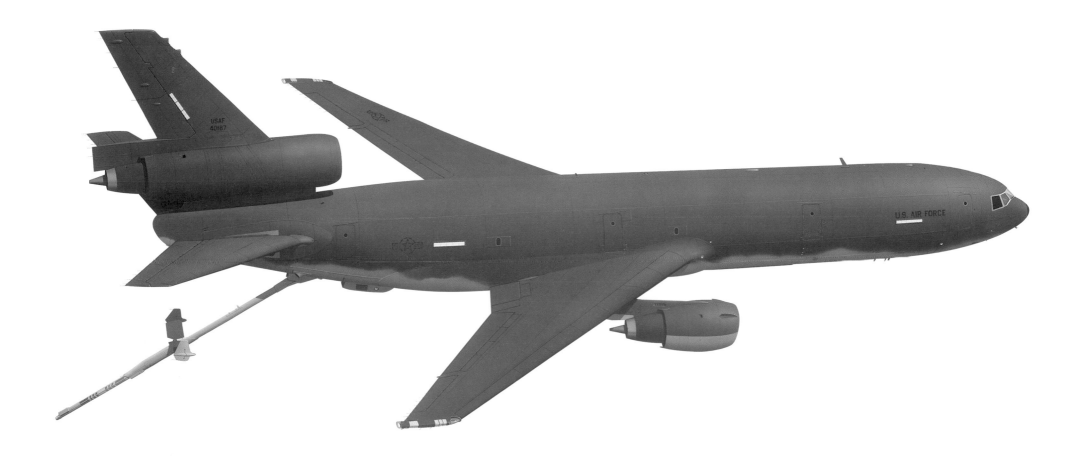

MIKOYAN-GUREVICH MIG-17 FRESCO-A

Forca Popular Aérea de Liberataco de Mocambique (Mozambique Air Force) 1980

Thought at first by Western observers to be just an improved MiG-15, the MiG-17 was in fact a new design, incorporating a number of aerodynamic refinements that included a new tail on a longer fuselage and a thinner wing with different section and planform, and with three boundary layer fences to improve handling at high speed. The prototype flew in January 1950, and the basic version of the MiG-17, known to Nato as Fresco-A, entered service in 1952; this was followed by the MiG-17P all-weather interceptor (Fresco-B), and then the major production variant, the MiG-17F (Fresco-C), which had structural refinements and was fitted with an afterburner. The last variant, the MiG-17PFU, was armed with air-to-air missiles.

Full-scale production of the MiG-17 in the Soviet Union lasted only five years before the type was superseded by the supersonic MiG-19 and MiG-21, but it has been estimated that around 8800 were built in that time, many of these being exported. MiG-17s saw action in the Congo, in the Nigerian civil war, in the Middle East and over North Vietnam, where they they were used in considerable numbers and proved tough and nimble opponents even for more modern types such as the F-4 Phantom. The MiG-17 was built in China as the J-5.

The example seen here, 'Red 21', was one of 48 examples which were delivered to Mozambique in the late 1970s and early 1980s. Several aircraft were shot down by anti-government Renamo guerrillas, and one was flown to South Africa by a defecting pilot.

MIKOYAN-GUREVICH MIG-17 FRESCO-A

Specification
- **Type** fighter
- **Crew** 1
- **Powerplant** one 3383kg (7452lb) thrust Klimov VK-1F turbojet
- **Performance** max speed 1145km/h (711mph); service ceiling 16,600m (54,560m); range 1470km (913 miles)
- **Dimensions** wing span 9.45m (31ft); length 11.05m (36ft 3in); height 3.35m (11ft)
- **Weight** 6000kg (14,770lb) loaded
- **Armament** one 37mm (1.46in) N-37 and two 23mm (0.91in) NS-23 cannon; up to 500kg (1102lb) of underwing stores

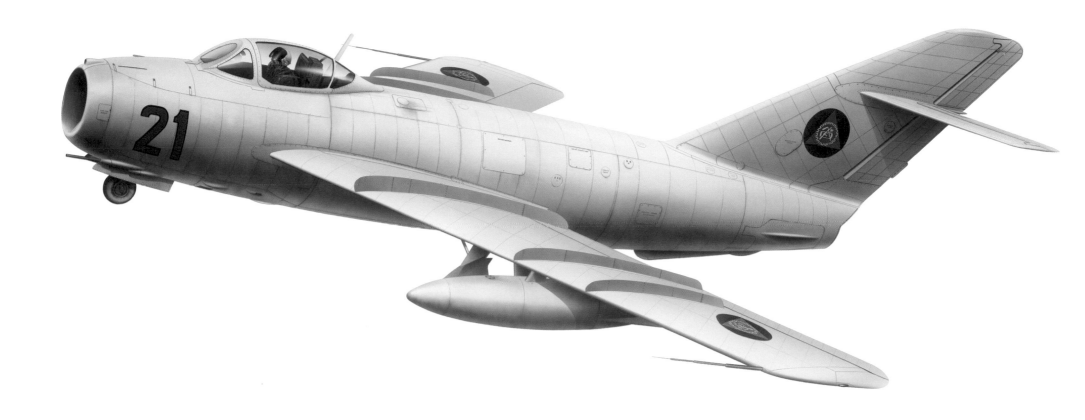

MIKOYAN-GUREVICH MIG-19 FARMER (SHENYANG F-6)

No 37 Wing, Pakistan Air Force, Miawali, late 1980s

MIKOYAN-GUREVICH MIG-19

Specification
- **Type** fighter
- **Crew** 1
- **Powerplant** two 3250kg (7165lb) thrust Klimov RD-9B turbojets
- **Performance** max speed 1480km/h (920mph); service ceiling 17,900m (58,725ft); range 2200km (1367 miles)
- **Dimensions** wing span 9.00m (29ft 6in); length 13.58m (44ft 7in); height 4.02m (13ft 2in)
- **Weight** 9500kg (20,944lb)
- **Armament** three 30mm (1.18in) cannon; four air-to-air missiles on underwing pylons

Designed as a successor to the MiG-17, the MiG-19, which flew for the first time in September 1953, was the first operational Soviet aircraft capable of exceeding Mach 1 in level flight. The first production model proved to have stability problems, and after modifications a second variant, MiG-19S, went into service in 1956. Both were known to Nato as Farmer-A.

In 1958, an all-weather fighter variant appeared, designated MiG-19P (Farmer-B), followed by the MiG-19C (Farmer-F) with more powerful engines. The MiG-19PF was a missile-armed all-weather variant, while the MiG-19PM was a night fighter. Like its predecessors, the MiG-19 was built under licence in China, Poland and Czechoslovakia. Chinese-built aircraft, designated Shenyang F-6, were exported to Pakistan and Vietnam, seeing combat with the air forces of both countries.

The most intensive use of the MiG-19 in combat was in the war between India and Pakistan, which flared up in December 1971. At that time the MiG-19, in its F-6 guise, formed the backbone of Pakistan's fighter force, serving with Nos 15, 19 and 25 Squadrons in the counter-air and ground-attack roles. The Pakistan Air Force was pleased with the type's performance in combat and bought a second batch from China, increasing the number in service to 130.

In November 1980, a large overhaul plant was built with Chinese assistance to handle repair and upgrade work on the F-6; this included the installation of British Martin-Baker ejection seats and pylons for Sidewinder missiles. The illustration shows a Chinese-built MiG-19 (Shenyang F-6) of the Pakistan Air Force.

MIKOYAN-GUREVICH MIG-21MF FISHBED-J

No. 7 'Battle Axes' Squadron,
Indian Air Force, Gwalior, 1980s

MIKOYAN-GUREVICH MIG-21MF FISHBED-J

Specification
- **Type** fighter
- **Crew** 1
- **Powerplant** one 6600kg (14,553lb) thrust Tumanski R-13-300 turbojet
- **Performance** max speed 2230km/h (1384mph); service ceiling 15,250m (50,000ft); range 1800km (1118 miles)
- **Dimensions** wing span 7.15m (23ft 5in); length 15.76m (51ft 9in); height 4.02m (14ft 9in)
- **Weight** 9400kg (20,727lb) loaded
- **Armament** one 23mm (0.9in) GSh-23 cannon; two K-13A air-to-air missiles on underwing pylons

Known by the Nato reporting name Fishbed, the MiG-21 was a child of the Korean War, where Soviet air combat experience had identified a need for a light, single-seat target defence interceptor with high supersonic manoeuvrability. Two prototypes were ordered, both appearing early in 1956; one, code-named Faceplate, featured sharply swept wings and was not developed further.

The initial production versions (Fishbed-A and Fishbed-B) were built in only limited numbers, being short-range day fighters with a comparatively light armament of two 30mm (1.18in) NR-30 cannon. The next variant, however, the MiG-21F Fishbed-C, carried two K-13 Atoll infrared homing air-to-air missiles, and had an uprated Tumansky R-11 turbojet as well as improved avionics.

The MiG-21F was the first major production version; it entered service in 1960 and was progressively modified and updated over the years that followed. In the early 1970s, the MiG-21 was virtually redesigned, re-emerging as the MiG-21B (Fishbed-L) multi-role air superiority fighter and ground-attack version. In its several versions, the MiG-21 became the most widely used jet fighter in the world, being licence-built in India, Czechoslovakia and China, where it was designated Shenyang F-8, and equipping some 25 Soviet-aligned air forces. In Vietnam, the MiG-21 was the Americans' deadliest opponent.

One of the major customers was India, the MiG-21MFs of which were equipped to carry a wide range of weaponry, reflecting their multi-role capability. For air-to-air combat, the Indian Air Force used the Soviet K-13A Atoll and R-60 Aphid, as well as the French Matra R550 Magic. The MiG-21MF Fishbed-J here is seen in the markings of the Indian Air Force's No. 7 'Battle Axes' Squadron.

MIL MI-24 HIND-D

16th Air Army, Group of Soviet Forces, German Democratic Republic, early 1980s

The Mil Mi-24, given the Nato reporting name Hind, was the first helicopter to enter service with the Soviet Air Force as a dedicated assault transport and gunship. Its missions included direct air support, anti-tank, armed escort and air-to-air combat.

The helicopter, which can carry eight fully armed troops, was used extensively during the Soviet involvement in Afghanistan in the 1980s. The Russians deployed significant numbers of Hinds to Europe and exported the type to many developing countries.

The Hind-A fuselage consisted of a large, oval-shaped body with a glassed-in cockpit, tapering at the rear to the tail boom. The Hind-D fuselage featured nose modification with tandem bubble canopies and a chin-mounted turret. The swept-back tapered tail fin had a rotor on the right on some models, with tapered flats on a boom just forward of the fin. External stores were mounted on underwing external stores points. Each wing had three hardpoints for a total of six stations. The Hind's wings provided 22– 28 per cent of its lift in forward flight. Nearly all of the older Hind-A, Hind-B and Hind-C variants were upgraded or modified to Hind-D or Hind-E standard.

The early model Mi-24 Hind-A was deployed to East Germany in strength in 1974, equipping two helicopter assault regiments at Parchim and Stendahl. The improved Hind-D began to reach the frontline units by 1976; it was supplanted and all but replaced by the Mi-24V Hind-E from 1979. Almost all the Hind-Ds had been replaced by the time the Russians withdrew from Germany in 1992.

MIL MI-24 HIND-D

Specification
- **Type** assault helicopter
- **Crew** 2
- **Powerplant** two Klimov (Isotov) TV3-117 Series III turboshaft engines each rated at 1641kW (2200hp)
- **Performance** max speed 310km/h (192mph); service ceiling 4500m (14,765ft); range 750km (466 miles)
- **Dimensions** rotor diameter 17.30m (56ft 9in); length 17.51m (57ft 5.5in); height 4.44m (14ft 6.25in)
- **Weight** 12,500kg (27,557lb) loaded
- **Armament** one four-barrelled 12.7mm (0.50in) rotary gun in remotely controlled undernose turret; various combinations of anti-armour missiles, rocket pods, gun pods etc

NORTH AMERICAN RA-5C VIGILANTE

*Reconnaissance Attack Squadron 7
(RVAH-7), United States Navy,
USS* Kitty Hawk, *1974*

NORTH AMERICAN RA-5C VIGILANTE

Specification
- **Type** reconnaissance aircraft
- **Crew** 2
- **Powerplant** two 8101kg (17,860lb) thrust General Electric J79-GE-10 turbojets
- **Performance** max speed 2230km/h; service ceiling 20,400m (67,000ft); range 5150km (3200 miles)
- **Dimensions** wing span 16.15m (53ft); length 23.11m (75ft 10in); height 5.92m (19ft 5in)
- **Weight** 36,285lb (80,000lb) loaded
- **Armament** none

First flown as the YA-5A on 31 August 1958, the North American RA-5 Vigilante supersonic naval attack bomber completed its carrier trials in July 1960. The aircraft was designed to carry either conventional or nuclear weapons in a linear bomb bay consisting of a tunnel inside the fuselage, the bombs being ejected rearwards between the two jet pipes. Fifty-seven A-5As were built, followed by 20 examples of the A-5B, an interim long-range variant.

The Vigilante's career as an attack bomber was relatively short-lived, the majority of A-5A and A-5B airframes being converted to RA-5C reconnaissance configuration. First service deliveries of the RA-5C to the US Navy were made in January 1964 to VAH-3, the training squadron for Heavy Attack Wing One; Reconnaissance Attack Squadron 5 (RVAH-5) became operational on the USS *Ranger* in the South China Sea in June that year.

Of the 10 RA-5C squadrons activated, eight saw service in Vietnam. Indeed, the RA-5C proved so successful in action over Vietnam that the production line was reopened in 1969 and an additional 48 aircraft were built. Eighteen aircraft were lost on operations.

RA-5C 149290 seen here was originally built as an A-5A, embarking on the aircraft carrier USS *Independence* with Heavy Attack Squadron 1 (VAH-1) in 1963. After being converted to RA-5C standard, the aircraft served aboard the carriers *John F. Kennedy*, *Forrestal*, *Independence*, *Kitty Hawk* and *Enterprise*. It was retired and stricken off US Navy charge on 3 August 1979.

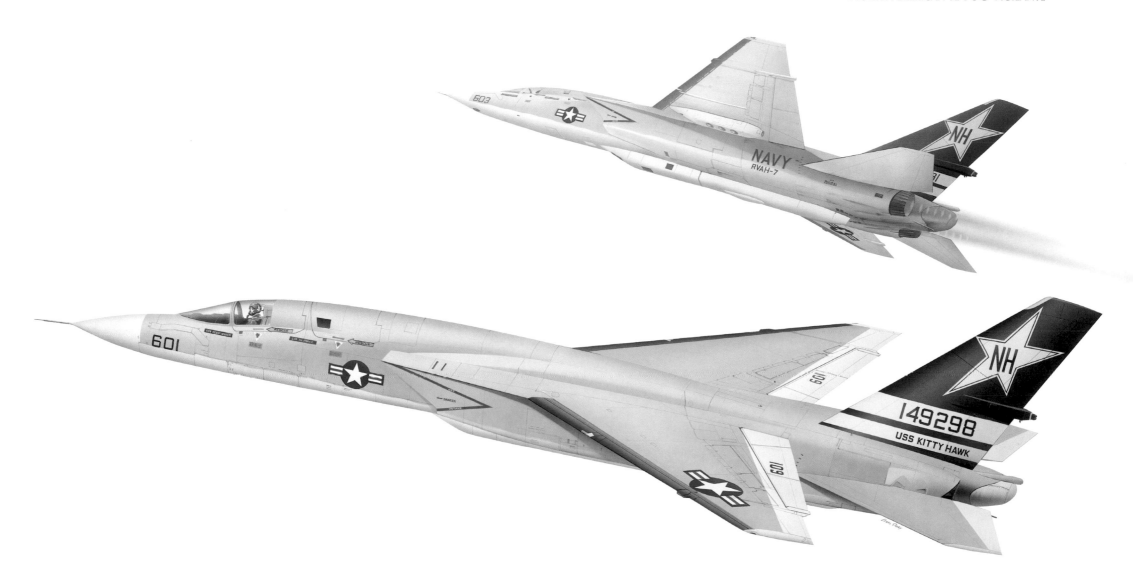

NORTH AMERICAN (ROCKWELL) OV-10 BRONCO

No. 411 Squadron, No. 41 Wing,
Royal Thai Air Force,
Chiang Mai Air Base, Thailand
1980s

NORTH AMERICAN (ROCKWELL) OV-10 BRONCO

Specification
- **Type** armed reconnaissance and counterinsurgency aircraft
- **Crew** 2
- **Powerplant** two 533kW (715hp) AiResearch T76-410/411 turboprops
- **Performance** max speed 452km/h (281mph); service ceiling 9150m (30,000ft); range 960km (600 miles)
- **Dimensions** wing span 12.19m (40ft); length 12.67m (41ft 7in); height 4.62m (15ft 2in)
- **Weight** 6536kg (14,466lb) loaded
- **Armament** two 7.62mm (0.30in) machine guns in sponsons on lower fuselage; up to 1632kg (3600lb) of bombs and/or rockets

---

In August 1964, it was announced that North American Aviation had won a US Navy competition for a light armed reconnaissance and coounterinsurgency aircraft. Originally designated NA-300, the first of seven prototypes flew on 16 July 1965 as the YOV-10A Bronco, powered by two AirResearch T76 turboprop engines. The first production OV-10A battlefield support aircraft entered service with the US Marine Corps (USMC) and US Air Force (USAF) in 1968, with 270 examples being built.

Many were employed in Vietnam for light armed reconnaissance, helicopter escort and forward air control. The type could also act in the ground support role until tactical fighters were called in. Fifteen aircraft were modified for night forward air control. The OV-10B was a target-towing version supplied to Federal Germany (24 examples), while the OV-10C was a version for the Royal Thai Air Force (36 delivered). Other variants were the OV-10E for Venezuela (16) and the OV-10F for Indonesia (6).

The Royal Thai Air Force (RTAF) acquired its first batch of 16 OV-10Cs in 1971. Concentrated on Chiang Mai in northern Thailand, the aircraft were responsible for counterinsurgency and patrol duties along the Burmese and Laotian borders. One aircraft was lost to a Laotian SA-7 missile in February 1988. In mid-1999, six of the 15 Broncos still surviving were retired, and plans were laid for the conversion of some aircraft into rain-makers. At that time, No. 411 Squadron was preparing to become the RTAF's first Alpha Jet unit.

NORTHROP F-5E TIGER II

*1° Esquadrão, 1° Grupo de Aviação
de Caça, Força Aérea Brasileira,
Base Aérea de Santa Cruz, Brazil
late 1970s*

NORTHROP F-5E TIGER II

Specification
- **Type** tactical fighter (F-5E Tiger II)
- **Crew** 1
- **Powerplant** two 2268kg (5000lb) thrust General Electric J85-GE-21B turbojets
- **Performance** max speed 1741km/h (1082mph); service ceiling 15,790m (15,800ft); combat radius 306km (190 miles)
- **Dimensions** wing span 8.13m (26ft 8in); length 14.45m (47ft 4.75in); eight 4.07m (13ft 4.25in)
- **Weight** 11,214kg (24,722lb) loaded
- **Armament** two 20mm (0.79in) M39 cannon; up to 3175kg (7000lb) of external stores

In the 1980s, Northrop pinned a great deal of hope in the potential of an advanced version of the F-5, the F-20 Tigershark. Although a superb aircraft, the F-20 attracted no customers, which left Northrop short of military contracts. The company therefore began design work on an upgraded version of the F-5 for the potential market of current operators.

While a number of other companies were already offering upgrades, Northrop, which was not only the original equipment manufacturer, but which also had experience of advanced avionics on the B-2 and F/A-18, saw itself as the logical choice. Initial improvements were conducted under a structural upgrade programme funded by the United States; however, in 1993, Northrop embarked on a much more ambitious programme using an F-5E 'borrowed back' from the US Navy. With a new avionics suite, the F-5E Tiger IV first flew on 20 April 1995. Now offered with various other avionics and electronic warfare suites, Tiger upgrades have been initiated by several air forces, including Brazil, Chile, Indonesia and Singapore.

This F-5E Tiger II is in the markings of *1° Esquadrão, 1° Grupo de Aviação de Caça* (No 1. Squadron, 1st Fighter Group) of the *Força Aérea Brasileira* (Brazilian Air Force); the 'fighting ostrich' insignia was originally used when the unit flew P-47D Thunderbolts with the 350th Fighter Group of the US Army Air Forces (USAAF) in Italy during World War II. Brazil's three Tiger squadrons share the surviving examples of the 36 F-5Es and four F-5Bs delivered from 1975, and the 22 ex–US Air Force F-5Es and four F-5Fs delivered in 1989.

PANAVIA TORNADO F.MK.3

*No. 229 Operational Conversion Unit,
Royal Air Force, RAF Coningsby,
Lincolnshire, late 1980s*

PANAVIA TORNADO F.MK.3

Specification

- **Type** long-range interceptor
- **Crew** 2
- **Powerplant** two 7493kg (31,970lb) thrust Turbo-Union RB.199-34R Mk 104 turbofans
- **Performance** max speed 2337km/h (1452mph); service ceiling 21,335m (70,000ft); intercept radius about 1853km (1000 miles)
- **Dimensions** wing span 13.91m (45ft 7in) spread and 8.6m (28ft 2in) swept; length 18.68m (61ft 3in); height 5.95m (19ft 6in)
- **Weight** 27,987kg (61,700lb) loaded
- **Armament** two 27mm (1.06in) IWKA-Mauser cannon; six external hardpoints with provision for up to 5806kg (12,800lb) of stores, including short- and medium-range air-to-air missiles, and drop tanks

In 1971, the UK Ministry of Defence issued Air Staff Target 395, which called for a minimum-change, minimum-cost but effective interceptor to replace the British Aerospace Lightning and the F.4 Phantom in the air defence of the United Kingdom. Primary armament was to be the British Aerospace Dynamics XJ521 Sky Flash medium-range air-to-air missile, and the primary sensor a Marconi Avionics pulse-Doppler radar. The result was the Air Defence Variant (ADV) of the Panavia Tornado interdictor/strike (IDS) aircraft. Three Tornado ADV prototypes were built.

The first squadron, No. 29, formed at RAF Coningsby in May 1987 and was declared operational at the end of November. The aircraft eventually armed seven squadrons in addition to No. 229 Operational Conversion Unit (OCU), 18 F.Mk.2s being followed by 155 F.Mk.3s, with improved radar. The Tornado ADV also serves with the air forces of Italy and Saudi Arabia.

This No. 229 OCU Tornado F.3 also carries the markings of No. 65 Squadron, which was formed as the OCU's 'shadow' squadron on 1 January 1987 in keeping with the Royal Air Force (RAF) practice of maintaining the identities of famous units. No. 65 Squadron's badge depicts 15 swords and a lion, and recalls a memorable combat in which its pilots destroyed 15 enemy aircraft. The Tornado also bears the crossed sword and torch badge of No. 229 OCU on its fin. This unit disbanded on 1 August 1992 and immediately re-formed as No. 56 (Reserve) Squadron. It moved to RAF Leuchars, Scotland, in March 2003.

PANAVIA TORNADO IDS

36° Stormo, 156° Gruppo, Aeronautica Militare Italiana, Gioia del Colle, 1984

PANAVIA TORNADO IDS

Specification
- **Type** tactical reconnaissance and defence suppression aircraft
- **Crew** 2
- **Powerplant** two 7292kg (16,075lb) thrust Turbo-Union RB.199-34R Mk 103 turbofan engines
- **Performance** max speed 2337km/h (1452mph); service ceiling 15,240m (50,000ft); combat radius 1390km (864 miles)
- **Dimensions** wing span 13.91m (45ft 7in) spread and 8.6m (28ft 2.5in) swept; length 16.72m (54ft 10in); height 5.95m (19ft 6.25in)
- **Weight** 27,216kg (60,000lb) loaded
- **Armament** up to 9000kg (19,840lb) of stores, including AGM-88 HARM anti-radiation missiles

A major departure from the basic Tornado IDS (Interdictor/Strike) aircraft is the Tornado ECR (Electronic Combat & Reconnaissance) version, known in Germany as EKA (Elektronische Kampfführung und Aufklärung), which entered service with both the *Luftwaffe* and *Aeronautica Militare Italiana* (Italian Air Force) as a combined defence suppression aircraft and a reconnaissance platform. A total of 35 new Tornado ECRs were delivered to the *Luftwaffe*, with Italy converting 16 of its IDS aircraft to the standard.

Italian aircraft are known as the Tornado IT-ECR and differ from their German counterparts in lacking a reconnaissance pod. The aircraft features an emitter-locator system which is capable of locating enemy radar sites, and then employs the AGM-88A High Speed Anti-Radiation Missile (HARM) to destroy it. The aircraft is externally distinguishable from the IDS in several ways, the most notable of these being the loss of the 27mm (1.06in) Mauser cannon, an Infrared Linescanner and the addition of a FLIR (forward-looking infrared) sensor next to the nose landing gear. Internally the aircraft also features the Operational Data Interface (ODIN) system, which enables the aircraft to pass video images in near real time from the Linescanner to either other ODIN-equipped aircraft or friendly ground forces.

The 36th *Stormo*'s 156th *Gruppo* converted to the Tornado in 1984, becoming operational at Gioia del Colle in August that year. The unit's primary task was maritime strike and interdiction. It later relinquished its IDS Tornados and switched to the Tornado Air Defence variant.

REPUBLIC F-105D THUNDERCHIEF

17th (Wild Weasel) Squadron, 388th Fighter Wing, United States Air Force, Korat, Thailand, 1973

REPUBLIC F-105D THUNDERCHIEF

Specification refers to the F-105D
- **Type** fighter-bomber
- **Crew** 1
- **Powerplant** one 11,113kg (24,500lb) thrust Pratt & Whitney J75-19W turbojet
- **Performance** max speed 2382km/h (1480mph); service ceiling 15,850m (52,000ft); combat radius 370km (230 miles)
- **Dimensions** wing span 10.65m (34ft 11in); length 19.58m (64ft 3in); height 5.99m (19ft 8in)
- **Weight** 23,834kg (52,546lb) loaded
- **Armament** one 20mm (0.79in) M61 cannon; provision for up to 3629kg (8000lb) of bombs internally and 2722kg (6000lb) externally

The first of two YF-105 Thunderchief prototypes flew on 22 October 1955, with deliveries of operational F-105Bs beginning in May 1958 to the 4th Tactical Fighter Wing (TFW) of the US Air Force (USAF). Only 75 F-105Bs were built, this variant being replaced on the production line in 1959 by the all-weather ground-attack F-105D version.

Production of the F-105D totalled 610 aircraft, and the aircraft proved its worth over Vietnam, where it flew more than 70 per cent of USAF strike missions with an abort rate of less than 1 per cent. Although it showed an astonishing ability to absorb tremendous battle damage and still get back to base, 397 F-105s were lost on operations in Vietnam, an attrition rate that earned the F-105 the nickname of 'Thud', this representing the noise a crashing aircraft makes when it hits the ground.

The F-105F, a two-seater variant, first flew on 11 June 1963. The F-105F, of which 143 were built, had full operational capability and was assigned in small numbers to each F-105D squadron. In Vietnam, F-105Fs frequently led strikes, providing accurate navigationto the target. F-105Fs were the first Thunderchiefs to assume the 'Wild Weasel' defence suppression role. F-105Fs fitted with improved defence suppression equipment were designated F-105G.

Activated at Korat, Thailand, on 1 December 1971 specifically for the defence suppression role, the 17th Wild Weasel squadron was one of the last USAF units to be withdrawn from Southeast Asia, in November 1974. The F-105G pictured here, 'White Lightning', is preserved at Liberal, Kansas, as a memorial to F-105 crews who lost their lives over Vietnam.

SAAB J-35 DRAKEN

*Eskadrille 729, Royal Danish Air Force,
Karup Air Base, Denmark, 1988*

SAAB J-35 DRAKEN

Specification for reconnaissance version, RF-35
- **Type** tactical reconnaissance aircraft
- **Crew** 1
- **Powerplant** one 7830kg (17,262lb) thrust Svenska Flygmotor RM6C (licence-built Rolls-Royce Avon 300 series) turbojet
- **Performance** max speed 2125km/h (1320mph); service ceiling 20,000m (65,000ft); range 3250km (2020 miles) with max fuel
- **Dimensions** wing span 9.40m (30ft 10in); length 15.40m (50ft 4in); height 3.90m (12ft 9in)
- **Weight** 16,000kg (35,274lb) loaded
- **Armament** one 30mm (1.18in) Aden cannon

Designed from the outset to intercept transonic bombers at all altitudes and in all weathers, the Swedish-designed Draken was, at the time of its service debut, a component of the finest fully integrated air defence system in western Europe. The first of three prototypes of this unique 'double delta' fighter flew for the first time on 25 October 1955, and the initial production version, the J-35A, entered service early in 1960.

The major production version of the Draken was the J-35F, which was virtually designed around the Hughes HM-55 Falcon radar-guided air-to-air missile and was fitted with an improved S7B collision-course fire control system, a high-capacity datalink system integrating the aircraft with the STRIL 60 air defence environment, an infrared sensor under the nose and PS-01A search and ranging radar. The J-35C was a two-seat operational trainer, while the last new-build variant, the J-35J, was a development of the J-35D with more capable radar, collision-course fire control and a Hughes infrared sensor to allow carriage of the Hughes Falcon air-to-air missile. The Saab RF-35 was a reconnaissance version.

Total production of the Draken was around 600 aircraft, equipping 17 Royal Swedish Air Force (RSAF) squadrons; the type was also exported to Finland and Austria, as well as Denmark. The Draken was the first fully supersonic aircraft in western Europe to be deployed operationally.

The Saab RF.35 continued to serve with *Eskadrille* 729 of the Royal Danish Air Force until the unit was disbanded as an economy measure and its task was taken over by the F-16s of *Esk* 726 in January 1994.

SUKHOI SU-7BMK FITTER-A

5th 'Pomorski' Fighter-Bomber Regiment, Polish Air Force, Bydgoszcz, Poland 1980s

SUKHOI SU-7BMK FITTER-A

Specification
- **Type** tactical fighter-bomber
- **Crew** 1
- **Powerplant** one 9008kg (19,842lb) thrust Lyulka AL-7F turbojet
- **Performance** Max speed 1700km/h (1065mph); service ceiling 15,200m (49,865ft); combat radius 320km (199 miles)
- **Dimensions** wing span 8.93m (29ft 3.5in); length 18.75m (61ft 6in); height 5.00m (16ft 5in)
- **Weight** 13,500kg (29,750lb) loaded
- **Armament** two 30mm (1.18in) NR-30 cannon; four external pylons with provision for two 750kg (1653lb) and two 500kg (1102lb) bombs; one RU-57 tactical free-fall nuclear bomb

The Sukhoi Su-7, which was first seen in public in 1956, remained the Soviet Air Force's standard tactical fighter-bomber throughout the 1960s and was also issued to the Polish Air Force. The Su-7U, code-named 'Moujik', was a two-seat trainer version.

The Su-7 saw a good deal of action with the Egyptian Air Force, initially during the Six-Day War of 1967, when two aircraft were shot down during a bombing raid on El Arish. In the so-called War of Attrition of 1969–70, an Egyptian Su-7 belly-landed intact near the Ghidi Pass in November 1969, providing Israel with a valuable intelligence coup. Three Su-7s were lost during a hit-and-run raid across the Suez Canal in April 1970, and on 11 September 1970 one example was lost during a reconnaissance sortie.

Eight squadrons of Egyptian AF Su-7BMs (backed up by three Algerian units) were involved in the Yom Kippur War of 1973, supporting the 900-tank assault on the Golan Heights on 6 October, and strafing Israeli columns in concert with MiG-17s and Iraqi Hunters during the opening phase. The Su-7 was credited with a good combat record during the conflict, proving remarkably resistant to ground fire. Indian Air Force Su-7s also saw action in the 1971 war with Pakistan.

Polish Su-7s with the 5th 'Pomorski' Fighter-Bomber Regiment were trained to deliver the RU-57 tactical nuclear bomb. Polish AF Su-7s were based close to Torun, where tactical nuclear weapons were stored in Soviet bunkers. The Polish Su-7BMK and Su-7UMK were stationed at Bydgoszcz until shortly before the base was closed in 1969.

SUKHOI SU-15TM FLAGON-F

*Soviet Air Defence Forces,
Dolinsk-Sokol, Sakhalin, early 1980s*

SUKHOI SU-15TM FLAGON-F

Specification
- **Type** all-weather interceptor
- **Crew** 1
- **Powerplant** two 6205kg (13,668lb) thrust Tumanskii R-11F2S turbojets
- **Performance** max speed 2230km/h (1386mph); service ceiling 20,000m (65,615ft); combat radius 725km (450 miles)
- **Dimensions** wing span 8.61m (28ft 3in); length 21.33m (70ft); height 5.10m (16ft 8in)
- **Weight** 18,000kg (39,680lb) loaded
- **Armament** four external pylons for medium-range air-to-air missiles

The Sukhoi Su-15 Flagon traces its ancestry back to the Sukhoi Su-9, known to Nato as 'Fishpot'. Fishpot-A was a single-seat interceptor; to some extent, an Su-7 with a delta wing. It was armed with the first Soviet air-to-air missile, the semi-active radar homing Alkali, four of which were carried under the wings. In 1961, a new model, the Su-11 Fishpot-B, was developed from the Su-9, and was followed into service by the Fishpot-C, which had an uprated engine. A tandem two-seat trainer variant of the Su-9 was given the Nato reporting name 'Maiden'.

The Su-9 flew for the first time in 1955 and entered service in the following year. The follow-on to the Su-11 aircraft was the Su-15, a twin-engined delta-wing interceptor that first flew in 1965 and was in Soviet Air Force service by 1969. Capable of carrying two air-to-air missiles, the Flagon was numerically the Soviet Union's most important all-weather interceptor by the mid-1970s, some 1500 being produced in total.

The T-5 prototype from which the Su-15 was developed was basically an enlarged version of the Su-11 with the same nose intake, but the T-58 which followed had a 'solid' nose housing AI radar equipment and intakes on the fuselage sides. A number of Flagon variants were produced, culminating in the definitive Su-15TM Flagon-F of 1971.

On 1 September 1983, a Su-15TM like the aircraft illustrated here, and based at Dolinsk-Sokol on Sakhalin, achieved notoriety by shooting down a Korean Air Lines Boeing 747 over the Sea of Japan.

SUKHOI SU-22MF FITTER-K

Jagdbombergeschwader 77 'Gerhard Leberecht von Blücher', Luftstreitkräfte, Laage, Rostock, 1980s

SUKHOI SU-22MF FITTER-K

Specification
- **Type** fighter-bomber
- **Crew** 1
- **Powerplant** one 11,250kg (24,802lb) thrust Lyulka AL-21F-3 turbojet
- **Performance** max speed 2220km/h (1380mph); service ceiling 15,200m (49,865ft); combat radius 675km (419 miles)
- **Dimensions** wing span 13.80m (45ft 3in); length 18.75m (61ft 6in); height 5m (16ft 5in)
- **Weight** 19,500kg (42,990lb) loaded
- **Armament** two 30mm (1.18in) cannon; nine external pylons with provision for up to 4250kg (9370lb) of stores

In the early 1960s, the Sukhoi bureau redesigned the Su-7, giving it a more powerful engine, variable-geometry wings and increased fuel tankage. In this guise it became the Su-17/20 Fitter C, which was unique among combat aircraft in being a variable-geometry derivative of a fixed-wing machine. It was an excellent example of a remarkable Russian talent for developing existing designs to their fullest extent.

The development of the Fitter-C was a facet of the Russians' practice of constant development, enabling them to keep one basic design of combat aircraft in service for 30 or 40 years and foster long-term standardization. Also, the use of the same production facilities over a long period of time helped greatly to reduce costs, which is why the Soviet Union was able to offer combat types on the international market at far more competitive rates than the West.

The Su-22 was an updated version with terrain-avoidance radar and other improved avionics. A principal Su-22M user was the Syrian Arab Air Force, which took delivery of some 50 aircraft from 1978; another important user was Vietnam. The Su-22 remains in service with former Warsaw Pact air forces, such as the Czech Republic and Slovakia.

Two East German units were armed with the Su-22M; the other was a naval wing, *Marinefliegergeschwader* 28 'Paul Wieczoreck'. As well as performing the tactical reconnaissance mission, East German Fitter crews were trained to use S-25L laser-guided rocket projectiles and the Kh-58U (As-11 Kilter) anti-radar missile in the defence suppression role.

SUKHOI SU-24 FENCER-D

149th Bomber Air Division, 67th Bomber Air Regiment, Siverskiy, Poland, 1985

SUKHOI SU-24 FENCER-D

Specification
- **Type** interdictor/strike aircraft
- **Crew** 2
- **Powerplant** two 11,250kg (24,802lb) thrust Lyulka AL-21F3A turbojets
- **Performance** max speed 2316km/h (1439mph); service ceiling 17,500m (57,415ft); combat radius 1050km (650 miles)
- **Dimensions** wing span 17.63m (57ft 10in) spread and 10.36m (34ft) swept; length 24.53m (80ft 5in); height 4.97m (16ft 0in)
- **Weight** 39,700kg (87,520lb) loaded
- **Armament** one 23mm (0.91in) GSh-23-6 six-barrelled cannon; nine external pylons with provision for up to 8000kg (17,635lb) of stores

In 1965, the Soviet government instructed the Sukhoi design bureau to begin design studies of a new variable-geometry strike aircraft in the same class as the General Dynamics F-111. One of the criteria was that the new aircraft must be able to fly at very low level in order to penetrate increasingly effective air defence systems. The resulting aircraft, the Su-24, made its first flight in 1970, and deliveries of the first production version, the Fencer-A, began in 1974.

Several variants of the Fencer were produced, culminating in the Su-24M Fencer-D, which entered service in 1986. It features an advanced nav/attack targeting system which, combined with the Kaira-24 laser ranger/designator, enables the use of laser-guided and TV-guided weapons. Navigation and radio communication systems were also upgraded. The addition of an in-flight refuelling system greatly improved the aircraft's range and flexibility.

The Su-24MR is a tactical reconnaissance version. The Su-24MK is the export variant of the Su-24M which was developed for friendly Arabian nations. Reportedly 20 aircraft were exported to Syria, 15 to Libya, and 24 to Iraq. There are almost no differences between the Su-24MK and the original Su-24M. The Ukrainian Air Force also inherited two regiments of Su-24s.

From 1982, two regiments of Fencer B/Cs were based at Brand and Grossenhain in East Germany, while three further regiments were installed at a clutch of bases in southwest Poland. In 1989, the two Germany-based units were withdrawn, but the Poland-based units remained in place until 1992.

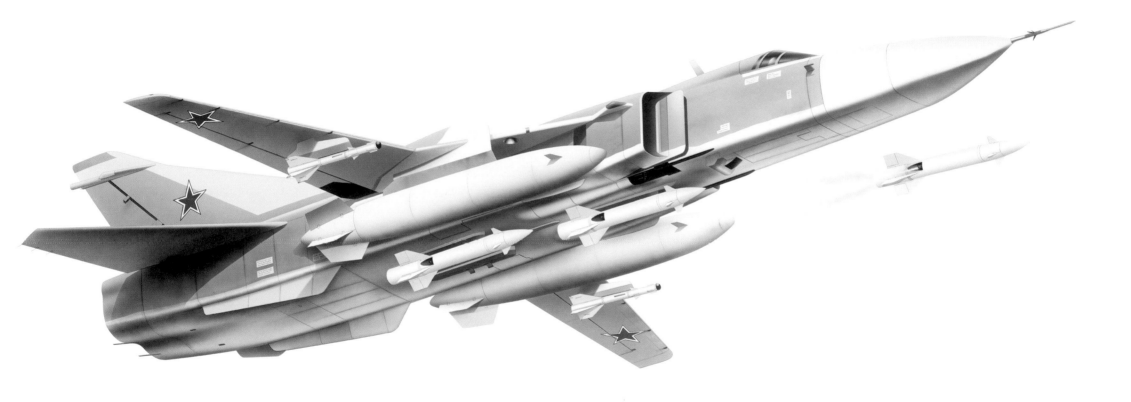

SUKHOI SU-25 FROGFOOT

*State Flight Test Centre, Akhtubinsk, Russia
1980s*

SUKHOI SU-25 FROGFOOT

Specification
- **Type** close support aircraft
- **Crew** 1
- **Powerplant** two 4500kg (9921lb) Tumanskii R-195 turbojets
- **Performance** max speed 975km/h (606mph); service ceiling 7000m (22,965ft); combat radius 750km (466 miles)
- **Dimensions** wing span 14.36m (47ft 1in); length 15.53m (50ft 11in); height 4.80m (15ft 9in)
- **Weight** 17,600kg (38,800lb) loaded
- **Armament** one 30mm (1.18in) GSh-30-2 cannon; eight external pylons with provision for up to 4400kg (9700lb) of stores

A Russian requirement for an attack aircraft in the A-10 Thunderbolt II class materialized in the Sukhoi Su-25 Frogfoot, which was selected in preference to a rival design, the Ilyushin Il-102. As a result of lessons learned during the Afghan conflict, an upgraded version known as the Su-25T was produced, with improved defensive systems to counter weapons such as the Stinger.

The improvements included the insertion of steel plates, several millimetres thick, between the engine bays and below the fuel cell. After this modification, no further Su-25s were lost to shoulder-launched missiles. In total, 22 Su-25s were lost in the nine years of the Afghan conflict.

The Su-25UBK is a two-seat export variant, while the Su-25UBT is a navalized version with a strengthened undercarriage and arrester gear. The Su-25UT (Su-28) was a trainer version, lacking the weapons pylons and combat capability of the standard Su-25UBK, but retaining the original aircraft's rough field capability and endurance. Only one aircraft was flown in August 1985, appearing in the colours of DOSAAF, the Soviet Union's paramilitary 'private flying' organization.

In service with the Soviet Air Force, the Su-25 was nicknamed 'Grach' ('Rook'), and most aircraft deployed to Afghanistan featured a cartoon rook design. Russian infantrymen called the aircraft *Rascheska* ('The Comb') because of its 10 weapon pylons.

Operated by the Sukhoi OKB Flight Test Department, this Su-25TM was detached to the State Flight Test Centre at Akhtubinsk, situated between Volgograd and Astrakhan. Known as 'Blue 10', the aircraft was used for weapons trials and also undertook overseas demonstration flights on behalf of potential customers.

TUPOLEV TU-95/TU-142 BEAR

135th Long-Range ASW Regiment, 206th Soviet Naval Air Division, Volgodskaya, 1985

TUPOLEV TU-95/TU-142 BEAR

Specification
- **Type** strategic bomber/maritime warfare aircraft
- **Crew** 10
- **Powerplant** four 11,186kW (15,000hp) Kuznetsov NK-12MV turboprop engines
- **Performance** max speed 805km/h (500mph); service ceiling 13,400m (44,000ft); range 12,550km (7800 miles)
- **Dimensions** wing span 48.50m (159ft); length 47.50 (155ft 10in); height 11.78m (38ft 8in)
- **Weight** 154,000kg (340,000lb) loaded
- **Armament** six 23mm (0.91in) cannon; weapons load of up to 11,340kg (25,000lb)

Given the Nato reporting name 'Bear', the Tupolev Tu-95 flew for the first time on 12 November 1952. The type entered service with the Soviet Strategic Air Forces (*Dal'naya Aviatsiya*) in 1957, early examples having played a prominent part in Soviet nuclear weapons trials.

The initial Tupolev Tu-95M Bear-A freefall nuclear bomber was followed by the Tu-95K-20 Bear-B of 1961, this being a maritime attack and reconnaissance version with a large radome under the nose and a Kh-20 (AS-3 Kangaroo) cruise missile. The Tu-95KD was similar, but was fitted with a flight refuelling probe. The Tu-95KM Bear-C, thought to be a new-build variant, was a specialized maritime reconnaissance version, as was the similar Bear-D, while the Bear-E and Bear-F were upgraded variants with a new electronics suite. These and later aircraft were designated Tu-142.

Later models include the Bear-H, equipped to carry up to four cruise missiles, and the Tu-142MR Bear-J, a very long frequency (VLF) communications platform based on the Bear-F. This variant is tasked with providing a secure communications link with Russian submarines using an 8km (5-mile) long antenna which is stowed in a container beneath the fuselage. Eight Tu-142s were supplied to the Indian Navy.

The 206th Naval Air Division, based on airfields on the Murmansk Peninsula, was responsible for long-range maritime reconnaissance and anti-submarine warfare operations throughout the Cold War era. It was also equipped with Tupolev Tu-16 and Ilyushin Il-38 aircraft.Pictured here is a Tu-142M Bear-F Mod 3 of the division's 135th Long-Range ASW Regiment.

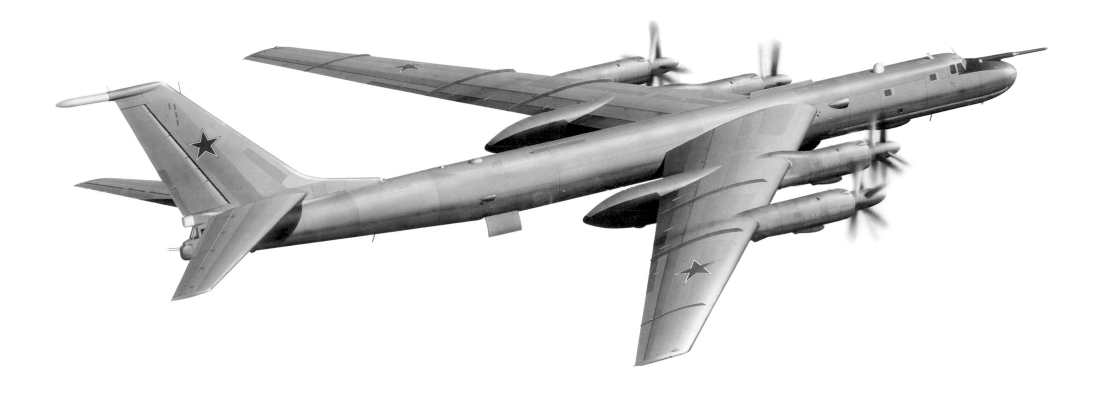

WESTLAND WESSEX

No. 28 Squadron, Royal Air Force, Kai Tak, Hong Kong, 1978

WESTLAND WESSEX

Specification
- **Type** transport helicopter
- **Crew** 3
- **Powerplant** two Rolls-Royce (Bristol Siddeley) Gnome Mk 110/111 coupled turboshafts each rated at 1007kW (1350hp)
- **Performance** max speed 212km/h (132mph); service ceiling 3658m (12,000ft); range 1040km (645 miles)
- **Dimensions** rotor diameter 17.07m (56ft); length 11.73m (48ft 4.5in); height 4.93m (16ft 2in)
- **Weight** 6123kg (13,500lb) loaded
- **Armament** optional door-mounted 7.62mm (0.30in) general-purpose machine gun

In 1956, Westland, which held the licence to build the Sikorsky S-55, acquired the licence for the more modern S-58, but modified the aircraft to take a turbine engine. The Royal Navy immediately ordered the new helicopter as the Wessex HAS Mk.1, to replace the older Whirlwind HAS Mk.7.

The aircraft was basically similar to the Sikorsky S-58; however, the nose profile was altered as a result of the installation of the turbine which, in the first production version, was a 1081kW (1450hp) Gazelle NGa.13. Later Wessex helicopters (Mk.2 and 5) were powered by twin Rolls-Royce Gnome engines and employed as troop transports.

Westland built 356 Wessex helicopters in all (including those for the civil market): the HAS Mk.1 version for the Royal Navy; the HC Mk.2 tactical transport version for the Royal Air Force (RAF); the HAS Mk.3 anti-submarine version with 1156kW (1550hp) Gazelle NGa.18 turbine; the HCC.Mk.4 for the Queen's Flight; the HU. Mk.5 for various roles on the Royal Navy's commando carriers; the HAS Mk.31 for the Royal Australian Navy; the Wessex Mk.52 for the Iraqi Navy (12); the Wessex Mk.53 for Ghana (3); the Wessex Mk.54 for Borneo and the Wessex Mk.60 commercial version.

No. 28 Squadron RAF was the last to use the Wessex HC.Mk.2, which replaced the Westland Whirlwind HAR.10 in 1972. The squadron was based at Kai Tak, Hong Kong, until 1978, when it moved to Sek Kong. The squadron disbanded in June 1997 (its refurbished helicopters going to Uruguay) and was re-formed three years later at RAF Benson, Oxfordshire, with the Merlin HC.3 helicopter.

THE POST-COLD WAR ERA: 1990–

With the collapse of Communism and the increased threat from terrorists aided by regimes hostile to the West, combat aircraft have played a key role in conflicts in the former Yugoslavia, Afghanistan, and Iraq. As these wars have demanded a greater ground-attack component, 'stealth' and flexibility have become a priority over speed and agility.

A USAF F-16C based at Incirlik Air Base, Turkey, involved in policing the United Nations no-fly zone over northern Iraq in 2002.

AERO L-39ZA ALBATROS

Vzdusné Síly ACR,
Kosice, Czechoslovakia, 1990s

The Aero L-39 Albatros was developed in Czechoslovakia to meet the needs of the Soviet Union and Warsaw Pact to replace the L-29 Delphin as the main jet training aircraft. The Soviet Union had considerable input into the design and took the great bulk of production. More than 2800 examples were built, making it the most numerous jet trainer ever produced.

The prototype flew in November 1968 and was followed by the L-39C unarmed trainer, the L-39ZO weapons trainer and the L-39ZA ground-attack and reconnaissance aircraft. Czechoslovakia itself introduced the Albatros to service in 1974, but was only one of more than 20 nations around the world to fly the type.The L-39 is simple to maintain and can carry a wide range of weapons for training and light attack missions.

The Czechoslovakian Air Force (*Ceskoslovenske Letectvo*) became the Air Force of the Army of the Czech Republic (*Vzdusné Síly ACR*) after the dissolution of the union of the Czech Republic and Slovakia in 1993. Many bases were closed and aircraft types retired, and the Czech Republic chose to concentrate in the future on two combat aircraft types. These will be the SAAB Gripen and the L-159 ALCA (Advanced Light Combat Aircraft), a much more capable derivative of the L-39.

Depicted in service in the mid-1990s, L-39ZA 2418 was still active in 2003 with 322 *Taktika Letka* (tactical squadron) at Namest nad Oslavou in the southeast of the country. This unit keeps some aircraft on quick-reaction alert to protect the local nuclear power plant. Around 30 L-39s remain in Czech service, with the L-159A single-seat and L-159B two-seat aircraft slowly entering arriving to replace the remaining MiG-21s.

AERO L-39ZA ALBATROS

Specification
- **Type** advanced trainer and light attack/reconnaissance aircraft
- **Crew** 2
- **Powerplant** one 16.87kN (3792lb thrust) Ivchencko AI-25TL turbofan engine
- **Performance** max speed 755km/h (486mph); service ceiling 11,000m (36,090ft); range 1100km (683 miles)
- **Dimensions** wing span 9.46m (31ft 0.5in); length 12.13m (39ft 9.5in); height 4.77m (15ft 8in)
- **Weight** 4700kg (10,362lb) loaded
- **Armament** one GSh-23 twin-barrel 23mm (0.91in) cannon; weapons load of up to 907lb (2000kg) of bombs or rockets

BEECH RC-12D GUARDRAIL V

2nd Military Intelligence Battalion,
Intelligence and Security Command,
US 7th Army Corps, US Army Europe,
Al Qaysumah, Saudi Arabia, 1991

BEECH RC-12D GUARDRAIL V

Specification
- **Type** twin-engined communications/electronic intelligence aircraft
- **Crew** 2
- **Powerplant** two 634kW (850hp) Pratt & Whitney PT-6A-42 turboprop engines
- **Performance** max speed 541km/h (336mph); service ceiling 10,668m (35,000ft); range 2220km (1380 miles)
- **Dimensions** wing span 16.61m (54ft 6in) without pods; length 13.3m (43ft 10in); height 4.57m (15ft 0in)
- **Weight** 6356kg (14,000lb) loaded
- **Armament** none

The first Beech Model 90 King Air was introduced onto the civil market in 1964 as an eight-seat passenger aircraft for the business user. This was later followed by the Super King Air 200 with a 'T'-tail. Versions of the original King Air served with the US military in Vietnam as the U-21, some of which were 'Guardrail' communications intelligence (Comint) aircraft. The first C-12s, military versions of the Beech Super King Air 200, were delivered to the US Army in 1975.

As well as a variety of transport and light cargo versions, the C-12 appeared in many Comint and Elint (electronic intelligence) forms, including the RC-12G, RC-12K, RC-12N, RC-12P and RC-12Q. There were 13 RC-12D Improved Guardrail V aircraft produced for the US Army's Military Intelligence Battalions and based in Germany. These were part of Intelligence and Security Command (INSCOM) and were filled with specialized receivers to listen in on Warsaw Pact communications and those of other potential enemies. The wingtip pods are thought to contain communications jammers, while the large and small wing antennas are for VHF and UHF systems, respectively.

Many of the other Guardrail variants are based in South Korea, and Israel has a small number of aircraft equivalent to the RC-12D. During Desert Shield and Desert Storm, the US Army's 2nd Military Intelligence Battalion (MIB) at Stuttgart, Germany, deployed RC-12Ds, including the example illustrated, to Saudi Arabia, where they intercepted Iraqi transmissions before and during the 1991 conflict.

After the war, the 2nd MIB was deactivated and its aircraft were redistributed to other units. By 1999, the example here was one of six RC-12Ds assigned to the 15th MIB at Robert Gray Army Air Field, Fort Hood, Texas.

BOEING AH-64D LONGBOW APACHE

1st Battalion, 14th Aviation (Training) Brigade, US Army Training and Doctrination Command, US Army Fort Rucker, Alabama, 1996

BOEING AH-64D LONGBOW APACHE

Specification
- **Type** attack helicopter
- **Crew** 2
- **Powerplant** two 1342kW (1800hp) General Electric T700-GE-701C turboshaft engines
- **Performance** max speed 293km/h (182mph); Hovering ceiling in ground effect 4172m (13,690 ft); range 428km (300 miles)
- **Dimensions** main rotor diameter 14.63m (48ft 0in); fuselage length 14.97m (49ft 1.5in); height 4.66m (15ft 3.5in)
- **Weight** 9525kg (21,000lb) loaded
- **Armament** one M230 Chain Gun 30mm (1.18in) cannon with 1200 rounds; 2841kg (6263lb) of ordnance, including unguided rockets and AGM-114 Hellfire missiles

Originally developed by Hughes, the AH-64 Apache has been produced under the McDonnell Douglas and McDonnell Douglas Helicopters banners and is now a Boeing product, following the 1997 merger of the two aerospace giants. The first YAH-64 flew in September 1975 and, after a long evaluation, was selected for production as the AH-64A Apache, which entered US Army service in April 1986.

The Apache offered a significant capability improvement over the AH-1 Cobra with its sophisticated night vision and target acquisition/designation system and laser-guided Hellfire missiles. The helmet-mounted sighting system is linked to the powerful Chain Gun cannon under the nose, allowing the pilot (in the aft seat) or co-pilot/gunner to aim the gun by looking at it. The A model Apache was exported to Israel, Egypt, the UAE, Saudi Arabia and Greece. In the 1991 Gulf War it flew the first missions in the conflict and destroyed large numbers of Iraqi vehicles.

Lessons from the war led to the development of the AH-64D, most but not all of which are fitted with the Longbow millimetre-wave radar in a mast-mounted radome. A new radar-guided version of the Hellfire allows firings from outside a line-of-sight position and identification and selection of targets at much greater ranges than previously. The US Army is to upgrade 500 of its 800-plus AH-64As to Longbow standard.

The first Longbow Apache flew in April 1992. This aircraft, 90-0423. was an AH-64A rebuilt as the fourth of six development AH-64Ds, and first flew as such in October 1993. It was later given the new serial 98-5083 and assigned to the 1st Battalion of the 14th Aviation (Training) Brigade (1/14 AVN) at Fort Rucker. The AH-64D has been exported to the Netherlands, Singapore and the United Kingdom. All of the British Army's will be supplied to the full specification.

BOEING B-52H STRATOFORTRESS

20th Bomb Squadron, 2nd Bomb Wing,
Air Combat Command,
United States Air Force,
Barksdale Air Force Base, Louisiana
1999

BOEING B-52H STRATOFORTRESS

Specification
- **Type** strategic bomber
- **Crew** 5
- **Powerplant** eight 75.62N (17,000lb thrust) Pratt & Whitney TF-33 turbofans
- **Performance** max speed 957 km/h (595 mph); service ceiling 15765m (55,000ft); range over 16,093 km (10,000 miles)
- **Dimensions** wing span 56.39m (185ft 9in); length 49.05m (160ft 11in); height 12.40m (40ft 8in)
- **Weight** 148,325kg (327,000lb) max take-off
- **Armament** up to 20 nuclear or conventional cruise missiles, conventional or nuclear free-fall bombs, AGM-142 Have Nap and AGM-84 Harpoon missiles; total payload about 22,680kg (50,000lb)

The Boeing B-52 was designed to replace the B-47 with an aircraft which had intercontinental range and less need to rely on aerial refuelling. The first example flew in April 1952, and its descendants are still in service more than 50 years later.

The XB-52 and YB-52 prototypes had a tandem cockpit similar to that of the B-47; however, production aircraft reverted to a more conventional flight deck arrangement. The B-52 was in some ways similar to the B-47, but had two more engines and much greater reliance on electronic countermeasures. Most models had quad tail machine guns, but the B-52H had a 20mm (0.79in) cannon, which was deleted in the 1990s. B-52s were used in the conventional bombing role in the Vietnam War against Vietcong concentrations in the south and strategic targets in the north. More than 30 were lost in action. The B-52 next saw action over Iraq and Kuwait in 1991, dropping nearly 30 per cent of the bombs used in operation Desert Storm.

This B-52H was ordered in 1960 and was built by Boeing's plant in Wichita, Kansas. It has gone through many updates and configuration changes over the years, not least becoming a cruise missile carrier, able to fire the AGM-86 ALCM as seen here. A conventional weapons upgrade saw the addition of such munitions as the JDAM satellite-guided bomb, the JSOW stand-off weapon and the AGM-142 Have Nap missile.

The Mad Bolshevik fired 20 cruise missiles and made 10 conventional bombing raids over Kosovo in 1999 and saw more action in Afghanistan and Iraq. It is currently one of 94 active B-52 remaining in the US inventory.

BOEING KC-135E STRATOTANKER

314th Air Refueling Squadron,
940th Air Refueling Wing, US Air Force
Reserve, McClellan Air Force Base,
California, 1993

BOEING KC-135E STRATOTANKER

Specification
- **Type** air refuelling tanker
- **Crew** 4
- **Powerplant** four 320.3kN (72,000lb thrust) Pratt & Whitney TF-33-PW-102 turbofan engines
- **Performance** max speed 850km/h (530mph); service ceiling 15,240m (50,000ft); range 2400km (1500 miles)
- **Dimensions** wing span 39.88m (130ft 10in); length 41.53m (136ft 3in); height 12.7m (41ft 8in)
- **Weight** 146,285kg (322,500lb) loaded
- **Payload** up to 37,650kg (83,000lb) fuel and/or freight

Derived from Boeing's 367-80 demonstrator of 1954, the KC-135 Stratotanker has become one of the longest-served aircraft in US Air Force (USAF) history. The massive build-up of US strategic jet bomber forces in the 1950s required an equally large number of tankers able to support the legions of B-47s and B-52s, and their constant airborne alert posture. The initial production version, the KC-135A, entered service with Strategic Air Command (SAC) in 1957. In 1965, the last of 732 was handed over. Many specialized intelligence, command post and other versions have followed, but the basic tankers have provided sterling service in every conflict from Vietnam to the 2003 Iraq war; about 500 remain in service.

The 940th Air Refueling Group was the 940th Tactical Airlift Group until 1977, when it moved to Mather Air Force Base, California, and acquired KC-135A tankers. By the end of 1986, all its aircraft had been converted into KC-135Es, their original J57 turbojet engines replaced by the more efficient TF33 turbofan. It was the first reserve unit to deploy to Saudi Arabia following the Iraqi invasion of Kuwait in 1990. In 1993 it moved to temporary facilities at McClellan Air Force Base and in 1994 was redesignated the 940th Air Refueling Wing. In 1998 it moved to a new permanent home at Beale Air Force Base and a year later was active during Operation Allied Force over the former Yugoslavia, being praised as the most productive tanker unit of the Kosovo war. Between October 2001 and April 2002, its KC-135s had their 1950s-era instrumentation replaced by a new 'glass' cockpit with electronic displays and the cockpit crew reduced to three.

Stratotanker 58-0001, depicted here refuelling an RF-4C Phantom reconnaissance aircraft, was built as a KC-135A and later converted to E standard. Assigned to the 904th for many years, it supported operations over the former Yugoslavia in 1999.

BRITISH AEROSPACE HAWK T.1A

No. 92 (Reserve) Squadron, No. 7 Flying Training School, Royal Air Force, RAF Chivenor, Devon, 1994

BRITISH AEROSPACE HAWK T.1A

Specification
- **Type** advanced jet trainer
- **Crew** 2
- **Powerplant** one 23.13kN (5200lb thrust) Rolls-Royce/Turboméca Adour Mk 1151-01turbofan engine
- **Performance** max speed 1040km/h (646mph); service ceiling 15,240m (50,000ft); range 2400km (1491 miles)
- **Dimensions** wing span 9.39m (30ft 10in); length 11.85m (38ft 11in); height 4.00m (13ft 1in)
- **Weight** 8340kg (18,390lb) loaded
- **Armament** one 30mm (1.18in) ADEN Mk. 4 cannon with 120 rounds in underfuselage pod; two AIM-9 Sidewinders or bombs or rockets up to 680kg (1580lb)

The first British Aerospace (originally Hawker Siddeley) Hawk flew in August 1974, the culmination of a lengthy process to create a subsonic aircraft to replace the Gnat, Hunter T.7 and some two-seat Jaguars for advanced and weapons training. In various versions, the Hawk has been a great export success, selling to Abu Dhabi, Australia, Canada, Dubai, Finland, Indonesia, Kenya, Kuwait, Saudi Arabia, South Africa, South Korea, Switzerland and Zimbabwe.

XX157 was the third Hawk built and, after evaluation, was delivered to the Royal Air Force (RAF) in December 1979. It was one of 88 updated to T.1A standard between 1983 and 1986. The modifications saw the wing pylons wired for Sidewinder air-to-air missiles, allowing the Hawk to undertake an emergency point defence role to supplement the Phantom and Tornado F.3. Even the Hawks used by the Red Arrows have this wartime capability.

No. 92 Squadron formed in 1917, with mostly Canadian personnel. It saw heavy action in both world wars and was the top-scoring RAF squadron in the Battle of Britain. In 1941, it moved to the Mediterranean and fought in Malta, Sicily and Italy. From 1947 to 1968, No. 92 was a home-based fighter squadron, flying Meteors, Sabres, Hunters and Lightnings in turn. In 1968, it moved to Wildenrath, Germany, and re-equipped with Phantoms in 1977, before disbanding in 1991. On 23 September 1992, 151 (Reserve) Squadron of 7 Flying Training School (No. 7FTS) at Chivenor, Devon, was renumbered No. 92 (Reserve) Squadron. This 'shadow identity' system allowed continuity of famous squadron 'numberplates'. In 1994, No. 7FTS was disbanded, Chivenor was closed and No. 92 Squadron once again went into limbo. With its distinguished history, it is a strong candidate for re-forming as a Eurofighter Typhoon unit in the next few years.

DASSAULT MIRAGE 50CN PANTERA

Grupo 4, IV Brigada Aérea,
Fuerza Aérea de Chile,
Punta Arenas, Chile
1990s

DASSAULT MIRAGE 50CN PANTERA

Specification
- **Type** single-seat fighter
- **Crew** 1
- **Powerplant** one 70.60kN (15,873lb thrust) Snecma Atar 9K-50 turbojet engine
- **Performance** max speed 2338km/h (1453mph); service ceiling 18,000m (59,055ft); range over 2630km (1635 miles)
- **Dimensions** wing span 8.22m (16ft 11.5in); length 15.56m (51ft 0.5in); height 4.50m (14ft 9in)
- **Weight** 14,700kg (32,407lb) loaded
- **Armament** two 30mm (1.18in) DEFA 534 cannon with 125 rounds each; up to 4000kg (8818lb) of weapons including bombs, rockets or Matra Magic air-to-air missiles

The Mirage 50 has its origins in the Mirage IIIC fighter, which entered French service in 1961. The multi-role Mirage IIIE led to the Mirage 5, which was essentially a ground-attack version intended for Israel. France embargoed their sale in 1967 after the Six-Day War and used the initial Mirage 5F in its own air force. It had a longer and slimmer nose than the Mirage III, and this contained an ESD Aida ranging radar.

The Mirage 50 first flew in April 1979 and introduced the Mirage F1's Atar 9K-50 engine, endowing better airfield performance, faster acceleration, a larger weapon load and improved manoeuvrability. Sixteen new examples were acquired by the Fuerza Aérea de Chile between 1979 and 1983, Chile becoming the first customer for the Mirage 50C.

These are not to be confused with the 24 ex-Belgian Mirage 5s delivered in the 1990s and upgraded as the 'Elkan'. The Elkans are operated by Grupo 8 of IV Brigada Aérea at Cerro Moreno in the north, while the Mirage 50s are based in the far south at Punta Arenas, having moved there from Santiago in 1986. Local aerospace company ENAER has been upgrading the Mirage 50s as the 'Pantera' (panther) since the mid-1980s, with FACh 514 being the first prototype.

With the help of Israel Aircraft Industries, ENAER has rebuilt the Mirage 50s with all-new avionics, including an Elta radar and a wide-angle head up display (HUD). Canard foreplanes as fitted on the Kfir have been added to improve turning ability, load carrying and take-off/landing performance. The first group of upgraded aircraft entered service in 1993, but upgrading has been at a very slow pace due to budgetary and technical difficulties.

DASSAULT MIRAGE 2000H VAJRA

No. 1 Squadron, Central Air Command, Bharatiya Vayu Sena, Maharajpura Air Force Base, Gwailor, India
1990s

DASSAULT MIRAGE 2000H VAJRA

Specification
- **Type** single-seat interceptor fighter
- **Crew** 1
- **Powerplant** one 64.3kN (14,462lb thrust) SNECMA M53-P2 turbofan engine
- **Performance** max speed 2338km/h (1453mph); service ceiling 18,000m (59,055ft); range 1850km (1150 miles)
- **Dimensions** wing span 9.13m (28ft 11.5in); length 14.36m (47ft 1.25in); height 5.20m (17ft 0.75in)
- **Weight** 17,000kg (37,478lb) loaded
- **Armament** two DEFA 534 30mm (1.18in) cannon with 125 rounds each; weapons load of up to 6300kg (13,890kg), including Matra Magic 2 and Super 530F air-to-air missiles, conventional or laser-guided bombs or AS30L laser-guided missiles

The Mirage 2000 has been France's most important combat aircraft since the 1980s, with 136 of the original 2000C fighter variant delivered to the *Armée de l'Air*, plus 32 2000B trainers and 194 2000D and N two-seat strike aircraft. It will be many years before its replacement by the Rafale is complete. As with previous Dassault fighters, the Mirage '*deux mille*' has had considerable export success, being sold to Abu Dhabi, Egypt, Greece, Peru, Qatar, Taiwan and India.

India was the first foreign customer for the Mirage 2000, taking 42 2000H and seven 2000TH models. These were delivered between 1985 and 1988 to No. 1 and No. 7 Squadrons, both based at Gwailor near Agra. There was a plan for Hindustan Aeronautics (HAL) to build a further 110, but this was abandoned when MiG-29s became available from the Soviet Union. An attrition replacement batch of four single-seat and six two-seat Mirages was ordered in 2000.

In service with the *Bharatiya Vayu Sena* (Indian Air Force), the Mirage 2000 is known as the 'Vajra', which is the invincible thunderbolt of the god Indra. No. 1 'Tigers' Squadron is mainly an air defence squadron, but is also tasked with ground-attack missions such as airfield denial with Durandal runway-cratering bombs and defence suppression with the ARMAT anti-radar missile.

Most of the Indian aircraft are believed to have the basic Thompson-CSF RDM radar of most export Mirage 2000s; however, use of the Matra Super 530D semi-active radar-guided air-to-air missile (shown here) suggests the higher specification RDI radar is fitted to some. For short-range engagements, the Super 530D is partnered by the Magic 2 infrared guided air-to-air missile.

DOUGLAS C-47 SKYTRAIN

*Comando Aéreo de Transporte Militar,
Fuerza Aérea Colombiana, Colombia,
1990s*

DOUGLAS C-47 SKYTRAIN

Specification
- **Type** twin-engined transport aircraft
- **Crew** three plus up to 28 fully equipped troops
- **Powerplant** two 895kW (1200hp) Pratt & Whitney R-1830-92 Twin Wasp radial engines
- **Performance** max speed 370km/h (230mph); service ceiling 7315m (24,000ft); range 2340km (1510 miles)
- **Dimensions** wing span 28.96m (95ft 0in); length 19.66m (64ft 6in); height 5.16m (16ft 11.5in)
- **Weight** 12,701kg (28,000lb) loaded

The immortal C-47 first flew as the Douglas DST in December 1935 and, as the DC-3, was the most numerous airliner in US commercial service before World War II. From 1938, the US military took the first of many thousands of DC-3s with many different designations. The C-47 Skytrain was the main military transport version, which entered service in 1942. During and after the war, almost every Western air force acquired C-47s (often known by the British name Dakota), and a small number remain in service today, mainly in Africa and South America. The C-47 has had a new lease of life in recent years with the Basler Company at Oshkosh converting many to BT-67 Turbo Dakotas with PT6A-67R turboprops, lengthened fuselages and new instrumentation. Following the example of the AC-47 'Spooky' in Vietnam, several nations have converted some of their basic transports to gunships, with three 7.62mm (.30in) miniguns firing through the port-side windows.

C-47s have served with the Fuerza Aérea Colombiana since 1949, and over 60 have been used at one time or another. As well as delivering freight and personnel to remote army bases, the C-47 was the main platform for dropping paratroopers and other special forces fighting guerrillas in Colombia's long-running internal conflict. This aircraft was built at Douglas's Oklahoma City plant in 1944 and delivered to the US Army Air Forces (USAAF) as 44-76916. After many years as a standard transport, FAC 681 was converted to BT-67 configuration circa 1987, then equipped as a gunship. It received the new serial FAC 1681.

The transport C-47s have now been replaced with more modern types in the Fuerza Aérea Colombiana – although they are still used by the police service. The remaining gunships are concentrated with Escuadrón Aerotáctico 214 at Palanquero (Puerto Salgar).

GENERAL DYNAMICS F-111F

*492nd Tactical Fighter Squadron,
48th Tactical Fighter Wing, USAFE,
RAF Lakenheath, Suffolk
early 1990s*

GENERAL DYNAMICS F-111F

Specification
- **Type** variable-geometry tactical bomber
- **Crew** 2
- **Powerplant** two 116kN (25,100lb thrust) Pratt & Whitney TF30-P100 afterburning turbofan engines
- **Performance** max speed 2338km/h (1453mph); service ceiling 17,267m (56,650ft); range 5848km (3634 miles)
- **Dimensions** wing span (spread) 19.20m (63ft); length 22.4m (73ft 6in); height 5.18m (17ft)
- **Weight** 44,884kg (98,950lb) loaded
- **Armament** up to 11,600kg (25,000lb)

The early career of the F-111 was hugely controversial due to its protracted development and the failure of the F-111B version, which was intended for the US Navy's fleet defence role. The F-111A of the US Air Force (USAF) first flew in December 1964 and made its combat debut in Vietnam in 1968. The initial deployment was notable for its 50 per cent loss rate, but the F-111, nicknamed the 'Aardvark', soon proved the most effective long-range strike platform, using its terrain-following radar to navigate to and attack important targets at night and in bad weather.

The F-111 had no internal bomb bay, but could carry a very wide range of conventional and nuclear ordnance, including almost all the precision-guided weapons in the US inventory. The F-111F differed from the F-111E in having the Pave Tack installation. This large underfuselage pod allowed the aircraft to designate the target for its own laser-guided bombs (LGBs). In the 1991 Gulf War, the F-111F proved a far more effective tank buster than the F-16, destroying over ten times as many Iraqi vehicles, mainly by night using LGBs.

Wearing the markings of the commander of the 48th Tactical Fighter Wing (TFW), F-111F 72-1451 was one of 14 aircraft assigned to the 492nd Tactical Fighter Squadron (TFS) during Operation Desert Storm, as part of the 48th TFW(Provisional), which supplied 47 F-111Fs to the war effort. The 20th TFW, normally based at Upper Heyford in Oxfordshire, also deployed its F-111Es and electronic warfare EF-111A 'Spark Varks' to Turkey.

The USAF retired its F-111s in 1996 and EF-111As in 1998, leaving Australia the only user of the Aardvark, or 'Earth Pig', as Royal Australian Air Force (RAAF) crews call it.

GENERAL DYNAMICS F-111F

524th Fighter Squadron, 27th Fighter Wing, Air Combat Command, United States Air Force, Cannon Air Force Base, New Mexico, 1993

GENERAL DYNAMICS F-111F

Specification
- **Type** variable-geometry tactical bomber
- **Crew** 2
- **Powerplant** two 116kN (25,100lb thrust) Pratt & Whitney TF30-P100 afterburning turbofan engines
- **Performance** max speed 2338km/h (1453mph); service ceiling 17,267m (56,650ft); range 5848km (3634 miles)
- **Dimensions** wing span (spread) 19.20 m (63ft); length 22.4m (73ft 6in); height 5.18m (17ft)
- **Weight** 44,884kg (98,950lb) loaded
- **Armament** up to 11,600kg (25,000lb)

The 'CC' tailcode identifies this F-111F as based at Cannon Air Force Base, the main stateside home for 'Aardvarks' from 1969 until 1998. The 27th Tactical Fighter Wing (TFW) consisted of the 522nd, 523rd and 524th Tactical Fighter Squadrons (TFSs), and (from 1990) the 428th Tactical Fighter Training Squadron. The 'Tactical' prefix to wing and squadron designations was dropped soon after Tactical Air Command became Air Combat Command in 1991.

At this time, the remaining strategic nuclear FB-111s in Strategic Air Command were reworked to F-111G status and served briefly with the 27th Fighter Wing (FW) alongside the F-111F and the EF-111A, which was to be the last version in US service.

F-111F 70-2396 was assigned to the 492nd TFS, 48th TFW, at Lakenheath, England, in the mid-1980s and was launched as part of Operation El Dorado Canyon, the raid on Libya in April 1986. It was assigned to the second of four groups destined for the Al Azziziyah Barracks in Tripoli, but two of four aircraft suffered technical problems and all aborted the mission. In 1990, three of the wing's squadrons were deployed to Taif, Saudi Arabia, and took part in the Desert Storm campaign in early 1991. This aircraft then belonged to the 493rd TFS, which was the only squadron able to drop the GBU-15 imaging infrared guided bomb, and 71 of these 908kg (2000lb) weapons were expended during the war. No F-111Fs were lost in combat, although one 493rd TFS aircraft crashed before the war.

When the F-111s were replaced in Europe by F-15Es in 1992, 70-2396 was reassigned to the 27th FW at Cannon; in January 1996 was placed in desert storage. At the same time as the F-111 was retired, the US Air Force (USAF) finally made Aardvark the type's official name.

GRUMMAN A-6E INTRUDER

Attack Squadron 75, 'Sunday Punchers',
Carrier Air Wing 3, US Navy,
USS John F. Kennedy, 1991

The Intruder made its combat debut in Vietnam, but reached maturity with the A-6E model during the 1970s, having a new terrain avoidance radar and other improved electronics. It entered service too late, however, to be involved in Southeast Asia. By the time of its last conflict in 1991, it was a much more capable aircraft, able to carry a wide range of precision ordnance, as well as 'dumb' munitions such as the cluster bomb dispensers illustrated here on A-6E Bureau No. 162192 of Attack Squadron 75 (VA-75), the 'Sunday Punchers'.

VA-75 was the first fleet unit to receive the Intruder, using them in action in Vietnam and Lebanon, and against Iraq. Carrier Air Wing 3 (CVW-3) deployed on the USS *John F. Kennedy* two weeks after the Iraqi invasion of Kuwait in August 1990 and did not return to the United States until the end of March 1991, having participated in operations Desert Shield and Desert Storm. The Intruders of VA-75 flew nearly 300 combat sorties, with No, 162192 flying 25 of that total.

During the war, 10 Navy squadrons aboard six carriers flew Intruders, as did two land-based US Marine Corps squadrons. Four Intruders were lost to enemy action during the war, although none of them was from VA-75. The mission was long-range strike by day and night, suppression of enemy air defences and anti-ship strike. The Intruder was expected to carry on into the twenty-first century, but the improved A-6F was cancelled after prototypes had been flown and the last two A-6E squadrons were retired in 1997.

This Grumman A-6E was last reported as being stored at the depot at Norfolk, Virginia. It may be destined for dumping at 'Intruder Reef' off the coast of Florida, where a number of surplus A-6s have been placed to create an artificial reef to promote marine life.

GRUMMAN A-6E INTRUDER

Specification
- **Type** all-weather carrier-based attack bomber
- **Crew** 2
- **Powerplant** two Pratt & Whitney J52-P-8B turbojets rated at 41.4 kN (9300lb thrust)
- **Performance** max speed 1297 km/h (806mph); service ceiling 12,925m (42,200ft); range (fully loaded) 1627 km (1011 miles)
- **Dimensions** wing span 16.15m (53ft); length 16.69m (54ft 9in); height 4.93m (16ft 2in)
- **Weight** 27,397kg (60,400lb) loaded
- **Armament** up to 8165kg (18,000lb) of conventional or precision bombs, guided missiles including AGM-62 Walleye, AGM-84 Harpoon, AGM-88 HARM and AGM-123 Skipper

GRUMMAN F-14A TOMCAT

Fighter Squadron 111 'Sundowners',
Carrier Air Wing 15, US Navy,
NAS Miramar, 1990s

GRUMMAN F-14A TOMCAT

Specification
- **Type** carrier-based interceptor fighter
- **Crew** 2
- **Powerplant** two 96.78kN (21,750lb thrust) Pratt & Whitney TF30-P-414A afterburning turbofan engines
- **Performance** max speed 2485km/h (1544mph); service ceiling over 15,240m (50,000ft); ferry range 3800km (2360 miles)
- **Dimensions** wing span 19.54m (64ft 1.5in); length 19.10m (62ft 8in); height 4.88m (16ft 0in)
- **Weight** 33,724kg (74,349lb) loaded
- **Armament** one M61 Vulcan 20mm (0.79in) cannon; maximum ordnance of 6577kg (14,500 lb), including two AIM-9, four AIM-7 Sparrow and four AIM-54 Phoenix air-to-air missiles

Although often regarded as the ultimate 'superfighter', the F-14 Tomcat is nearing the end of its career with the US Navy. Many famous squadrons were disbanded in the 1990s, and others have since made the transition to the F/A-18F Super Hornet for the fleet defence role. Despite various avionics upgrades, the F-14 retains the AIM-7 Sparrow for medium-range hitting power, unlike most other US fighters which now employ the longer-range AIM-120 AMRAAM. The Tomcat's combination of cannon, Sidewinder, Sparrow and Phoenix missiles is thought adequate to cover threats at all ranges.

Fighter Squadron 111 (VF-111) was redesignated from VA-154 in 1959 and subsequently flew the F-11F Tiger, F-8 Crusader and F-4 Phantom, scoring several kills with the latter two types in Vietnam. The squadron became famous in those colourful days of US naval aviation for its red and white shark's mouth on the nose and sunburst on the rudder or tail fin. In 1978, the squadron made the transition from the F-4J to the F-14A, and took its Tomcats to sea aboard the USS *Kitty Hawk* in May 1979.

Remaining as part of Carrier Air Wing 15 (CVW-15), the squadron flew from the Pacific Fleet carriers *Kitty Hawk* and *Carl Vinson* for the following 16 years. When not on cruise, the squadron was based at Naval Air Station Miramar near San Diego. During the 'Sundowners' Tomcat period, the US Navy toned down its colour schemes and markings to reduce visual and infrared detection ranges. All colour disappeared and the famous shark's mouth and sunburst became all but invisible on VF-111's aircraft, although small areas of colour occasionally reappeared on the commanding officer's F-14. VF-111 was the victim of post–Cold War cutbacks and disbanded in 1995.

GRUMMAN F-14A+ TOMCAT

*Fighter Squadron 103 'Sluggers',
Carrier Air Wing 17 (CVW-17),
United States Navy, USS* Saratoga, *1991*

GRUMMAN F-14A+ TOMCAT

Specification
- **Type** carrier-based interceptor fighter
- **Crew** 2
- **Powerplant** two Electric F110-GE-400 turbofans rated at 62.27kN (14,000lb thrust) dry and 102.75kN (23,100lb thrust) in afterburner
- **Performance** max speed 1997km/h (1241mph); service ceiling over 16,150m (53,000ft); range 2965km (1842 miles)
- **Dimensions** wing span 19.54m (64ft 1.5in); length 19.10m (62ft 8n); height 4.88m (16ft)
- **Weight** 33,724kg (74,349lb) loaded
- **Armament** one M61 Vulcan 20mm (0.79in) cannon; maximum ordnance of 6577kg (14,500lb), including two AIM-9, four AIM-7 Sparrow and four AIM-54 Phoenix air-to-air missiles

Designed as a successor to the F-4 Phantom in the fleet air defence role, the Grumman F-14A Tomcat was conceived to engage and destroy targets at extreme range using the AWG-9 fire control system and AIM-54 Phoenix missiles. It remains the US Navy's standard carrier-based interceptor. The first development aircraft flew December 1970. Deliveries to the US Navy began in October 1972, with the first operational cruise in 1974. F-14s covered the evacuation of Saigon in 1975, but saw no combat at this time.

Problems with the F-14A's TF-30 turbofan were a key factor in the development of re-engined and upgraded Tomcat variants. Two re-engined variants with the GE F110 were proposed: the F-14A+ was to be an interim type, while the F-14D would introduce improved digital avionics. Subsequently, the F-14A+ was redesignated as the F-14B, of which there were 38 new-build examples and 32 rebuilt F-14As. The F-14A+/F-14B incorporated some avionics changes, including a modernized fire control system, new radios, upgraded radar warning syestem, and various cockpit changes.

The F-14A+ seen here was one of those converted from an F-14A, and it was assigned to Fighter Squadron 103 (VF-103) aboard USS *Saratoga* during the first US–Iraq Gulf War. On 21 January 1991, it was shot down by an SA-2 surface-to-air missile while on combat air patrol near Al Asad air base, Iraq. Its pilot, Lieutenant Devon Jones, was rescued by a US Air Force (USAF) helicopter, but the radar intercept officer (RIO), Lieutenant Ralph 'Rat' Slade, was captured by Iraqi forces. He was released at the end of hostilities. When Fighter Squadron 84 (VF-84), the famous 'Jolly Rogers' squadron, was disbanded in the mid-1990s, VF-103 adopted its identity and insignia. It remains operational with the Tomcat.

HANDLEY PAGE VICTOR K.MK 2

No. 55 Squadron, Strike Command, Royal Air Force, RAF Marham 1993

HANDLEY PAGE VICTOR K.MK 2

Specification
- **Type** air refuelling tanker
- **Crew** 5
- **Powerplant** four 80kN (17,250lb thrust) Rolls-Royce Conway 103 turbojets
- **Performance** max speed 1009km/h (627mph); service ceiling 18,288m (60,000ft); range 9656 km (6000 miles)
- **Dimensions** wing span 36.58m (120ft); length 35.02m (114ft 11in); height 8.15m (26ft 9in)
- **Weight** 92,988kg (205,000lb) max take-off
- **Payload** 55,780kg (123,000lb) of fuel

The Handley-Page Victor was the last of the V-bombers to fly in Royal Air Force (RAF) service, in December 1952, and the longest serving, from 1958–93. The initial Victor B.1 had Sapphire engines and primary armament of one Yellow Sun nuclear weapon. The engines were buried inside the 'crescent' wing, which was aerodynamically very sophisticated for its day. The B.2 had longer wings and Conway engines, and was designed for high-altitude bombing. In all, 86 Victors were built. When the Valiant was withdrawn in 1965 and B.2 numbers increased, many of the B.1s were converted to K.1 tankers. In turn, the Victor was withdrawn from bombing duties and converted to the K.2, as the Vulcan became the sole V-bomber in RAF service.

Originally 29 Mk 2 Victors were earmarked for conversion to K.2 standard, but only 24 were completed, all by Hawker Siddeley, which took over the programme when Handley Page went into receivership in 1970. The K.2 had two hose drum units (HDUs) on the wings and a centreline refuelling point. The centreline station was best for refuelling large aircraft, as it had a higher rate of flow, able to dispense 1814kg (4000lb) of fuel per minute.

Victor XL188, built as a B.Mk 2, was later converted to B.2R reconnaissance standard and finally became a K.2 tanker. During the 1982 Falklands War, it was used to refuel the Vulcan bombers which attacked Port Stanley Airfield as well as Victors operating in the maritime radar reconnaissance role. Eleven Victors were needed to support one Vulcan, some of them refuelling the bomber and some topping others up so they could reach and return from the farthest refuelling points. No. 55 Squadron operated the Victor tanker from 1975–93, when the Victor was retired from RAF service. XL188 was scrapped at Kinloss in 1997.

LOCKHEED C-130K HERCULES C.MK.1P

Lyneham Hercules Wing, Royal Air Force, RAF Lyneham, Wiltshire, 1990

LOCKHEED C-130K HERCULES C.MK.1P

Specification
- **Type** transport aircraft
- **Crew** 4
- **Powerplant** four 3017kW (4050hp) Allison T56-A-7 turboprop engines
- **Performance** max speed 547km/h (340mph); service ceiling 10,060m (33,000ft); range 6145km (3820 miles)
- **Dimensions** wing span 40.41m (132ft 7in); length 29.79m (97ft 9in); height 11.68m (38ft 4in)
- **Weight** 70,308kg (155,000lb) loaded
- **Payload** 19,051kg (42,000lb)

The Royal Air Force (RAF) took delivery of 66 C-130Ks Hercules C.Mk.1s, beginning in December 1966. These aircraft equipped four squadrons of what was then RAF Transport Command Nos 24 and 36 at Lyneham and Nos 30, and 47 Squadrons at Fairford. These squadrons were followed by No. 48 Squadron, deployed to Changi, Singapore, in October 1968, and No. 70 Squadron, which equipped in Cyprus in 1970. In 1971, all four UK-based Hercules squadrons were concentrated on Lyneham, where they were joined later by the two overseas-based squadrons.

RAF Lyneham is currently home to the entire RAF Hercules force, comprising four squadrons and the Operational Conversion Unit, which now bears the number plate of No. 57 (Reserve) Squadron. The Hercules fleet comprises 44 aircraft. One flight, No. 1312, is based on Port Stanley in the Falkland Islands. Thirty of the original Hercules were converted to C.Mk.3 (C-130H-30) standard between 1980 and 1985. All of the C.Mk.3s are also modified with inflight refuelling probes, as were 25 C.Mk.1s.

In 1995, the RAF placed an order for 25 C-130Js, as replacements for some of the current fleet of Hercules C1s and C3s. A total of 15 of the stretched version, the C-130J-30, and 10 standard C-130Js were ordered. These aircraft are known as the Hercules C.4 and C.5 in RAF service. The first new C-130J-30 was delivered on 24 August 1998 and the last on 21 June 2001. No. 24 Squadron was the first to become operational with the new variant.

The Hercules C.Mk.1P of the Lyneham Hercules Wing pictured here is fitted with ESM (Electronic Surveillance Measures) wingtip pods to detect, analyse and locate hostile radio and radar signals.

LOCKHEED MARTIN F-16C FIGHTING FALCON

52nd Tactical Fighter Wing, USAFE, Spangdahlem Air Base, Germany 1990s

The F-16 Fighting Falcon, originally designed by General Dynamics and now produced by Lockheed Martin, is the world's most prolific combat aircraft, with more than 2000 in service with the United States Air Force (USAF) and a further 2000 in service with 19 other air forces around the world.

The F-16 had its origin in a USAF requirement of 1972 for a lightweight fighter and first flew on 2 February 1974. It carries an advanced GEC-Marconi HUDWACS (HUD and Weapon Aiming Computer System) in which target designation cues, as well as flight symbols, are shown on the head-up display. The HUDWAC computer is used to direct the weapons to the target, as designated on the HUD. There are five ground-attack modes and four air-combat modes. The F-16's underwing hardpoints are stressed for manoeuvres up to 9g, enabling the aircraft to dogfight while still carrying weaponry.

The F-16B and F-16D are two-seat versions, while the F-16C, delivered from 1988, featured numerous improvements in avionics and was available with a choice of engine. F-16s have seen action in the Lebanon (with the Israeli Air Force), in the Gulf Wars and in the Balkans. The type has been upgraded constantly to extend its life well into the twenty-first century.

The F-16C shown here was the personal aircraft of Brigadier-General Glenn A. Proffitt II, Officer Commanding the 52nd Tactical Fighter Wing (TFW), which took over the 'Wild Weasel' defence suppression role following the retirement of the F-4G Phantom in the 1990s.

LOCKHEED MARTIN F-16C FIGHTING FALCON

Specification
- **Type** air superiority, strike, and defence suppression aircraft
- **Crew** 1
- **Powerplant** either one 10,800kg (23,770lb) thrust Pratt & Whitney F100-PW-200 or one 13,150kg (28,984lb) thrust General Electric F110-GE-100 turbofan
- **Performance** max speed 2142km/h (1320mph); service ceiling 15,240m (50,000ft); combat radius 925km (525 miles)
- **Dimensions** wing span 9.45m (31ft); length 15.09m (49ft 6in); height 5.09m (16ft 8in)
- **Weight** 16,057kg (35,400lb) loaded
- **Armament** one General Electric M61A1 multi-barrelled cannon; seven external hardpoints for up to 9276kg (20,450lb) of ordnance

LOCKHEED MARTIN YF-22 RAPTOR

United States Air Force
Edwards AFB, 1990

LOCKHEED MARTIN F-22 RAPTOR

Specification
- **Type** advanced tactical fighter
- **Crew** 1
- **Powerplant** two 15,872kg (35,000lb) thrust Pratt & Whitney F119-P-100 turbofans
- **Performance** max speed 2335km/h (1450mph); service ceiling 19,812m (65,000ft); combat radius 1285km (800 miles)
- **Dimensions** wing span 13.1m (43ft); length 19.55m (64ft 2in); height 5.39m (17ft 8in)
- **Weight** 27,216kg (60,000lb) loaded
- **Armament** AIM-9X and AMRAAM air-to-air missiles; GBU-32 Joint Direct Attack Munition and other advanced weapons

The Lockheed proposal was selected, and the first definitive F-22 flew on 7 September 1997. The second prototype first flew on 29 June 1998. By late 2001, there were eight F-22s flying.

The F-22 combines many stealth features. Its air-to-air weapons, for example, are stored internally; three internal bays house advanced short-range, medium-range and beyond-visual-range air-to-air missiles. Following an assessment of the aircraft's combat role in 1993, it was decided to add a ground-attack capability, and the internal weapons bay can also accommodate 454kg (1000lb) GBU-32 precision guided missiles.

The F-22 is designed for a high sortie rate, with a turnaround time of less than 20 minutes, and its avionics are highly integrated to provide rapid reaction in air combat, much of its survivability depending on the pilot's ability to locate a target very early and kill it with a first shot. The F-22 was designed to meet a specific threat, which at that time was presented by large numbers of highly agile Soviet combat aircraft, its task being to engage them in their own airspace with beyond-visual-range weaponry. It will be a key component in the Global Strike Task Force, formed in 2001 to counter any threat worldwide. The United States Air Force (USAF) requirement is for 438 aircraft.

In September 1983, the USAF awarded Advanced Tactical Fighter (ATF) concept definition study contracts to six American aerospace companies. Of these, two – Lockheed and Northrop – were selected to build demonstrator prototypes of their respective proposals. Each produced two prototypes, the Lockheed YF-22, one of which is seen here, and the Northrop YF-23.

LOCKHEED F-117A NIGHTHAWK

49th Fighter Wing, United States Air Force, Holloman Air Force Base, New Mexico, 1992

LOCKHEED F-117A NIGHTHAWK

Specification
- **Type** fighter-bomber
- **Crew** 1
- **Powerplant** two 4899kg (10,800lb) thrust General Electric F404-GE-F1D2 turbofan engines
- **Performance** max speed Mach 0.92; service ceiling classified; range classified
- **Dimensions** wing span 13.20m (43ft 4in); length 20.08m (65ft 11in); height 3.78m (12ft 5in)
- **Weight** 23,814kg (52,500lb) loaded
- **Armament** provision for 2268kg (5000lb) of stores on rotary dispenser in weapons bay, including the AGM-88 HARM anti-radiation missile, AGM-65 Maverick air-to-surface missile, GBU-19 and GBU-27 optronically guided bomb, BLU-109 laser-guided bombs, and B61 free-fall nuclear bomb

The amazing F-117A 'Stealth' aircraft began life in 1973 as a project called 'Have Blue', launched to study the feasibility of producing a combat aircraft with little or no radar and infrared signature. Two Experimental Stealth Tactical (XST) 'Have Blue' research aircraft were built and flown in 1977 at Groom Lake, Nevada (Area 51). The evaluation of the two Have Blue aircraft led to an order for 65 production F-117As. Five of these were used for evaluation, and one crashed before delivery. The type made its first flight in June 1981 and entered service in October 1983.

F-117As of the 37th Tactical Fighter Wing played a prominent part in the 1991 Gulf War, making first strikes on high-priority targets; since then, they have been used in the Balkans and Afghanistan. The last of 59 F-117As was delivered in July 1990. The F-117's primary role is to attack high-value command, control and communications targets. Such targets include leadership bunkers, command posts and air defence and communications centres.

The 49th Fighter Wing has a long and distinguished record. Activated on 18 August 1948 at Misawa, Japan, with F-51 Mustangs and F-80 Shooting Stars, it rearmed with F-84 Thunderjets, with which it carried out many notable ground-attack missions during the Korean War. Armed successively with the F-86 Sabre, F-100 Super Sabre, F-105 Thunderchief and F-4 Phantom, it saw combat in Vietnam in 1972. It used F-15A Eagles from 1977–92, when it rearmed with the F-117A.

LOCKHEED U-2R

*99th Strategic Reconnaissance Squadron,
100th Strategic Reconnaissance Wing,
Beale AFB, California, 1990s*

LOCKHEED U-2R

Specification
- **Type** high-altitude reconnaissance and surveillance aircraft
- **Crew** 1
- **Powerplant** one 7711kg (17,000lb) thrust Pratt & Whitney J75 P-13B turbojet (U-2R)
- **Performance** max speed 796km/h (495mph); service ceiling 27,430m (90,000ft); range 4183km (2600 miles)
- **Dimensions** wing span 31.39m (103ft); length 19.13m (62ft 9in); height 4.88m (16ft)
- **Weight** 18,733kg (41,300lb) loaded
- **Armament** none

One of the most controversial and politically explosive aircraft of all time, the Lockheed U-2 high-altitude reconnaissance aircraft made its first flight in August 1955, with an order for 52 production aircraft following quickly. Overflights of the Soviet Union and Warsaw Pact territories began in 1956 and continued until 1 May 1960, when a Central Intelligence Agency pilot, Francis G. Powers, was shot down near Sverdlovsk by a Soviet SA-2 missile battery.

U-2s were used to overfly Cuba during the missile crisis of 1962, one being shot down, and the type was also used by the Chinese Nationalists to overfly mainland China, all four aircraft being subsequently lost. U-2s also operated over North Vietnam in 1965–66.

The last U-2 variant was the U-2R, but in 1978 the production line was reopened for the building of 29 TR-1A battlefield surveillance aircraft, developed from the U-2R. All TR-1As were re-designated U-2R in the 1990s.

The U-2's cockpit featured a manually operated canopy that hinged to one side in the same way as the F-104's, and there was no ejection seat. The U-2 pilot worked in a unique environment. An unusual feature was the food heater, which prepared astronaut-type meals for consumption via a tube.

This U-2R is configured to carry the 'Senior Span' pod above the rear fuselage. This system allows the aircraft to transmit gathered data into a satcom link, from where it is transmitted by an upward-facing dish antenna to a satellite, for onward transmission to users in real time.

MCDONNELL DOUGLAS F-4G 'WILD WEASEL' PHANTOM II

35th Tactical Fighter Wing (Provisional), United States Air Force, Sheikh Isa Air Base, Bahrain, January 1991

As a result of the lessons learned in Vietnam, the provision of airborne equipment to fulfil the defence suppression role, and the modification of aircraft to carry it, assumed top priority in US Air Force (USAF) Tactical Air Command planning in 1975. What Tactical Air Command needed was a self-contained weapon system – an aircraft capable of carrying both the necessary electronics and the weaponry to hit enemy surface-to-air missile radars effectively, and the F-4 Phantom was the best choice available.

'Wild Weasel' trials had alredy been carried out with two F-4Ds in 1968, but later studies showed that the F-4E variant was easier to modify. USAF funding was consequently obtained to convert 116 F-4Es to F-4G standard under the Advanced Wild Weasel Programme. Modfications included the addition of a torpedo-shaped fairing on top of the fin to house APR-38 radar antennae, and the F-4E's M61A1 cannon installation was deleted to permit the installation of the computer systems associated with the F-4G's sensory radar. With this equipment, the Wild Weasel crew could detect, identify and locate hostile radar emitters and select the appropriate weapons package for use against them.

The F-4G pictured here, normally based at Spandahlem in Germany with the 23rd Tactical Fighter Squadron (TFS), 52nd Tactical Fighter Wing (TFW), was assigned to the 35th TFW for operations during Desert Storm in 1991. It carries 27 mission marks in the form of a 'spook' figure. The 'Night Stalker' artwork is an allusion to the 'Rhino' nickname adopted by the Phantoms.

MCDONNELL DOUGLAS F-4G 'WILD WEASEL' PHANTOM

Specification

- **Type** defence suppression aircraft
- **Crew** 2
- **Powerplant** two 8119kg (17,900lb) thrust General Electric J79-GE-17 turbojets
- **Performance** max speed 2390km/h (1485mph); service ceiling 26,308km/h (58,000lb); range 2817km (1750 miles)
- **Dimensions** wing span 11.70m (38ft 5in); length 17.76m (58ft 3in); height 4.96m (16ft 3in)
- **Weight** 26,308kg (58,000lb) loaded
- **Armament** up to 5888kg (12,980lb) of ordnance and stores on underwing pylons, including AGM-88 HARM anti-radiation missiles

MCDONNELL DOUGLAS F-15C EAGLE

318th Fighter Interceptor Squadron, Tactical Air Command, United States Air Force, Washington, 1990s

MCDONNELL DOUGLAS F-15C EAGLE

Specification
- **Type** air superiority fighter
- **Crew** 1
- **Powerplant** two 10,885kg (23,810lb) thrust Pratt & Whitney F100-PW-220 turbofans
- **Performance** max speed 2655km/h (1650mph); service ceiling 30,500m (100,000ft); range 5745km (3570 miles) with conformal fuel tanks
- **Dimensions** wing span 13.05m (42ft 9in); length 19.43m (63ft 9in); height 5.63m (18ft 5in)
- **Weight** 30,844kg (68,000lb) loaded
- **Armament** one 20mm (0.79in) M61A1 cannon; four AIM-7 or AIM-120 and four AIM-9 air-to-air missiles

The United States Air Force (USAF) and various aircraft companies in the United States began discussions on the feasibility of an advanced tactical fighter to replace the F-4 Phantom in 1965. Four years later it was announced that McDonnell Douglas had been selected as prime airframe contractor for the new aircraft, then designated FX; as the F-15A Eagle, it flew for the first time on 27 July 1972, and first deliveries of operational aircraft were made to the USAF in 1975.

The tandem-seat F-15B was developed alongside the F-15A, and the main production version was the F-15C. The latter was built under licence in Japan as the F-15J. The F-15E two-seat dedicated strike/attack variant was supplied to Israel as the F-15I and to Saudi Arabia as the F-15S. Saudi Arabia also purchased a further 62 F-15C/D aircraft to replaced its BAe Lightning F.Mk.53 interceptors, which had been withdrawn from use. In all, the USAF took delivery of 1286 F-15s (all versions), Japan 171, Saudi Arabia 98 and Israel 56.

F-15s saw much action in the 1991 Gulf War, and Israeli aircraft were in combat with the Syrian Air Force over the Bekaa Valley in the 1980s. F-15s have also been operational over the Balkans and other trouble spots.

The 318th Fighter Interceptor Squadron (FIS) converted to the F-15C from the Convair F-106A in 1983. The squadron was deactivated in 1989, its Eagles being assigned to the Oregon Air National Guard.

MCDONNELL DOUGLAS F-15DJ EAGLE

204th Hikotai, 7th Kokudan,
Japanese Air Self-Defence Force,
Hyakuri Air Base, Ogawa, Japan
1990s

MCDONNELL DOUGLAS F-15DJ EAGLE

Specification
- **Type** air superiority fighter
- **Crew** 2
- **Powerplant** two 10,885kg (23,810lb) thrust Pratt & Whitney F100-PW-220 turbofans
- **Performance** max speed 2655km/h (1650mph); service ceiling 30,500m (100,000ft); range 5745km (3570 miles) with conformal fuel tanks
- **Dimensions** wing span 13.05m (42ft 9in); length 19.43m (63ft 9in); height 5.63m (18ft 5in)
- **Weight** 30,844kg (68,000lb) loaded
- **Armament** one 20mm (0.79in) M61A1 cannon; four AIM-7 or AIM-120 and four AIM-9 air-to-air missiles

Japan has been a major F-15 customer, purchasing a total of 223 F-15Js and F-15DJs, the latter a two-seat combat training variant with the full capability of the single-seat F-15. The F-15J/DJ is Japan's principal air superiority fighter, most examples having been built by Mitsubishi.

The Japanese aircraft differ from the F-15C/D with the deletion of sensitive ECM, radar warning, and nuclear delivery equipment. The AN/ALQ-135 is replaced by indigenous J/ALQ-8 and the AN/ALR-56 RHAWS is replaced by J/APR-4. Like the F-15C, the F-15J/DJ has a wing loading of only 25kg/0.9m² (54lb per sq ft) and this, together with two 10,782kg (23,770lb) thrust Pratt & Whitney F100-PW-220 advanced technology turbofans, gives it an extraordinary turning ability and the combat thrust-to-weight ratio (1.3:1) necessary to retain the initiative in a fight.

The high thrust-to-weight ratio permits a scramble time of only six seconds, using 183m (600ft) of runway, and a maximum speed of more than Mach 2.5 gives the pilot the margin he needs if he has to break off an engagement. To increase the Eagle's survivability, redundancy is incorporated in its structure; for example, one vertical fin, or one of three wing spars, can be severed without causing the loss of the aircraft.

The illustration shows a McDonnell Douglas F-15DJ Eagle of the 204th Hikotai (Squadron), which forms part of the 7th Kokudan (Wing) at Hyakuri Air Base, together with the 305th Hikotai. The aircraft is depicted launching an AIM-9 Sidewinder air-to-air missile.

MCDONNELL DOUGLAS
F-15E STRIKE EAGLE

*48th Fighter Wing, 3rd Air Force,
USAFE, Lakenheath, Suffolk, 1994*

MCDONNELL DOUGLAS F-15E STRIKE EAGLE

Specification

- **Type** strike/attack aircraft and air superiority fighter
- **Crew** 2
- **Powerplant** two 10,885kg (23,810lb) thrust Pratt & Whitney F100-PW-220 turbofans
- **Performance** max speed 2655km/h (1650mph); service ceiling 30,500m (100,000ft); range 5745km (3570 miles) with conformal fuel tanks
- **Dimensions** wing span 13.05m (42ft 9in); length 19.43m (63ft 9in); height 5.63m (18ft 5in)
- **Weight** 36,741kg (81,000lb) loaded
- **Armament** one 20mm (0.79in) M61A1 cannon; four AIM-7 or AIM-120 and four AIM-9 air-to-air missiles; many combinations of underwing ordnance

The F-15E Strike Eagle, which was originally developed as a private venture, is the latest development of the McDonnell Douglas F-15 Eagle air superiority fighter. The prototype first flew in 1982.

The Strike Eagle carries a two-man crew, the pilot and back-seat weapons and defensive systems operator. The avionics suite is substantial, and to accommodate it one of the fuselage tanks has been reduced. More powerful engines have been fitted without the need for extensive airframe modifications. Strengthened airframe and landing gear allow a greater weapons load. The F-15E can be fitted with FAST (fuel and sensor tactical) packs, now called conformal fuel tanks (CFTs), attached to the side of the fuselage outside each air intake. CFTs carry extra fuel and also sensors such as reconnaissance cameras, infrared equipment, radar warning receivers and jammers.

A feature of the F-15 is its large wing area and correspondingly low wing loading. While this makes for a more uncomfortable low-level ride than that experienced by the crews of dedicated attack aircraft such as the Su-24 or Tornado, it confers superb air-to-air capability on the F-15E, enabling it to put up a highly credible defence if attacked. F-15E units were at the forefront of precision bombing during the 1991 Gulf War.

The McDonnell Douglas F-15E Strike Eagle pictured here bears the markings of the 48th Fighter Wing (FW) of the 3rd Air Force, based at Lakenheath (code letters LN) in the United Kingdom. Formerly equipped with F-111Fs, the 48th FW has deployed its F-15Es to both the Middle East and the former Yugoslavia as part of multinational peacekeeping forces.

MCDONNELL DOUGLAS CF-18 HORNET

No 3 Tactical Fighter Wing, Canadian Air Force, Cold Lake, Alberta, 1990s

MCDONNELL DOUGLAS CF-18 HORNET

Specification
- **Type** fighter-bomber
- **Crew** 1
- **Powerplant** two 7264kg (16,000lb) thrust General Electric F404-GE-400 turbofans
- **Performance** max speed 1912km/h (1183mph); service ceiling 15,240m (50,000ft); combat radius 1065km (662 miles)
- **Dimensions** wing span 11.43m (37ft 6in); length 17.07m (56ft); height 4.66m (15ft 3´in)
- **Weight** 25,401kg (56,000lb) loaded
- **Armament** one 20mm (0.79in) M61A1 Vulcan cannon; external hardpoints with provision for up to 7711kg (17,000lb) of stores

The McDonnell Douglas Hornet also serves with the Canadian Armed Forces as the CF-18, equipping No. 3 Wing (Nos 425 and 433 Tactical Fighter Squadrons at Bagotville, Quebec); No. 4 Wing (No 410 Tactical Fighter Operational Training Squadron; and Nos 416 and 441 Tactical Fighter Squadrons at Cold Lake, Alberta.

Three Canadian Hornet squadrons served in Germany as part of Canada's contribution to Nato; these were Nos 409, 421 and 439. All were disbanded following their withdrawal from Europe. The aircraft of all three squadrons were reassigned to Hornet units in Canada.

During the Gulf War of 1991, 24 CF-18s were sent to Qatar to participate in the American-led Desert Shield and Desert Storm campaigns. Canadian pilots flew more than 5,700 hours — about 2,700 combat air patrol missions — to protect Canadian naval forces in the Gulf.

During Operation Allied Force, the 79-day Nato air campaign in former Yugoslavia from March to June of 1999, Canada committed 18 CF-18s to Task Force Aviano, flying from Aviano Air Base in northern Italy. CF-18s flew 678 sorties, in the air-to-ground and air-to-air roles using both precision guided munitions and unguided 'iron' bombs. With much less than 10 per cent of the aircraft committed to the campaign, Canadian aircraft conducted 10 per cent of the Nato strike sorties during the campaign.

The CF-18 can carry a Nitehawk pod that incorporates a forward-looking infrared sensor that allows pilots to see targets at night. It also has a laser designator to guide precision bombing. A CF-18 Hornet of the Canadian Armed forces is seen here launching an AIM-7 Sparrow air-to-air missile.

MCDONNELL DOUGLAS/BRITISH AEROSPACE HARRIER GR.7

No, IV (AC) Squadron, Royal Air Force,
RAF Cottesmore, Rutland
1990s

MCDONNELL DOUGLAS/BRITISH AEROSPACE HARRIER GR.7

Specification
- **Type** short take-off, vertical landing (STOVL) strike aircraft
- **Crew** 1
- **Powerplant** one 10,796kg (23,800lb) thrust Rolls-Royce Pegasus Mk 105 vectored thrust turbofan
- **Performance** max speed 1065km/h (661mph); service ceiling 15,240m (50,000ft); combat radius 277km (172 miles) with 2722kg (6000lb) payload
- **Dimensions** wing span 9.25m (30ft 4in); length 14.12m (46ft 4in); height 3.55m (11ft 7in)
- **Weight** 14,061kg (31,000lb) loaded
- **Armament** two 25mm (0.98in) Aden cannon in under-fuselage pods; six external hardpoints with provision for up to 7711kg (17,000lb) or 3175kg (7000lb) of stores (short and vertical take-off, respectively)

The Harrier GR.7 is a further development of the Harrier GR.5, the Royal Air Force (RAF) equivalent of the US Marine Corp (USMC) AV-8B Harrier II. Delivery of the Harrier GR5 began in 1987, production GR5s being later converted to GR7 standard. This version, generally similar to the USMC's night-attack AV-8B, has FLIR, a digital moving map display, night-vision goggles for the pilot and a modified head-up display.

Britain originally pulled out of the collaborative advanced Harrier programme because the RAF's requirement was for only 94 aircraft compared with a USMC requirement for more than 300. Hence, when the UK government decided to rejoin, British Aerospace (BAe) became the junior partner, responsible for only 40 per cent of airframe work on aircraft for the United States and Spain, and 50 per cent on RAF aircraft.

BAe makes the rear and centre fuselages of all aircraft, the fins and rudders of all aircraft, and tailplanes of RAF aircraft. It also assembles all RAF aircraft from the respective McDonnell Douglas and BAe subassemblies.

The Harrier GR.9, which first flew in 2003, is a further upgrade; all GR.7 aircraft are to undergo this upgrade and will then be redesignated GR.9.

After a lengthy deployment to RAF Gütersloh, Germany, No. IV Squadron moved to Laarbruch, where it was co-located with No. 3 Squadron. No. IV Squadron was the last to relinquish the Harrier GR.3, but the first to equip with the GR.7. Both Laarbruch units subsequently redeployed to RAF Cottesmore, Rutland, United Kingdom.

MIKOYAN-GUREVICH MIG-27L FLOGGER-J

*No. 9 'Wolfpack' Squadron,
Indian Air Force, Hindan, 1990*

The MiG-23, which flew in prototype form in 1967 and which entered service with the Frontal Aviation's attack units of the 16th Air Army in East Germany in 1973, was a variable-geometry fighter-bomber with wings sweeping from 23 to 71 degrees, and was the Soviet Air Force's first true multi-role combat aircraft. The MiG-23M Flogger-B was the first series production version and equipped all the major Warsaw Pact air forces; a simplified version for export to Libya and other Middle East air forces was designated MiG-23MS Flogger-E.

The MiG-23UB Flogger-C was a two-seat trainer, retaining the combat capability of the single-seat variants, while the MiG-23BN/BM Flogger-F and Flogger-H were fighter-bomber versions for export. The MiG-27, which began to enter service in the late 1970s, was a dedicated battlefield support variant known to Nato as Flogger-D; the MiG-27D and MiG-27K Flogger-J were improved versions, while the MiG-23P was a dedicated air defence variant.

About 5000 MiG-23/27s were built, and in the 1990s the type was in service with 20 air forces. The service debut of the MiG-23/27 was not without its share of problems, though, many accidents in the early days having resulted from failure of the wing sweep mechanism.

The Indian Air Force's MiG-27s were designated MiG-27L. The first aircraft were assembled from Soviet-supplied kits by Hindustan Aeronautics Ltd, but at a later stage in the programme major Indian sub-ssemblies were incorporated. In Indian Air Force service, the type is known as Bahadur (Valiant).

MIKOYAN-GUREVICH MIG-27L FLOGGER-J

Specification
- **Type** battlefield support aircraft
- **Crew** 1
- **Powerplant** one 10,000kg (22,046lb) thrust Tumanskii R-27F2M-300 turbojet
- **Performance** max speed 2445km/h (1520mph); service ceiling 18,290m (60,000ft); combat radius 966km (600 miles)
- **Dimensions** wing span 13.97m (45ft 10in) spread and 7.78m (25ft 6in) swept; length 16.71m (54ft 10in); height 4.82m (15ft 9in)
- **Weight** 18,145kg (40,000lb) loaded
- **Armament** one 23mm (0.91in) GSh-23L cannon; underwing pylons for various combinations of air-to-air missiles and offensive stores

TS 537

PALE

MIKOYAN MIG-29 FULCRUM-A

237th Gvradeyskaya Tsentr Pokaza Aviatsionnoy Tekniki, Air Forces Moscow Military District (VVS MVO), Kubinka, Russia, early 1990s

MIKOYAN MIG-29 FULCRUM-A

- **Crew** 1
- **Powerplant** two 81.39kN (18,298lb) Klimov/Leningrad RD-33 afterburning turbo fan engines
- **Performance** max speed 2445km/h (1,519mph); combat radius 750km (466miles) service ceiling 17000m (55,775ft)
- **Dimensions** span 11.36m (37ft 3.25in); length 17.32m (56ft 10in); height 4.73m (15ft 6.2in)
- **Weight** loaded 18,500kg (40,785lb)
- **Armament** one GSh-301 30-mm cannon, maximum stores of 3000kg (6,614lb)

During the Great Patriotic War, as Russians call World War II, many Soviet army and air units were awarded the 'Guards' prefix for exceptional performance. The 234th *Istrebeitel'nyi Aviatsionny Polk* (Fighter Aviation Regiment) flew Lavochkin fighters during the war, but was not honoured as a Guards Unit. In 1952, it was redeployed to Kubinka near Moscow to replace units sent to Korea. Kubinka has long been used for demonstrating advanced combat aircraft to national and foreign leaders. Its personnel were the first in the Soviet Union to fly solo and jet aerobatic displays, and led May Day and other fly-pasts over Moscow from 1946. The success of these demonstrations led to the awarding of the coveted 'Guards' title and the right to display the Guards banner on the unit's aircraft.

Post-war Soviet and Russian unit histories remain largely obscure, but it seems the 234th was later redesignated the 237th GTsPAT (*Gvradeyskaya Tsentr Pokaza Aviatsionnoy Tekniki*, or Guards Aircraft Demonstration Centre), named after Ivan Kozhedub. Kozhedub was the leading Soviet ace of the war, with 62 victories, and later became leader of the Soviet air units in Korea. By 1989, the flying unit at Kubinka was designated the 237th Composite Air Regiment and its 1st Squadron received the Su-27 'Flanker', leading to the formation in 1991 of the Russian Knights display team. The 237th's MiG-29 unit also formed a display team from its complement of 'Fulcrums', and this became known as the 'Swifts'.

The MiG-29 makes an exceptional aerobatic platform with its ability to fly at high angle-of-attack and its relatively light weight combined with powerful engines. Both teams have made a number of foreign visits and demonstrations in Europe and beyond. The 237th is Russia's main aerobatic school and is equipped with Su-24 and Su-25 attack aircraft as well as MiG and Sukhoi fighters.

MIKOYAN MIG-29 FULCRUM-A

968th Istrebeitel' nyi Aviatsionny Polk,
16th Air Army, Soviet Frontal Aviation,
Nobitz (Altenburg), German Democratic
Republic, 1990s

MIKOYAN MIG-29 FULCRUM-A

Specification
- **Crew** 1
- **Powerplant** two 81.39kN (18,298lb thrust) Klimov/Leningrad RD-33 afterburning turbofan engines
- **Performance** 2445km/h (1519mph); service ceiling 17,000m (55,775ft); combat radius 750km (466 miles)
- **Dimensions** wing span 11.36m (37ft 3.25in); length 17.32m (56ft 10in); height 4.73m (15ft 6.2in)
- **Weight** 18,500kg (40,785lb) loaded
- **Armament** one GSh-301 30mm (1.18in) cannon; maximum stores of 3000kg (6614lb)

The MiG-29 (Nato code name 'Fulcrum') was developed to meet a requirement for a lightweight fighter to replace MiG-21s, MiG-23s and Su-17s in the battlefield air superiority and ground-attack roles. The first prototype flew in October 1977, and deliveries to Soviet Frontal Aviation began in 1983.

The powerful pulse-Doppler radar is backed up with a passive infrared search-and-track (IRST) system. This can detect, track and engage a target while leaving the radar in a non-emitting mode. The IRST sensor is mounted in front of the windscreen. For close-in engagements, a helmet-mounted sight can be used to cue infrared-homing missiles onto an off-boresight target.

Early production MiG-29s such as this one did not have the tailfin extensions with the chaff and flare dispensers. They also retained the small ventral fins under the tailplanes omitted from later production aircraft. Various upgrades brought the early aircraft up to the same capability levels as later batches, but few, if any, remain in service in Russia.

Until the early 1990s, significant Soviet forces were based with the 16th Air Army in East Germany. The 968th *Istrebeitel' nyi Aviatsionny Polk* (IAP, or Fighter Aviation Regiment) was based at Altenburg, near Leipzig, for a brief period. The 968th's Fulcrums replaced a regiment of MiG-27 'Floggers', which in turn had replaced Su-24 'Fencers' in 1989. The particular squadron that operated this MiG-29 is unknown, but it was the only one to wear a squadron badge at Altenburg and flew earlier-production Fulcrums than its sister units. The winged star badge originated with Yak fighters in World War II.

In April 1992, the 968th IAP withdrew to Lipetsk in Russia. Altenburg is now a civil airport, served by budget airline Ryanair, among others.

MITSUBISHI F-1

3 Hikotai, 3 Kokudan, Northern Air Defence Force, Air Defence Command, Japan Air Self-Defence Force, Misawa Air Base, Japan, early 1990s

Influenced by the SEPECAT Jaguar, the Mitsubishi F-1 was developed from the two-seat T-2 trainer, which was Japan's first indigenous supersonic aircraft. The T-2 flew in July 1971 and incorporated many 'off the shelf' components built under licence in Japan. These included the M61 cannon, Weber ejection seats and the Ishikawajima-Harima TF40 engines, which were licence-built versions of the Rolls-Royce/Turboméca Adour engines as used in the Jaguar.

Ninety were built in total and two were converted into development aircraft for the F-1 combat aircraft. The rear seat of the T-2 is deleted and a new air-to-air and air-to-ground radar replaces the search and ranging set in the T-1. Optimized for the maritime strike role, the Japan Air Self-Defence Force (JASDF) defines the F-1 as an 'anti-landing craft' aircraft, although it has a significant secondary fighter role. For surface attack, the F-1 employs the radar-guided ASM-1 with a range of about 50km (31 miles) or the longer-ranged imaging-infrared guided ASM-2, of which up to four can be carried. Bombs and rockets can also be carried.

The first converted T-2 flew in 1975, and the production F-1 entered service in 1978, replacing the F-86 Sabre with the 3 Hikotai (3rd Squadron) of 3 Kokudan (3rd Wing) at Misawa Air Base in northern Honshu. Originally plans called for more than 160 T-1s to be built, but budgetary constraints reduced this number to 77.

The 3rd Kokudan has now swapped its F-1s for the Mitsubishi F-2A, which is derived from the F-16, and this particular F-1 has moved on to Tsukui on Kyushu with 6 Hikotai, 8 Kokudan.

MITSUBISHI F-1

Specification
- **Type** maritime strike aircraft
- **Crew** 1
- **Powerplant** two 32.49kN (7305lb thrust) Ishikawajima-Harima TF40–IHI-801 afterburning turbofan engines
- **Performance** max speed 1708km/h (1061mph); service ceiling 15,240m (50,000ft); range (loaded) 1300km (808 miles)
- **Dimensions** wing span 7.88m (25 ft 10.5in); length 17.86m (58ft 7in); height 4.39m (14ft 5in)
- **Weight** 13,700kg (30,203lb) loaded
- **Armament** one 20mm (0.79in) JM61 Vulcan cannon; ASM-1 or ASM-2 radar-guided air-to-surface missiles, AIM-9L Sidewinder air-to-air missiles

NORTHROP GRUMMAN B-2A SPIRIT

393rd Bomb Squadron,
509th Bombardment Wing, United States
Air Force, Whiteman Air Force Base,
Missouri, mid-1990s

NORTHROP GRUMMAN B-2A SPIRIT

Specification
- **Type** strategic bomber
- **Crew** 4
- **Powerplant** four 8618kg (19,000lb) thrust General Electric F118-GE-110 turbofans
- **Performance** max speed 764km/h (475mph); service ceiling 15,240m (50,000ft); range 11,675km (7255 miles)
- **Dimensions** wing span 52.43m (172ft); length 21.03m (69ft); height: 5.18m (17ft)
- **Weight** 181,437kg (400,000lb) loaded
- **Armament** 16 AGM-129 Advanced Cruise Missiles, or alternatively 16 B.61 or B.83 free-fall nuclear bombs, 80 Mk 82 227kg (500lb) bombs, 16 Joint Direct Attack Munitions, 16 Mk84 907kg (2000lb) bombs, 36 M117 340kg (750lb) fire bombs, 36 CBU-87/89/97/98 cluster bombs, and 80 Mk36 304kg (560lb) or Mk 62 sea mines

Development of the B-2, originally known as the Advanced Technology Bomber (ATB), was begun in 1978 and the US Air Force (USAF) originally wanted 133 examples; however, by 1991, successive budget cuts had reduced this to 21 aircraft. The prototype flew on 17 July 1989, and the first production B-2 was delivered to the 393rd Bomb Squadron of the 509th Bomb Wing at Whiteman Air Force Base, Missouri, on 17 December 1993.

In designing the ATB, Northrop decided on an all-wing configuration from the outset. The all-wing approach was selected because it promised to result in an exceptionally clean configuration for minimizing radar cross-section, including the elimination of vertical tail surfaces, with added benefits such as span-loading structural efficiency and high lift/drag ratio for efficient cruise. Outboard wing panels were added for longitudinal balance, to increase lift/drag ratio and to provide sufficient span for pitch, roll and yaw control.

The original ATB design had elevons on the outboard wing panels only, but as the design progressed additional elevons were added inboard, giving the B-2 its distinctive 'double-W' trailing edge. The aircraft is highly manoeuvrable, with fighter-like handling characteristics. In addition to the 'stealth' properties of its design, the B-2 is coated with radar-absorbent materials.

The 509th Bombardment Wing, which began life as the 509th (Composite) Bomb Group, was formed in 1944 to drop the world's first atomic bombs. Since then, it has pioneered the operational use of new strategic weapons and systems for the USAF.

NORTHROP F-5E TIGER II

No. 144 'Black Kite' Squadron,
Republic of Singapore Air Force,
Paya Lebar, Singapore, late 1990s

NORTHROP F-5E TIGER II

Specification
- **Type** lightweight tactical fighter
- **Crew** 1
- **Powerplant** two 2267kg (5000lb) thrust General Electric J85-GE-21B turbojets
- **Performance** max speed 1700km/h (1056mph); service ceiling 15,550m (51,800ft); combat radius 1405km (875 miles)
- **Dimensions** wing span 8.13m (26ft 8in); length 14.45m (47ft 5in); height 4.08m (13ft 5in)
- **Weight** 11187kg (24,664lb) loaded
- **Armament** two M-39 20mm (0.79in) cannon; up to 2494kg (5500lb) of stores on external pylons

The Northrop N156 was conceived as a relatively cheap and simple aircraft capable of undertaking a variety of tasks. After nearly three years of intensive testing and evaluation, it was announced on 25 April 1962 that the N156 had been selected as the new all-purpose fighter for supply to friendly nations under the Mutual Aid Pact, and the aircraft entered production as the F-5A Freedom Fighter, the first example flying in October 1963.

The F-5A entered service with US Air Force (USAF) Tactical Air Command in April 1964. The first overseas customer was the Imperial Iranian Air Force, which formed the first of seven F-5A squadrons in February 1965. The Royal Hellenic Air Force also received two squadrons in 1965, and Norway received 108 aircraft from 1967, these being fitted with arrester hooks and rocket assisted take-off for short field operations.

Between 1965 and 1970, Canadair built 115 aircraft for the Canadian Armed Forces as CF-5A/Ds, these using Orenda-built J85-CAN-15 engines. Other nations using the type were Ethiopia, Morocco, South Korea, the Republic of Vietnam, Nationalist China, the Philippines, Libya, the Netherlands, Spain, Thailand and Turkey. An improved version, the F-5E Tiger II, was selected in November 1970 as a successor to the F-5A series. It served with a dozen overseas air forces, and also in the 'aggressor' air combat training role with the USAF.

Other Singaporean F-5 units based at Paya Lebar in 2004 were No. 141 'Merlin' and No. 149 Shikra (Lynx) Squadrons. All are now equipped with the upgraded F-5S/T.

PANAVIA TORNADO GR.MK.1A

No. 13 Squadron, Royal Air Force,
RAF Marham, Norfolk, early 1990s

PANAVIA TORNADO GR.MK.1A

Specification
- **Type** tactical reconnaissance aircraft
- **Crew** 2
- **Powerplant** two 7292kg (16,075lb) thrust Turbo-Union RB.199-34R Mk 103 turbofan engines
- **Performance** max speed 2337km/h (1452mph); service ceiling 15,240m (50,000ft); combat radius 1390km (864 miles)
- **Dimensions** wing span 13.91m (45ft 7in) spread and 8.6m (28ft 2.5in) swept; length 16.72m (54ft 10in); height 5.95m (19ft 6.25in)
- **Weight** 27,216kg (60,000lb) loaded
- **Armament** up to 9000kg (19,840lb) of stores; Vinten Linescan infrared sensors and TIALD (Thermal Imaging and Laser Designator)

T he variable-geometry Tornado was the result of a 1960s requirement for a strike and reconnaissance aircraft capable of carrying a heavy and varied weapons load and of penetrating foreseeable Warsaw Pact defensive systems by day and night, at low level and in all weathers. To develop and build the aircraft, a consortium of companies was formed under the name of Panavia; it consisted principally of the British Aircraft Corporation (later British Aerospace), Messerschmitt-Bölkow-Blohm (MBB) and Aeritalia, as well many subcontractors. Another consortium, Turbo-Union, was formed by Rolls-Royce, MTU of Germany and Fiat to build the Tornado's Rolls-Royce RB-199 turbofan engines.

The first of nine Tornado IDS (Interdictor/Strike) prototypes flew in Germany on 14 August 1974, aircrews of the participating nations having been trained at RAF Cottesmore in the United Kingdom, which received the first Tornado GR.1s in July 1980. The Royal Air Force (RAF) took delivery of 229 GR.1 strike aircraft, the *Luftwaffe* 212, the German Naval Air Arm 112, and the *Aeronautica Militare Italiana* (Italian Air Force) 100. RAF and Italian Tornados saw action in the 1991 Gulf War.

The Tornado GR.1A is a variant with a centreline reconnaissance pod, deliveries beginning in 1990, while the GR.4, armed with Sea Eagle anti-shipping missiles, is an anti-shipping version; the GR.4A is the tactical reconnaissance equivalent. Forty-eight Tornado IDS were delivered to Saudi Arabia.

The Tornado GR.Mk.1A was developed to meet the RAF's reconnaissance needs in the 1990s and beyond. It retains virtually full air-to-ground strike capability, although the 23mm (0.91in) Mauser cannon were deleted to make room for the recce pod. The GR.Mk.1A also served with No. 2 Squadron, also at Marham.

ROCKWELL B-1B

34th Bomb Squadron, 366th Wing,
United States Air Force,
Ellsworth Air Force Base, South Dakota
1990s

ROCKWELL B-1B

Specification
- **Type** strategic bomber
- **Crew** 4
- **Powerplant** four 13,962kg (30,780lb) thrust General Electric F101-GE-102 turbofans
- **Performance** max speed 1328km/h (825mph); service ceiling 15,240m (50,000ft); range 12,000km (7455 miles)
- **Dimensions** wing span 1.67m (136ft 8in); length 44.81m (147ft); height 10.36m (34ft)
- **Weight** 216,634kg (477,000lb) loaded
- **Armament** up to 84,500lb (38,320kg) of Mk 82 or 24,200lb (10,974kg) of Mk 84 iron bombs in the conventional role, 24 SRAMs, 12 B-28 and B-43 or 24 B-61 and B-83 free-fall nuclear bombs, eight ALCMs on internal rotary launchers and 14 more on underwing launchers, and various combinations of other underwing stores; low-level operations are flown with internal stores only

Designed to replace the B-52 and FB-111 in the low-level penetration role, the Rockwell B-1 variable-geometry supersonic bomber prototype flew on 23 December 1974, and on 2 December 1976 the US Air Force (USAF) was authorized to proceed with production of the aircraft. In June 1977, however, President Jimmy Carter, in a nationwide television address, reversed this decision and stated that the B-1 would not be produced, but on 2 October 1981 President Ronald Reagan's new US administration took the decision to resurrect the supersonic bomber programme.

The operational designation of the supersonic bomber, 100 of which were to be built for Strategic Air Command, was to be B-1B. The two prototypes already built, and which had undergone a substantial evaluation programme, were now to be known as B-1As. The first B-1B flew in October 1984, and the first operational B-1B was delivered to the 96th Bomb Wing at Dyess Air Force Base on 7 July 1985. The last B-1B was delivered on 2 May 1988, since when the type has taken part in offensive operations in the Balkans and elsewhere. The B-1B equips five USAF squadrons assigned to the 8th Air Force, and two of the Air National Guard.

The 366th Wing, to which this B-1B belongs, is the USAF's rapid deployment air intervention wing, which also comprises F-16Cs, F-15C/Es and KC-135R tankers. Known as 'The Gunfighters', the wing's function is to deploy at very short notice for operations in any part of the world.

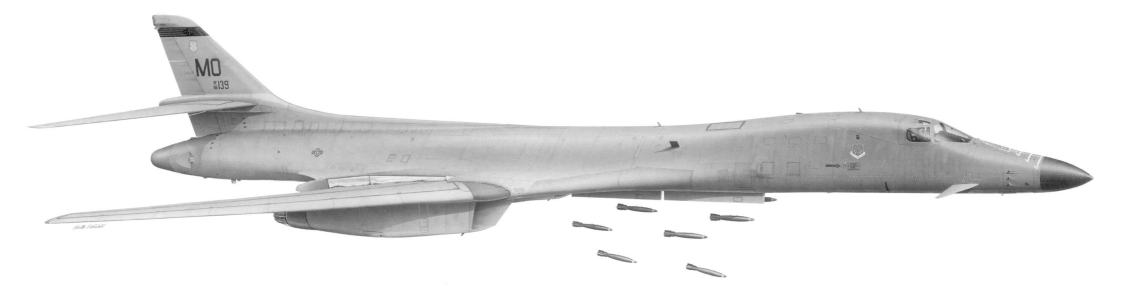

SAAB AJ 37 VIGGEN

Flygflottilj 6, Västgöta Flygflottilj,
Svenska Flygvapnet, Karlsborg,
Sweden, 1992

SAAB AJ 37 VIGGEN

Specification
- **Type** ground-attack fighter
- **Crew** 1
- **Powerplant** one 125.04kN (28,110lb thrust) Volvo Flygmotor RM8B afterburning turbofan engine
- **Performance** max speed 2126km/h (1321mph); service ceiling 18,000m (59,055ft); range 2000km (1243 miles)
- **Dimensions** wing span 10.60m (34ft 9.25in); length 16.40m (53ft 9.75in); height 5.6m (18ft 3in)
- **Weight** 17,000kg (37,478lb) loaded
- **Armament** up to 5897kg (13,000lb) of bombs, rockets or air-to-surface missiles

Saab's Viggen (named for the Norse god Thor's thunderbolt) was developed as a relatively low-cost Mach 2 fighter for the *Svenska Flygvapnet* (Royal Swedish Air Force), capable of operating from dispersed airfields and even sections of highway. The design pioneered the use of flap-equipped canards with a stable delta-wing configuration. The engine was based on the commercial Pratt & Whitney JT8D-22 turbofan, but equipped with a thrust reverser and Swedish-designed afterburner.

The initial AJ 37 Viggen all-weather attack variant featured sophisticated navigation/attack multi-role radar. The first of seven Viggen prototypes initially flew in February 1967, and deliveries began in 1971. The primary armament comprised Saab Rb 04E anti-ship missiles (replaced by the far more capable long-range Rbs 15) and licence-built AGM-65 Maverick air-to-surface missiles. A total of 108 attack Viggens was built, out of 319 of all variants. For most of their careers, the AJ 37s wore the spectacular 'fields and meadows' splinter camouflage pattern seen here.

Flygflottilj (Wing) 6 was based at Karlsborg and consisted of two squadrons, numbered 1 and 2 *Attackflygdivisionen*. Only comparatively recently have squadron badges appeared on Viggens; otherwise the only unit identifier was usually the wing number on the nose. *Flygflottilj* 6 (F6) disbanded at the end of 1993, the first *Flygvapnet* wing to go in a wave of post–Cold War cuts. The unit's Viggens, which were the oldest in service by that time. were either transferred to F10 or F15, or relegated to instruction duties, scrapped or preserved.

AJ 37 37034 is on display at Uppsala in northern Sweden, home of the last Viggen unit not disbanded or re-equipped with the JAS 39 Gripen.

SAAB JA 37 VIGGEN

Flygflottilj 4, Jämtlands Flygflottilj, Svenska Flygvapnet, South Norrland Military Command, Östersund, Sweden, 1990s

Until the debut of the Panavia Tornado, it may be argued that the Saab Viggen was the most advanced combat aircraft ever produced in Europe, possessing as it did a far more advanced radar, greater speed range and a more comprehensive avionics fit than its contemporaries. Certainly one of the most potent combat aircraft of the 1970s, the Saab 37 Viggen (Thunderbolt) was designed to carry out the four roles of attack, interception, reconnaissance and training.

Like the earlier J-35 Draken, it was fully integrated into the STRIL 60 air defence control system. Powered by a Swedish version of the Pratt & Whitney JT8D turbofan engine, with a powerful Swedish-developed afterburner, the aircraft had excellent acceleration and climb performance. Part of the requirement was that it should be capable of operating from sections of Swedish motorways. The first of seven prototypes flew for the first time on 8 February 1967, followed by the first production AJ-37 single-seat all-weather attack variant in February 1971.

Deliveries of the first of 110 AJ-37s to the *Svenska Flygvapnet* (Royal Swedish Air Force) began in June that year. The JA-37 interceptor version of the Viggen, 149 of which were built, replaced the J35F Draken; the SF-37 (26 examples delivered) was a single-seat armed photo reconnaissance variant; and the SH-37 (26 delivered) was an all-weather maritime reconnaissance version, replacing the S-32C Lansen. The SK-37 (18 delivered) was a tandem two-seat trainer, retaining a secondary attack role. Some Viggens were expected to remain in service until 2010.

SAAB JA 37 VIGGEN

Specification
- **Type** interceptor
- **Crew** 1
- **Powerplant** one 11,899kg (26,015lb) thrust Volvo Flygmotor RM8B turbofan
- **Performance** max speed 2124km/h (1320mph); service ceiling 18,290m (60,000ft); combat radius 1000km (621 miles)
- **Dimensions** wing span 10.60m (34ft 9in); length 16.30m (53ft 5in); height 5.60m (18ft 4in)
- **Weight** 20,500kg (45,194lb) loaded
- **Armament** BAe Sky Flash and AIM-9L Sidewinder air-to-air missiles

SEPECAT JAGUAR GR.MK.1A

RAF Jaguar Detachment, Royal Air Force, Muharraq, Bahrain, 1991

SEPECAT JAGUAR GR.MK.1A

Specification
- **Type** tactical strike aircraft
- **Crew** 1
- **Powerplant** two 3313kg (7305lb) thrust Rolls-Royce/Turbomeca Adour Mk 102 turbofans
- **Performance** max speed 1593km/h (990mph); service ceiling 14,000m (50,000ft); combat radius 557km (357 miles)
- **Dimensions** wing span 8.69m (28ft 6in); length 16.83m (55ft 2in); height 4.89m (16ft)
- **Weight** 15,500kg (34,172lb) loaded
- **Armament** two 30mm (1.18in) DEFA cannon five external hardpoints with provision for 4536kg (10,000lb) of underwing stores; two overwing-mounted AIM-9L Sidewinders for self-defence

Developed jointly by the British Aircraft Corporation and Breguet (later Dassault-Breguet) under the banner of SEPECAT (Société Europeanne de Production de l'Avion Ecole de Combat et Appui Tactique), the Jaguar emerged from protracted development as a much more powerful and effective aircraft than originally envisaged. The first French version to fly, in September 1968, was the two-seat E model, 40 being ordered by the *Armée de l'Air*, followed in March 1969 by the single-seat Jaguar A tactical support aircraft.

Service deliveries of the Jaguar E began in May 1972, the first of 160 Jaguar As following in 1973. The British versions, known as the Jaguar S (strike) and Jaguar B (trainer), flew on October 12 1969 and 30 August 1971, respectively, being delivered to the Royal Air Force (RAF) as the Jaguar GR.Mk.1 (165 examples) and T.Mk.2 (38 examples). *Armée de l'Air* Jaguars were fitted with a stand-off bomb release system, while British Jaguars were fitted with two weapon guidance systems: a Laser Ranging and Marked Target Seeker (LRMTS) and a Navigation and Weapon Aiming Subsystem (NAVWASS).

The Jaguar International, first flown in August 1976, was a version developed for the export market. It was purchased by Ecuador (12), Nigeria (18) and Oman (24), and was licence-built in India by HAL (98, including 40 delivered by BAe).

When Britain and France decided to contribute personnel and material to Operation Desert Storm in 1991, it was inevitable that the Jaguar, which was capable of rapid deployment with minimal support and which could function in relatively primitive conditions, should be included in the Coalition Forces' Order of Battle. In the event, the aircraft performed extremely well.

SIKORSKY CH-53D

*118 Tayeset Ha'Yassuriet Ha'Rishona,
Israeli Defence Force/Air Force, Tel Nof,
Israel, 1990s*

SIKORSKY CH-53D

Specification
- **Type** transport and recue helicopter
- **Crew** 3/4
- **Powerplant** three General Electric T64-GE-416 engines rated at 2756kW (3696hp)
- **Performance** max speed 315km/h (196mph); service ceiling 5640m (18,500ft); range 2075km (1290 miles)
- **Dimensions** rotor diameter 24.08m (79ft); length 22.35m (73ft 4in); height 8.97m (29ft 5in)
- **Weight** 31,640kg (69,750lb) loaded
- **Armament** up to three 7.62mm (0.30in) Miniguns

It was the shortcomings of other helicopter types in the Vietnam War that provided the impetus for the development of the Sikorsky H-53, a large and powerful helicopter whose range of missions would eventually embrace heavy-lift operations, military transport, search and rescue, vertical replenishment, vertical onboard delivery, airborne mine countermeasures, early warning, minesweeping, special duties, humanitarian aid and disaster relief.

Entering US Air Force (USAF) service in 1967, the CH-53A and the HH-53B which followed – the latter famous as the 'Jolly Green Giant' – quickly proved their worth in transporting supplies and rescuring downed aircrew. Two years later, the HH-53C 'Super Jolly', fitted with an external cargo hook and a rescue hoist, also made its combat debut.

Other variants of the basic design are the CH-53D Sea Stallion, designed for the transportation of equipment, supplies and personnel during the assault phase of an amphibious operation and subsequent operations ashore; the MH-53J Pave Low III, which is fitted with terrain-following, terrain-avoidance radar and forward-looking infrared sensor, along with a projected map display, and is optimized for low-level penetration; and the MH-53E Sea Dragon, used primarily for Airborne Mine Countermeasures (AMCM), with a secondary mission of shipboard delivery.

The Israeli Air Force acquired 33 S-65C-3 helicopters (basically CH-53Ds) from the United States and two more from Austria in 1981; 10 more ex-US Marine Corps CH-53As were delivered after the 1991 Gulf War. The helicopters have been substantially ugraded to keep them effective well into the twenty-first century.

SIKORSKY SH-60B SEAHAWK

Fleet Replenishment Squadron, Helicopter Anti-Submarine Squadron Light 41, United States Navy, Naval Air Station North Island, San Diego, California, 1990s

SIKORSKY SH-60B SEAHAWK

Specification
- **Type** ASW and general purpose helicopter
- **Crew** 4
- **Powerplant** two General Electric T700-GE-401 turboshaft engines each rated at 1260kw (1690hp)
- **Performance** max speed 272km/h (169mph); service ceiling classified; range 704km (437 miles)
- **Dimensions** rotor diameter 16.36m (53ft 8in); length 15.26m (50ft 1in); height 3.63m (11ft 11in)
- **Weight** 9182kg (20,244lb)
- **Armament** two Mk 46 lightweight homing torpedoes

The Sikorsky SH-60 Seahawk is the US Navy's version of the well-proven UH-60 Black Hawk, which entered service with the US Army in 1979. First deliveries of the SH-60B Seahawk, whose tasks encompass anti-submarine warfare, search and rescue, drug interdiction, anti-ship warfare, cargo lift, and special operations, were made in 1983. The SH-60F, which is the carrier-based variant, was first delivered in 1988.

The US Navy's SH-60B Seahawk is an airborne platform based aboard cruisers, destroyers and frigates, and deploys sonobouys (sonic detectors) and torpedoes in an anti-submarine role. It can also act as an extension to its parent vessel's radar capabilities.

Some versions, such as the US Air Force (USAF) MH-60 G Pave Hawk and the US Coast Guard HH-60J Jayhawk, are equipped with a rescue hoist with a 75m (250ft) cable that has a 270kg (600lb) lift capability, and a retractable inflight refuelling probe. The US Army's UH-60L Black Hawk is capable of carrying 11 soldiers or 1170 kg (2600lb) of cargo, or of hoisting a load of 4050kg (9000lb). In 1982, the USAF took delivery of its first MH-60G Pave Hawk, while the US Coast Guard received the HH-60J Jayhawk in 1992.

The SH-60B Seahawk seen here is towing a brightly coloured Magnetic Anomaly Detector (MAD) serving the Texas Instruments ASQ-81(V)2 system, which detects submarines by measuring disturbances in the earth's magnetic field caused by the presence of a large metallic mass such as a submarine.

The Seahawk is primarily used in the anti-submarine role and also serves with Australia, Greece, Japan, Spain, Taiwan and Turkey. The Seahawk depicted here is with Helicopter Anti-Submarine Squadron Light 41 (HSL-41 Seahawks).

SUKHOI SU-27 FLANKER-B

582nd Guards Fighter Air Regiment,
Fourth Air Army, Frontal Aviation,
Chojna, Poland, 1990

SUKHOI SU-27 FLANKER-B

Specification
- **Type** air superiority fighter and long-range interceptor
- **Crew** 1
- **Powerplant** two 12,500kg (27,557lb) thrust Lyulka AL-31M turbofans
- **Performance** max speed 2500km (1500mph); service ceiling 18,000m (59,055ft); combat radius 1500km (930 miles)
- **Dimensions** wing span 14.70m (48ft 2in); length 21.94m (71ft 11in); height 6.36m (20ft 10in)
- **Weight** 30,000kg (66,138lb) loaded
- **Armament** one 30mm (1.18in) GSh-3101 cannon; 10 external hardpoints with provision for various combinations of air-to-air missiles

The Sukhoi Su-27, like the F-15, is a dual-role aircraft; in addition to its primary air superiority task, it was designed to escort Su-24 Fencer strike aircraft on deep-penetration missions. The prototype, designated T-10, flew for the first time in May 1977, the type being allocated the code name 'Flanker' by Nato.

Full-scale production of the Su-27P Flanker-B air defence fighter began in 1980, but the aircraft did not become fully operational until 1984. Like its contemporary, the MiG-29 Fulcrum, the Su-27 combines a wing swept at 40 degrees with highly swept wing root extensions, underslung engines with wedge intakes, and twin fins. The combination of modest wing sweep with highly swept root extensions is designed to enhance manoeuvrability and generate lift, making it possible to achieve quite extraordinary angles of attack.

The Su-27UB Flanker-C is a two-seat training version, while the Su-27K Flanker-D is a navalzsed version, serving in small numbers aboard the Russian carrier *Kutnetzov* (formerly *Tbilisi*). The Su-27 serves with the air forces of China, where it is designated J-11, and Vietnam, and some were inherited by states such as Belarus and Kazakhstan, created by the collapse of the Soviet Union. The Su-30K export version of the Flanker is operated by No. 24 Squadron of the Indian Air Force.

The 582nd Guards Fighter Air Regiment was one of two Poland-based Su-27 units withdrawn to Russia in 1992 as part of the general withdrawal of Russian forces from former Warsaw Pact countries. The aircraft illustrated here, of the 582nd Guards Fighter Air Regiment, is Sukhoi Su-27 Flanker-B 'Blue 24'.

TRANSALL C-160NG

*64e Escadre de Transport, Armée de l'Air,
Evreux/Fauville, France, 1990s*

TRANSALL C-160NG

Specification
- **Type** transport aircraft
- **Crew** 4
- **Powerplant** two 6100hp Rolls-Royce Tyne RTy.20 Mk 22 turboprop engines
- **Performance** max speed 536km/h (333mph); service ceiling 8500m (27,900ft); range 4558km (2832 miles)
- **Dimensions** wing span 40m (131ft 3in); length 32.40m (106ft 3in); height 11.65m (38ft 5in)
- **Weight** 16,000kg (35,270lb) loaded
- **Payload** 93 troops, 68 paratroops, 62 stretchers

The Transall C-160 tactical transport was designed and produced as a joint venture between France and Federal Germany, Transall being an abbreviation of the specially formed consortium Transporter Allianz, comprising the companies of MBB, Aerospatiale and VFW-Fokker. The prototye flew for the first time on 25 February 1963, and series production began four years later.

The principal variants were the C-160A, consisting of six pre-series aircraft; the C-160D for the *Luftwaffe* (90 built); the C-160F for France (60 built); the C-160T (20 built for export to Turkey); and the C-160Z (nine built for South Africa). Production of a second series was authorized in 1977 following an additional French order and requests by other countries including Turkey and South Africa. The new version was designated the C.160NG (Nouvelle Generation) and was fitted with improved avionics and a reinforced wing with additional fuel tanks for extended range, as well as flight refuelling equipment. S

Six second-generation French Transalls were specially modified for two types of special duty; two were equipped for electronic intelligence (Elint) and jamming operations, and four were fitted with VLF transmission equipment, including a long, trailing aerial which enabled the aircraft to communicate with nuclear submarines of France's *Force Océanique Stratégique* without the need for them to surface. The aerial platform was known as ASTARTE (*Avion STAtion Relais de Transmissions Exceptionelles* – aircraft relay station for special transmissions). This system was due to be replaced by a ground-based communication system.

TUPOLEV TU-22M BACKFIRE

924th Reconnaissance Air Regiment, Northern Fleet, Olenya, Russia, 1998

Allocated the NATO reporting name 'Backfire', the Tupolev Tu-22M first flew in 1971, reached initial operational capability (IOC) in 1973 and, during the years that followed, replaced the Tu-16 Badger in Soviet service. The mission of the new bomber, peripheral attack or intercontinental attack, became one of the most fiercely contested intelligence debates of the Cold War, and it was a long time before the true nature of the threat it posed – anti-shipping attack – became known.

The original design (Backfire-A) underwent major modifications and re-emerged as the Tu-22M2 Backfire-B. About 400 Tu-22Ms were produced, 240 of them being M-2s/3s. The M3 (Backfire-C) variant had reduced defensive armament and the flight refuelling probe was deleted; a reconnaissance version, the Tu-22MR, entered service in 1985, and the Tu-22ME is the latest of the attack variants.

The variable-geometry Tu-22M Backfire's design was based on that of the earlier Tu-22 Blinder, which had many shortcomings and which saw operational service in Afghanistan during the Soviet intervention there.

The 924th Reconnaissance Air Regiment is sometimes referred to as the 924th Missile Carrier Regiment. Its role during the Cold War would have been to attack Nato ships in the North Atlantic and North Sea, or any naval unit that was approaching the Russian coast. To do this, large numbers of Backfires would have been deployed to make saturation attacks on Nato naval forces, using the Kh-22M (AS-4 Kitchen) air-to-surface missile. Backfires also serve with the Northern Fleet's 574th Air Reconnaissance Regiment, and with units of the Black Sea Fleet.

Seen here is a Tu-22M3 Backfire-C of the 924th Reconnaissance Air Regiment.

TUPOLEV TU-22M BACKFIRE

Specification

- **Type** maritime strike aircraft
- **Crew** 4
- **Powerplant** two 20,000kg (44,092lb) thrust Kuznetsov NK-144 turbofans
- **Performance** max speed 2125km/h (1321mph); service ceiling 18,000m (59,055ft); range 4000km (2485 miles)
- **Dimensions** wing span 34.30m (112ft 6in) spread and 23.40m (76ft 9in) swept; length 36.90m (129ft 11in); height 10.80m (35ft 5in)
- **Weight** 130,000kg (286,596lb) loaded
- **Armament** one 23mm (0.91in) GSh-23 twin-barrel cannon in radar controlled tail barbette; up to 12,000kg (26,455lb) of stores in weapons bay, or one S-4 missile, or three AS-16 missiles

VICKERS (BAC) VC-10

Aeroplane and Armament Experimental Establishment, Boscombe Down, Wiltshire 1990s

VICKERS (BAC) VC-10

Specification
- **Type** flight refuelling tanker
- **Crew** 4
- **Powerplant** four 9905kg (21,800lb) thust Rolls-Royce Conway 301 turbofans
- **Performance** max speed 935km/h (580mph); service ceiling 11,600m (38,000ft); range 7600km (4725 miles)
- **Dimensions** wing span 55.60m (182ft 5in); length 52.30m (171ft 9in); height 12m (39ft 6in)
- **Weight** 152,000kg (335,000lb) loaded
- **Armament** none

Designated VC-10 C.Mk.1, 14 examples of this four-jet long-range airliner were delivered to No. 10 Squadron, Royal Air Force (RAF) Air Support Command, between 1966 and 1968. Four standard VC-10s and five Super VC-10s were later converted to the flight refuelling role and delivered to the RAF in 1984 and 1985 as VC-10 K.Mk.2s and VC-10 K.Mk.3s. A final batch of ex-British Airways Super VC-10s, converted in the early 1990s, received the designation VC-10 K.Mk.4.

All the RAF's VC-10 tankers were operated by No. 101 Squadron, a former V-Force unit which re-formed in 1984 to undertake the new task and saw intensive action during Operation Desert Storm in 1991, refuelling RAF and US Navy aircraft. Each aircraft is a three-point tanker, fuel being dispensed from either the two wing hoses or from the single fuselage-mounted Hose Drum Unit (HDU). The wing hoses can transfer fuel at up to 1000kg (2200lb) per minute and are used to refuel tactical aircraft. The HDU can transfer fuel at up to 2000kg (4400lb) per minute and is usually used to refuel 'heavy' aircraft, although it can also be used by fighter types. Each tanker variant of VC-10 carries a different fuel load.

Vickers VC-10 ZA148 was the first VC-10 Mk.3 and was used for trials by the Aeroplane and Armament Experiment Establishment (A&AEE), so No. 101 Squadron's first delivery was the second conversion, ZA150, delivered to RAF Brize Norton on 1 February 1985.

VOUGHT A-7D CORSAIR II

*125th Tactical Fighter Squadron,
138th Tactical Fighter Group,
Oklahoma Air National Guard,
Kirtland Air Force Base, New Mexico,
1990s*

VOUGHT A-7D CORSAIR II

Specification
- **Type** tactical fighter-bomber
- **Crew** 1
- **Powerplant** one 6465kg (14,250lb) thrust Allison TF41-1 (Rolls-Royce Spey) turbofan engine
- **Performance** max speed 1123km/h (698mph); service ceiling 15,545m (51,000ft); range 1127km (700 miles)
- **Dimensions** wing span 11.80m (38ft 9in); length 14.06m (46ft 1in); height 4.90m (16ft 0in)
- **Weight** 19,050kg (42,000lb) loaded
- **Armament** one 20mm (0.79in) M61 Vulcan cannon; provision for up to 6804kg (15,000lb) of external stores

The prototype Corsair flew for the first time on 27 September 1965, and several versions were subsequently produced for the US Navy and US Air Force (USAF) by the Vought Corporation, a subsidiary of Ling-Temco-Vought.

The first attack variant was the A-7A, which made its combat debut in the Gulf of Tonkin on 4 December 1966 with Attack Squadron 147 (VA-147), operating from the USS *Ranger*. In all, 199 A-7As were delivered before production switched to the A-7B, which had an uprated engine. The first production model flew on 6 February 1968, the US Navy taking delivery of 198 examples.

The next variant was the A-7D tactical fighter for the USAF, which went into action in Vietnam in October 1972; 459 were built, many being allocated to Air National Guard (ANG) units. The final major Corsair variant, the two-seat A-7K, served only with the ANG. Corsair IIs were also operated by the Hellenic, Portuguese and Thai air forces.

The ANG took delivery of the A-7D from October 1975, when the 188th Tactical Fighter Squadron (TFS) at Kirtland Air Force Base received its first aircraft. In all, 14 ANG squadrons operated the type and achieved an enviably low accident rate. The last A-7D/K operators were Ohio, Iowa and Oklahoma ANG units, their aircraft being upgraded to Low-Altitude Navigation and Attack (LANA) configuration in 1987.

Prior to converting to the A-7D in July 1978, the Oklahoma ANG flew the North American F-100D Super Sabre, and began conversion to the F-16C in 1993.

WESTLAND LYNX AH.MK.1

No. 656 Squadron, British Army Air Corps, Netheravon, Wiltshire, early 1990s

WESTLAND LYNX AH.MK.1

Specification
- **Type** combat helicopter
- **Crew** 2
- **Powerplant** two Rolls-Royce Gem 41-2 turboshaft engines rated at 846kW (1135hp)
- **Performance** max speed 259km/h (161mph); service ceiling 3230m (10,600ft); endurance 3 hrs
- **Dimensions** rotor diameter 12.8m (42ft); length 15.16m (49ft 9in); height 3.6m (11ft 10in)
- **Weight** 4763 kg (10,500 lb) loaded
- **Armament** one of two 20mm (0.79in) cannon, 7.62mm (0.30in) Miniguns or rocket projectile pods; variety of air-to-surface missiles

First flown in March 1971, the Westland Lynx originated as a joint project between Westland (UK) and Aerospatiale (France) to produce a small military and naval helicopter based on Westland's WG13 design. The naval version was intended to replace the Wasp as a small ship-based anti-submarine helicopter and serve on the new Type 21, Type 22 and Type 42 frigates and destroyers.

The HAS2 entered service in 1977. The first HAS3, with uprated engines and a search radar, was delivered in July 1982. The latest version of the naval Lynx, the HMA8, has further uprated engines and a more capable search radar. In all, 60 HAS2 and 31 HAS3 were newly built for the Royal Navy. Fifty-three HAS2 have been upgraded to HAS3 standard, and a further 44 HAS3s are being converted to HMA8 standard.

Contemporary with the Lynx HAS.1 was the Lynx AH.Mk.1 for the British Army Air Corps (AAC), the first of a line of battlefield support Lynx helicopters culminating in the AH.Mk.9. Army Air Corps Lynxes have a primary anti-armour role and will be relegated to utility duties with the deployment of the Apache AH.Mk.1 from 2004.

Foreign countries using various marks of the Lynx are Brazil, Denmark, France, Germany, Netherlands, Norway, Pakistan, Portugal and South Korea.

The Westland Lynx pictured here was subsequently converted to AH.Mk.7 standard and serves with No. 671 Squadron of the AAC at Middle Wallop, Hampshire. Its original unit, No. 656 Squadron, was formed as an RAF unit in December 1942 and saw action in Burma and Malaya with fixed-wing Auster aircraft before being disbanded in 1947.

WESTLAND SEA KING

1 Staffel, Marinefliegergeschwader 5, Kiel, Germany, 1990s

WESTLAND SEA KING

Specification
- **Type** search and rescue/ASW helicopter
- **Crew** 4
- **Powerplant** two Rolls-Royce Gnome (Mks. 1 & 2 H1400-1, Mk. 4 onwards H1400-2) free power turbines – 1193kW (1600hp) maximum power each
- **Performance** max speed 226km/h (140mph); service ceiling 1980m (6500ft); range 1482km (921 miles)
- **Dimensions** rotor diameter 18.9m (62ft); length 16.69m (54ft 9in); height 5.2m (17ft 2in)
- **Weight** 9707 kg (21,400lb) loaded
- **Armament** HAS: four lightweight torpedoes or depth charges; optional door-mounted 7.62mm (0.30in) general-purpose machine gun. HC: door-mounted 7.62mm (0.30in) general-purpose machine gun. SAR: none

In 1959, Westland acquired the licence to build the Sikorsky S-61B to replace the Wessex in the anti-submarine role. The Royal Navy specification called for a British powerplant with different characteristics from the original one, different electronics and a wide range of mission capabilities.

Westland adopted a pair of Rolls-Royce Bristol Gnome turbines for its version of the Sea King, with fully computerized controls and largely British-made ASW equipment. The resultant helicopter is readily identifiable by the dorsal radome of the all-weather search radar. The first production Sea King HAS Mk.1 flew on 7 May 1969, and the first Royal Naval Squadron was formed the following August.

Versions of the Sea King include the HAS Mk.1, Mk.2 and Mk.5 for the Royal Navy; HAR Mk.3 (16 of the SAR version for the Royal Air Force); Sea King Mk.42 (24 for the Indian Navy); Mk.41 for the German Navy (22); Mk.43 for the Royal Norwegian Navy (11); Mk.45 for the Pakistani Navy (6); Mk.48 for the Belgian Air Force (5 of the SAR version); and Mk.50 for the Royal Australian Navy (12). A commando version has also been produced, serving with the Royal Navy, Egypt and Qatar.

The *Marineflieger*'s Sea King Mk.41s were based on the Royal Navy's HAS.Mk.1, with the same radar but with all anti-submarine warfare equipment removed. The helicopters were later upgraded to undertake ASV (air-to-surface vessel) missions as well as ASR duties.

Index